Representations of Poverty and Place

Laura L Paterson · Ian N Gregory

Representations of Poverty and Place

Using Geographical Text Analysis to Understand Discourse

palgrave
macmillan

Laura L Paterson
Languages and Applied Linguistics
The Open University
Milton Keynes, UK

Ian N Gregory
History
University of Lancaster
Lancaster, UK

ISBN 978-3-319-93502-7 ISBN 978-3-319-93503-4 (eBook)
https://doi.org/10.1007/978-3-319-93503-4

Library of Congress Control Number: 2018943637

Cover design by Fatima Jamadar

This Palgrave Macmillan imprint is published by the registered company Springer Nature Switzerland AG
The registered company address is: Gewerbestrasse 11, 6330 Cham, Switzerland

Acknowledgements

This work came out of a large number of collaborations and benefited from input from many colleagues. A particular mention should go to Dr. Andrew Hardie, from the Department of Linguistics and English Language, Lancaster University, for his technical wizardry in helping us manipulate such large amounts of material. Both authors would like to acknowledge the Economic and Social Research Council (ESRC) for supporting this work through the ESRC Centre for Corpus Approaches to Social Science (grant number ES/K002155/1). Ian Gregory would also like to acknowledge the contribution that the European Research Council (ERC) made to the work described in this book through funding from the European Union's Seventh Framework Programme (FP7/2007–2013)/ERC grant 'Spatial Humanities: Texts, GIS, places' (agreement number 283850).

Contents

About the Authors

Laura L Paterson is a Lecturer in English Language and Applied Linguistics at The Open University and editor of the *Journal of Language and Discrimination*. She is a corpus-based sociolinguist whose research concerns the discursive construction of UK poverty, audience response to poverty porn, media depictions of protest, and discourses of marriage.

Ian N Gregory is Professor of Digital Humanities at Lancaster University. His main area of expertise is in applying Geographical Information Science approaches in unconventional ways, particularly through the use of textual sources. He has published six books and nearly a hundred journal articles and book chapters.

List of Figures

List of Tables

Introduction

This book presents an entirely new, interdisciplinary method that we use to study the geographies associated with poverty in the UK. Bringing together corpus linguistics, critical discourse analysis (CDA), and geographical information systems (GIS), we interrogate the discourses surrounding poverty and place in two multimillion-word corpora of contrasting UK national newspapers. We demonstrate that the combination of these methods—henceforth geographical text analysis (GTA)—can be applied to large volumes of textual data, and use our analysis of poverty and place to show how the apparent division between quantitative and qualitative (i.e. textual) data is a false dichotomy. We also demonstrate the importance of considering geography—in particular the use of toponyms—within critical analyses of language.

Researchers wishing to study poverty have the option of drawing upon many different types of data. Economists, for example, are likely to use quantitative data related to GDP, wages, inflation, and/or wealth distribution to calculate who is (and who is not) in poverty. Ethnographers, on the other hand, may wish to focus on the lived experiences of those in poverty, concentrating their work on interactions with people experiencing homelessness or hardship. Historians may work systematically through census data or workhouse records to inform depictions of the development of poverty in a given place and/or time, and philosophers may consider poverty in the abstract in order to make conclusions about societal hierarchies. This range of data and approaches indicates that poverty is a wide-ranging, multifaceted, social issue, which can be realised in different forms and measured on different scales. The research presented here takes language as its primary data set and draws on techniques from linguistics in combination with techniques from the spatial humanities to present an innovative method for approaching the analysis of poverty.

Geographical approaches to poverty tend to be based on quantitative data, such as statistical measures of deprivation like Carstairs scores (Morris and Carstairs 1991), which have often been derived from census data. Such statistical data are well-suited to use with GIS. Quantitative analyses tend to be comprehensive, insofar as they can cover entire countries and provide robust data on macro-level trends, but they are less likely to show nuances within a data set. Smaller-scale qualitative studies can also have a geographical angle, such as the Open Society Foundations' report on the lived experiences of six white working-class communities across Europe (OSF 2014).[1] However, despite its fairly wide geographical reach, the focus on six locations means that, as with all small-scale studies, it is difficult to generalise from the OSF's data.

Significantly, linguists can work to a range of scales using a myriad of textual sources. CDA, for example, tends to focus on the detailed analysis of a relatively small number of texts, with the aim of accounting for the wider social context within which such texts are produced. At the other end of the scale, corpus linguistics facilitates the analysis of large bodies of texts spanning millions of words, which would be infeasible to analyse using manual analytical approaches alone. To this end, there is an established body of literature combining corpus linguistics with (critical) discourse analysis (Conrad 2002; Orpin 2005; Baker 2006;

[1]One of the locations chosen by the OSF was Higher Blackley in Manchester. Based on their findings, the authors of the report note the rise of 'a particular negative image of white working-class people' in the mass media which is 'most pronounced' in the UK (2014: 62).

Baker et al. 2008; Mautner 2009; Baker and McEnery 2015a, etc.) indicating that such methods are suitable and profitable for linguistic analysis. To date, however, existing work in corpus linguistics and CDA has tended to largely ignore geography.

However, all texts have some (implicit) reference to place insofar as they are constructed in a specific place and time for a given audience. Even large reference corpora, such as the British National Corpus (BNC), which was established to provide a snapshot of British English in the late twentieth century, are fixed in terms of the geographical locations of their texts' authors, publishing houses, and primary audiences. Yet, despite the implicit links between texts and their place of construction, publication, and consumption, corpus linguistics does not always acknowledge the potential role of geography in the analysis of language. The same criticism applies for analysis of explicit mentions of place, such as the occurrence of place-names. Nevertheless, mentions of place influence our understandings of the world: we may associate particular locations with being rich or poor, which may then translate to some areas being understood to be more desirable than others. Locations associated with poverty may also be associated with other factors, including particular types of (low-paid) jobs, the ethnicity of the people who live there, and/or lower life expectancies.

By combining corpus linguistics and CDA with GIS, we add a further dimension to the academic analysis and discussion of place. Thus we follow Cooper and Gregory's (2011: 90) argument that 'there is a move towards using GIS technology to highlight the imbricated relationship between the locatedness of everyday life and the spatialities of cultural practices'. Geographical text analysis has the capacity to aid the critical discourse analyst in facilitating a visual representation of biases evident in texts, as it allows the researcher to map and spatially analyse the use of place in relation to particular themes, such as poverty. To date, GTA has been used in humanities research, particularly in historical demography (Murrieta-Flores et al. 2015; Porter et al. 2015) and in literary studies (Gregory and Donaldson 2016; Donaldson et al. 2017). This book represents one of the first times that this approach has been used to study a modern topic in the social sciences.

Our decision to draw on linguistic data to analyse poverty, as opposed to the other data types noted above, is justified by the argument that language is a primary method of communication which allows us to come to a shared understanding of how the world is structured. Whatever nuances of meaning each reader attaches to the word *poverty*, there are some widespread interpretations that we obtain and reproduce through society and societal norms. Uncovering these norms, and interrogating how they came to represent common sense interpretations of UK poverty, is a valuable empirical endeavour. Our choice to focus on newspaper data stems from the accessibility and ubiquity of such texts. Members of the public are in regular contact with the mass media thus the messages carried have the capacity to reach and influence the opinions of huge audiences.[2] The fact that newspapers report on poverty indicates its social significance as a topic of debate and demonstrates its apparent newsworthiness (see Potts et al. 2015). However, newspapers are not neutral sources of language data; in line with their political leanings, they represent poverty in particular ways, both reflecting and shaping how it is conceptualised by the wider public. For example, if such outlets are shown to (re)produce negative discourses about people in poverty, those consuming the media may be misinformed and/or and may be less likely to support endeavours to eliminate poverty proposed by institutional agents, such as the government, charities, and food banks.

Bednarek (2006: 14) argues that readers are unlikely to assume that a single journalist is responsible for a given article, but rather, they will see the text as an example of an 'institutional voice', understanding the text as part of a larger whole, and 'identify the newspaper (as institution) as the definite, or ultimate sources of what why are reading'. Such sources 'are important objects of study because they further our understanding of how the legitimacy of activities [...] is formulated and contested' (Breit 2010: 622). The social power of these institutional voices is

[2]Bednarek (2006: 12) notes that Britain has more national daily and Sunday newspapers than any other country and that the British are the third biggest buyers of newspapers in the world. She also notes that tabloid papers outsell broadsheets by about four to one and that over 50% of the British population who read newspapers read a national tabloid in comparison with 13% for broadsheets (2006: 13).

measurable in wider society. To take one particular example, despite the fact that UK benefit fraud (a topic closely related to poverty by the mass media) accounted for only 0.8% of benefit expenditure in 2014/15 (DWP 2015), media depictions of benefit claimants paint welfare fraud as a wide-ranging epidemic: in 2012, the *Sun* newspaper unveiled a 'Beat the Cheat' campaign, encouraging its readers to report suspected benefit fraud. Furthermore, research by Ipsos MORI (2013) found that the British public believed 24% of benefits were fraudulently claimed, a figure thirty times higher than factual. Analysing the language used to by the media to discuss UK poverty is thus a worthy research topic.

In the first instance, we set out to identify which place-names are mentioned in relation to poverty in our corpora of two UK national newspapers. Our corpora comprise news and comment articles from the *Daily Mail* and the *Guardian* published between 2010 and 2015 (although the analysis presented herein focuses primarily on the news sections, see Chapter 4 for more details). We establish which place-names occur, and how frequently. We also note those locations which are seldom, if ever mentioned and consider their relative size. We consider whether place-names correlate with particular aspects of poverty discourses, such as unemployment or benefits receipt, and we use GIS software (ArcGIS) to investigate how media representations of place compare to official statistics.

Our analysis of the geographies of poverty in the UK includes a wide variety of place-names. To help guide the reader through these, Fig. 1 shows some of the most significant places referred to in subsequent chapters. The map illustrates that the two newspapers associate many different types of place with poverty. London and the large provincial cities such as Birmingham, Liverpool, Manchester, Newcastle, Belfast and Glasgow are, perhaps, predictable. There are also smaller cities and towns in former industrial areas, such as Merthyr Tydfil in south Wales, the Black Country (consisting of towns such as Wolverhampton and Walsall), Nottingham and Leicester in the Midlands, and Middlesbrough in the north-east of England. Seaside towns such as Margate in Kent and Torquay in Devon also feature, as do port cities such as Bristol, Hull, and Aberdeen. Finally, there are more affluent cities including Oxford, Cambridge, and York. In the course of the book, we will establish how and why these places are associated with poverty by one or both newspapers.

Fig. 1 Places that are frequently referred to in this book

To establish the terms of debate, Chapter 1 reviews how poverty is defined and measured in different disciplines. We consider the proxy measures that are used to estimate poverty rates, such as unemployment and overcrowding, and also review more qualitative approaches to poverty that are based on the lived experiences and access to resources of those living in poverty. The chapter also focuses on the difference between absolute poverty and relative poverty, with UK poverty tending to be conceptualised as the latter. As this book draws together methods and approaches from different disciplines, we have included two chapters which explain the basics of corpus linguistics, CDA, and GIS, in order to make GTA accessible to a range of readers from different fields. Chapter 2 focuses on analytical approaches to large volumes of text using corpus linguistics and CDA. Chapter 3 explores how geography can be modelled computationally using a geographical information system (GIS).

Chapter 4 brings these different analytical techniques together to provide a detailed description of GTA. To provide an exemplar of GTA, this chapter is based around the use of a single search term, the word *poverty*. Having established proof of concept for GTA at such a large scale, we then present a much broader analysis of the geographies associated with poverty in our chosen newspapers, which includes a comparison between the textual data from our corpora and more-established measures of poverty, such as census and worklessness statistics. Chapter 5 describes how corpus linguistics techniques were used to identify a much wider set of search terms that our newspapers associate with poverty. These are grouped under four main themes: employment, money, benefits, and housing. The following two chapters explore the geographies associated with these themes in more detail. Chapter 6 looks at employment and money, while Chapter 7 moves on to benefits and housing. It also briefly compares how the geographies of all four themes in our corpora compare with geographies of poverty as defined using quantitative sources.

Chapter 8 brings all of our poverty-related search terms together to present an overall analysis of the geographies of poverty as represented in our corpora. It focuses on how different areas of the UK are associated with poverty in different, nuanced ways by each newspaper. Taking a critical perspective we demonstrate that the newspapers' choice of place, and what aspects of poverty to focus on, provides supporting evidence for the overarching ideologies that they each endorse. Our extended conclusion draws out the main findings of our analysis and considers what GTA can tell us about representations of poverty. It also addresses some of the broader implications of the methods used and notes the limitations of this exemplar of GTA which should be addressed in future research.

References

Baker, P., & T. McEnery (eds.). 2015. *Corpora and Discourse Studies*. Basingstoke: Palgrave.

Baker, P. 2006. *Using Corpora in Discourse Analysis*. London: Continuum.

Baker, P., C. Gabrielatos, M. KhosraviNik, M. Kryzanowski, T. McEnery, & R. Wodak. 2008. A Useful Methodological Synergy? Combining Critical Discourse Analysis and Corpus Linguistics to Examine Discourses of Refugees and Asylum Seekers in the UK Press. *Discourse and Society* 19 (3): 273–306.

Bednarek, M. 2006. *Evaluation in Media Discourse: Analysis of a Newspaper Corpus*. New York: Continuum.

Breit, E. 2010. On the (Re)construction of Corruption in the Media: A Critical Discursive Approach. *Journal of Business Ethics* 92 (4): 619–635.

Conrad, S. 2002. Corpus Linguistic Approaches for Discourse Analysis. *Annual Review of Applied Linguistics* 22: 75–95.

Cooper, D., & I. Gregory. 2011. Mapping the English Lake District: A Literary GIS. *Transactions of the Institute of British Geographers* 36 (1): 89–108.

Donaldson C., I. N. Gregory, & J. E. Taylor. 2017. Locating the Beautiful, Picturesque, Sublime and Majestic: Spatially Analysing the Application of Aesthetic Terminology in Descriptions of the English Lake District. *Journal of Historical Geography* 56: 43–60.

Gregory, I. N., & C. Donaldson. 2016. Geographical Text Analysis: Digital Cartographies of Lake District Literature. In D. Cooper D., C. Donaldson, & P. Murrieta-Flores (eds.). *Literary Mapping in the Digital Age*. Abingdon: Routledge, pp. 67–87.

Mautner, G. 2009. Checks and Balances: How Corpus Linguistics can Contribute to CDA. In R. Wodak & M. Meyer (eds.). *Methods of Critical Discourse Analysis*. London: Sage, pp 122–143.

Morris, R., & V. Carstairs. 1991. Which Deprivation? A Comparison of Selected Deprivation Indexes. *Journal of Public Health Medicine*: 318–325.

Murrieta-Flores, P., A. Baron A., I. N. Gregory, A. Hardie, & P. Rayson. 2015. Automatically Analysing Large Texts in a GIS Environment: The Registrar General's Reports and Cholera in the Nineteenth Century. *Transactions* in GIS 19: 296–320.

Orpin, D. 2005. Corpus Linguistics and Critical Discourse Analysis: Examining the Ideology of Sleaze. *International Journal of Corpus Linguistics* 10 (1): 37–61.

Porter, C., P. Atkinson, & I. N. Gregory. 2015. Geographical Text Analysis: A New Key to Nineteenth-Century Mortality. *Health and Place* 36: 25–34.

Potts, A., M. Bednarek, & H. Cape. 2015. How can Computer-Based Methods Help Researchers to Investigate News Values in Large Datasets? A Corpus Linguistic Study of the Construction of Newsworthiness in the Reporting on Hurricane Katrina. *Discourse & Communication* 9 (2): 149–172.

1

Defining and Measuring Poverty

Any discussion of poverty and its related discourses must begin with a definition. One positive of taking an interdisciplinary approach to the analysis of poverty is the increase in the pool of potential resources that we can draw upon in defining the term. We must define poverty within the geographical boundaries of the UK and situate our definition within the twenty-first century. Fundamentally, we must question how to measure poverty. The very foundation of this book relies on comparing measurements of poverty and/or deprivation using census data (and its derivatives) with discursive depictions of poverty, using the tools of Geographical Text Analysis (GTA).

Lansley and Mack (2015: 3) argue that '[d]efinitions of poverty matter' because they act as a determinant of 'whether the incomes and living conditions of the poorest in society are acceptable or not'. This chapter discusses some of the many different ways of defining and measuring poverty, both quantitative and qualitative. Section 1.1 considers definitions of poverty and notes that, as there is no undisputed way to measure poverty, any definition (used implicitly and explicitly) likely performs an ideological function. Section 1.2 focuses on attempts to measure poverty both quantitatively and socioculturally,

L. L Paterson and I. N Gregory, *Representations of Poverty and Place*,
https://doi.org/10.1007/978-3-319-93503-4_1

using measures such as census statistics and Carstairs scores. Section 1.3 considers the wider social context within which this research sits, and summarises some of the major trends in discourses of poverty identified in existing research.

1.1 Key Components of Poverty

The *Oxford English* Dictionary's definition of poverty is 'Destitution: The condition of having little or no wealth or few material possessions' (OED 2017). Far from being absolute, references to 'little or no wealth' and 'few' possessions leaves the understanding of poverty somewhat open to interpretation. Following Chambers (2006: 3) it is important to note that 'What poverty is taken to mean depends on who asks the question, how it is understood, and who responds'. Perhaps even more importantly Chambers (2006: 3) notes that 'Our common meanings have all been constructed by us, non-poor people. They reflect our power to make definitions according to our perceptions'. It is therefore important to survey a range of definitions and be aware how the selection of definition(s) will act as a lens through which research is designed and carried out. Furthermore, research must be informed by an awareness of the social structure that facilitate non-poor people's definitions of poverty and which restrict the voices of those in poverty.

In their review of definitions of poverty in the late twentieth and early twenty-first centuries, Misturelli and Heffernan (2008: 670) note that there are seven key aspects of poverty: material, physical, economic, political, social, institutional, and psychological. Whilst they present an overview of developments in definitions of poverty from the 1970s onwards, they note that geographical influences began to appear in the 1980s, with distinctions being made between 'urban' and 'rural poverty' (2008: 674). In the early 2000s, 'concepts of poverty appeared to be moving from defining poverty to defining the poor themselves […] the focus was on grouping the poor into discrete categories often linked to the poverty line' (2008: 679). Yet, they argue that definitions of poverty that employ an in/out dichotomy have been rejected as being too simplistic; the life experiences of people close to either side of a 'poverty line' or threshold economic figure are not automatically dissimilar and, relatedly, those on either side of the line cannot be seen as two homogenous wholes. This is similar to Lee's (1999: 174) argument that poverty thresholds are somewhat arbitrary and are not absolute measures; there will be some people below the poverty line not 'experiencing poverty' and presumably the opposite holds true for those above the line. Yet, despite some inter-decade differences, including fluctuations in the relative weightings of the different elements of poverty, the fact that the seven elements Misturelli and Heffernan identified repeat across their dataset shows that the core of what constitutes poverty appears fairly stable.

Despite this apparent stability, Gordon (2006: 29) argues that 'there is still no official definition of poverty in the UK'. There is an EU definition (established in 1984) which includes 'persons, families and groups of persons whose resources (material, cultural and social) are so limited as to exclude them from the minimum acceptable way of life in the Member State in which they live' (2006: 30). By this definition, poverty is therefore conceptualised as a relative phenomenon, not an absolute state. Gordon (2006: 32) makes a distinction between the definition of poverty and the social realisation(s) of poverty when he suggests that 'Poverty is the lack of resources and deprivation is the consequence of poverty' and suggests that to be poor in Britain, in 'scientific terms', people must have 'both a low income *and* a low standard of living' (2006: 39). Lansley and Mack (2015: 3) note that the Child Poverty Act (2010) uses 60% of median household income as a threshold for measuring poverty, and thus it represents a 'statutory recognition that poverty is relative'.[1]

There is also a recognised definition of *absolute poverty* (see Gordon 2006: 31), endorsed by the United Nations, that references 'a condition characterised by severe deprivation of basic human needs, including food, safe drinking water, sanitation facilities, health, shelter, education,

[1]Lansley and Mack (2015) note this measure is sometimes reported as 60% of average household income (taken to imply the mean), which would make abolishing (child) poverty impossible. However, it is statistically possible for no one to live on a household income less than 60% of the median of the UK's household incomes.

and information' (UN 1995: 57). However, one can be in poverty without being in absolute poverty and, as such, some measures of poverty noted by the UN will be largely irrelevant in countries with systematic clean water supplies, public sanitation facilities, nationalised health provision, and free education. Lansley and Mack (2015: 3), however, argue that foregrounding the extremes of poverty and emphasising 'hunger and homelessness' can be used by powerful institutions 'as a way of underplaying the extent of poverty'. The fact that the UN's definition of *absolute poverty* is not universally applicable emphasises that the geography of poverty is significant; what is considered poverty in one socially-defined location (such as within a country's borders) may not be considered poverty in other locations.

To this end, Gordon (2006: 39) argues that 'low income and low standard of living can only be accurately measured relative to the norms' of individual societies, what he terms *objective poverty*. He proposes that deprivation measures relating to 'personal, physical and mental conditions, local and environmental facilities, social activities and customs, are more suitable for measuring poverty and deprivation than economic measures of consumption expenditure (Gordon 2006: 39). In measuring objective poverty, Gordon (2006: 40) notes that the variables of income and 'standard of living are correlated' and acknowledges that there 'will always be some ambiguities near the margins about whether a person should be defined as "poor" or not'. He suggests, therefore, that 'it is better to conceive the poverty threshold as a band of low income and standard of living rather than as a hard fixed line' (2006: 40).

Despite different interpretations of poverty, its manifestations as relative or absolute, the acceptance/rejection of an in/out dichotomy, and its geographical location, what all the definitions above have in common is an underlying sense that poverty is something which can be observed and scientifically measured. Language about poverty lines, margins, thresholds, standards, minimums, income levels, etc. and yes/no measures such as access to clean water and sanitation, treat poverty as something quantifiable and concrete. The possibility that poverty is unmeasurable is not considered; yet we cannot intrinsically measure poverty as it is an abstract, socially-determined concept. In order to address this, the following section discusses what is actually measured when determining the boundaries of poverty.

1.2 Poverty by Proxy

Measurements of poverty and deprivation in human geography, and specifically in existing research employing GIS (see Chapter 3), tend to be based on quantitative data,[2] including Carstairs scores (Morris and Carstairs 1991), the Index of Local Conditions (Lee 1999),[3] the Townsend Index (Townsend et al. 1988), and Indices of Multiple Deprivation (Noble et al. 2006). All of these indices are calculated using combinations of variables from census data or other statistical indicators, such as unemployment, overcrowded housing, or lack of amenities (see Morgan and Baker 2006; Morris and Carstairs 1991). However, none of these indices actually measure poverty, rather poverty is calculated using quantifiable proxies that are presumed to be symptomatic of poverty. Morgan and Baker (2006: 28) note that deprivation measures, such as Carstairs scores have been 'constructed to act as a proxy for data on personal/household income or wealth which have not routinely been collected in the UK census'.

The data used to calculate Carstairs scores—unemployment, overcrowded housing, lack of car ownership, and low social class—is problematic. In early calculations of Carstairs scores (at least) the unemployment statistics were based on male employment figures only. Wider social factors were also ignored. For example, the ownership of a car does not take into account the fact that cars vary greatly in both their monetary value and level of ownership (people may have company cars, lease their cars, purchase them with finance, own their vehicles outright, etc.) and so the assumption that two households who each have cars will be in some way statistically similar is questionable. Additionally, whilst overcrowding may appear more clear cut, as it measures the ratio

---

[2]See Lee (1999) and Morgan and Baker (2006) for a discussion of statistical measures of deprivation in the UK.

[3]The Index of Local Conditions (see Lee 1999) is based primarily on census data and includes unemployment, poor children, overcrowding, lack of amenities, no car, children in flats, education at 17, income support, low educational qualifications, standardised mortality rates, derelict land, and crime.

of people to rooms in a house, we have to consider political factors too, such as the Removal of the Spare Room Subsidy (Bedroom Tax) implemented by the UK Coalition government in 2013. Government guidelines on Housing Benefit determine that a two-bedroom home with a combined kitchen/living space occupied by an adult couple and two children of the same sex under 16 is appropriate housing. Thus, a definition of overcrowding that is 'more than one person per room' may need to be revisited, as the example given here leads to four people living in effectively three rooms.

Lee (1999: 172) argues that whilst the UK census 'is still the best source for spatial analysis, it is limited for the analysis of poverty or deprivation' because it does not sufficiently cover variables relating to poverty. He suggests that unemployment is used as a de facto measure of poverty (1999: 174) and posits two main problems with using unemployment rates as a single measure of poverty (or indeed any measures 'which use single proxy indicators'). He states that 'it is not possible to read off the whole range of possible circumstances' for individuals or households when using a single measure and he notes that although the relationship between a single measure and other variables may correlate well, nevertheless 'the relationship between any two indicators is far from dichotomous' (1999: 175).

Another proxy measure for poverty that has been used in the social sciences is social class. For example, Dorling et al. (2000) used measures of social class, based on occupation, within local government wards to indicate relative poverty. Here we have a three-part assumption: occupation = social class/economic status = poverty.[4] This is particularly problematic given that definitions of social class are as fluid as definitions of poverty (see Block 2013). Morgan and Baker (2006: 29)

[4]Dorling et al. (2000) estimate levels of poverty by calculating proportions of social class groups within a ward using the midpoint of each social class—assuming a normal distribution—to calculate a poverty index. Using data from Charles Booth's study of London poverty 1889–1903 and the 1991 UK census, their results show that historically, there has not been much change in poverty distribution in London boroughs between the nineteenth and twentieth centuries. They note some areas that have seen lots of immigrant settlement have 'moved down the social scale slightly' whilst others have been through the process of gentrification, but overall 'affluent places have remained affluent and poor places have remained relatively poor' (2000: 1549).

note that the 2001 UK Census included the now widely-used NS-SEC (National Statistics Socio-economic Classification) instead of the previously used 'social class'. However, the NS-SEC still relies predominantly on employment as a measure of socioeconomic status/groupings, and so Lee's (1999) criticisms (noted above) still stand.

Alternative measurements of poverty/deprivation are based on living standards. As such, they 'conceptualise poverty as a combination or series of deprivations, both material and social, such that resources are so seriously below those commandeered by the average individual or household that they are, in effect, excluded from ordinary living patterns, customs and activities' (Lee 1999: 174). Pantazis et al. (2006) discuss the construction and administration of the Poverty and Social Exclusion Survey—a UK-based initiative that was founded on earlier work by Mack and Lansley (1983/85) and the Breadline Britain Survey (see Meinhof and Richardson 1994). By asking members of the British public which possessions and activities they see as necessary to maintain a minimum acceptable standard of living, the aim of these surveys have been to 'try to discover whether there is a public consensus on what is an unacceptable standard of living for Britain' and to find out 'who, if anyone, falls below that standard' (Mack and Lansley 1985: 50 in Pantazis et al. 2006: 89). The results of these surveys have shown that there is a high level of consensus (50% of participants agreeing) across different social demographics (age, class, gender) on what items and social activities are necessary for an acceptable living standard. UK residents without access to three or more of these essentials—which include beds and bedding, a refrigerator, visits to friends/family, contents insurance, carpets in living rooms and bedrooms, television, and a holiday away from home—are deemed to be in poverty.

Updating the Breadline Britain surveys, Lansley and Mack (2015) asked respondents from over two thousand households whether seventy six different items/activities (including 30 measures relating to children) were a necessity in twenty-first century daily life: items tested include living in a damp-free home, possessing items such as curtains and a dining table, eating two meals a day, and attending weddings/funerals. Twenty-six adult items and twenty-four children's items met the 50% threshold for being considered necessities. Whilst Lansley and Mack acknowledge that responses to the tested items were not uniform, they point out that there was a relatively high level of consensus amongst their participants (2015: 25ff.). They note that, in comparison to previous studies with similar methodologies, the composition of this list of necessities has changed over time—a weekly roast dinner, for example, is less likely to be seen as a necessity now due to changes in eating habits, and carpets are less likely to be seen as a necessity due to the popularity of laminate/wooden floors—and they suggest that 'the public accept that minimum living standards need to reflect contemporary and not past styles of living. They believe that needs do not stand outside society as some kind of timeless given' (2015: 18). Thus there is consensus that poverty is not fixed and absolute, but relative (at least in a temporal sense). The items deemed necessities went beyond the basics of food and shelter and included telephones, a leisure activity, and visiting friends.

Lansley and Mack (2015: 26) argue that one of the most controversial items they tested was possession of a television. They suggest that a television, which 'has been a near-universal possession for decades' divided opinion amongst respondents in terms of educational background (71% of people without qualifications deemed it a necessity compared with 43% of those with a degree) and type of occupation (65% of manual workers to 48% of non-manual workers). Lansley and Mack also note a correlation between television ownership being seen as a necessity and restrictions affecting respondents' ability to go out (such as ill health, old age, and lack of income). However, what is telling is that they draw on a single quote from the 1983 survey:

> I watch TV from first thing in the morning till last thing at night, till the television goes off. That's all I've got: to watch television. I can't afford to do other things at all. (Lansley and Mack 2015: 27)

They generalise from this one participant, whom they describe as 'a young lone parent with a nine-month-old baby living in a damp and decaying attic in London' (2015: 27). Here the authors rely heavily on social stereotypes and do not provide sufficient evidence for their statements. Such generalisations run the risk of using individual experiences of poverty to attribute attitudes to a generic, homogenised class or social group. By drawing upon stereotypes Lansley and Mack (2015) use a thirty-year-old quote to characterise the pastimes of a homogenised poor.

Lansley and Mack (2015: 30) argue that their method of defining poverty through public consensus leads to 'a democratically defined standard, free of value judgements by experts, officials or the government' which represents the views of 'all groups in society, young and old, rich and poor, in and out of work – and, perhaps most significantly, across the political spectrum'. At least some of the responses in Lansley and Mack's study will have come from those in poverty, as the survey covered a range of social demographics. Thus, their measure addresses the issue of poverty not being defined by the poor (cf. Chambers 2006). Using their list of necessities, Lansley and Mack tested over five thousand households to estimate levels of poverty across the UK and Northern Ireland. They conclude that whilst there are high levels of deprivation across the UK, rates are higher in 'London, the North-East and North-West of England, the West Midlands, Wales and Northern Ireland, and slightly lower in Scotland and southern and eastern England (excluding London)' (Lansley and Mack 2015: 51). However, despite this regional variation, they argue that people who do not possess three of the household essentials 'form a distinct group' (even though they might have different combinations of missing essentials) and, furthermore, that the deprivation experienced by this group leads to 'severely restricted lifestyles and opportunities' (2015: 50). However, to homogenise those without three necessities is to ignore potential regional and intersectional differences, such as house prices, the variable cost of living, employment rates and the number of available jobs available, and the health and educational profiles of different areas. As the following analysis demonstrates, a consideration of place in conjunction with poverty can highlight different lived experiences of poverty and different economic stressors that vary according to location.

1.3 Conceptualisations of Poverty and the Poor

To conclude this chapter we focus on the language surrounding poverty, beginning with Kress' (1994: 29) observation that, despite its abstract nature, poverty can be a grammatical agent and act upon its subject: 'poverty can drive us into despair, poverty causes the breakup of families, and so on, as the media tell us every day'. Kress (1994: 28) argues that poverty 'is something that you are *in*' rather than something that you possess and, furthermore, the 'place that you are *in* when you are in poverty is an abstract place, like despair [...] a kind of mental place, an emotional state of affairs'. The use of an abstract concept as an agent acts to obscure any human input which could be (in)directly responsible for individuals experiencing poverty and performs an ideological function insofar as the structural inequality which could be to blame for (mass) poverty is not explicitly expressed. Further, due to its abstract nature, poverty is difficult to oppose.

Kress also argues that the term poverty 'is something with which you are afflicted' and is 'a characteristic which acts as a description of a person, a classification' (1994: 29). By conceptualising poverty as a label for a particular group of people we can begin to see how its use could be socially powerful; to label someone as 'poor' or 'in poverty' is to imbue them with a set of (negatively-loaded) characteristics that, presumably, they cannot escape. Indeed, the small number of reports of people escaping poverty that we find in our corpora (see Chapter 4) is evidence of the perceived rarity of moving out of poverty, and goes someway to explaining the apparent newsworthiness of such stories. Although it is possible to deny that one is in poverty, any denials are determined in the first instance by whether the person who has been labelled has a voice to protest. In media discourse those who are labelled as 'poor' tend not to have the right of reply.[5]

[5]Jo (2013: 516) notes how Lister's (2004: 7) definition of poverty includes 'shameful and corrosive social relation[s] ...characterized by a lack of voice, disrespect, humiliation and reduced dignity and self-esteem'.

In a US context, Lorenzo-Dus and Marsh (2012: 289) analysed two US National Security Strategy reports and found that poverty was also referred to through metaphor, particularly metaphors relating to disease. This is a linguistic choice where depicting 'poverty as an illness means classifying it as a biological entity—as a phenomenon from the natural, rather than the social, world'. Furthermore, they note that this characterisation of poverty fits with Kress' (1994) discussion of the passivity of poverty as a noun, as 'natural phenomena obey natural forces, over which societies ultimately have little control' (2012: 289). However, Gordon (2011, cited in Lansley and Mack 2015: 73) argues that poverty 'is not like syphilis or a biblical curse across a generation—poverty is not a disease and it cannot be caught and all credible evidence shows that it is not "transmitted" to children by their parents' genes or culture'.

The ideology of poverty as generational was expressed in the 'Troubled Families' strategy of the UK coalition government, which was launched in 2011 and is set to run to 2020. Lansley and Mack (2015: 67) argue that families in disadvantaged households were 'redefined by ministers first into families that are "troubled", and then into families that *are* or *cause* trouble'. Unlike Kress' analysis of poverty, such conceptualisations presuppose that the poor are somehow responsible for and/or complicit in their own poverty. Similar arguments can be found (implied) in media reports about benefit fraud or non-working parents with large numbers of children.[6] Relatedly, Lansley and Mack (2015: 147) argue that particular mass media outlets report that 'there are deprived areas of the UK with a "Benefits Street" culture based on generations of families choosing a life on benefits' but they note that such claims do 'not match the evidence', citing research by the Joseph Rowntree Foundation which found no families in high unemployment

[6]Lansley and Mack (2015: 147) claim the 'frequency with which the tabloid press and some television programmes feature very large families living on benefits' is disproportionate to reality, as reports from the DWP state that there were 'only 180 claiming households with ten or more children in 2010' and 91% of households claiming benefits 'have three or fewer children, and only one percent have six or more'.

areas in Middlesbrough and Glasgow where multiple generations had never worked. Nevertheless, negative evaluations of those in poverty, and the related assumptions about the roles people have played in their own poverty, carry social weight.

Pantazis et al. (2006), for example, show awareness of wider social characterisations of the poor. They note McKay's (2004) argument that 'families who cannot afford necessities often possess a number of non-necessities' and as a result 'they have atypical preferences and choose to spend their money on "luxuries" not "necessities"' (Pantazis et al. 2006: 114). They argue that McKay does not acknowledge that some 'luxuries' may have been purchased before the onset of poverty, but in any case, 'as deprivation increases, the average number of non-necessities a respondent possesses decreases' (2006: 114), showing that McKay's criticism is not realised in actuality. However, the authors do not consider in detail McKay's additional claim that 'such families may be classified as poor using deprivation indicators, when it might be more accurate to say that their consumption preferences deviate from the average' (McKay 2004: 220 cited in Pantazis et al. 2006: 114). What McKay is tapping into here is the notion of a 'flawed consumer': the ideology that the poor are responsible for their own fate because they are unable to manage money and are 'inadequate [...] consumers' (Bauman 2004: 38). McKay's use of the term 'atypical preferences' presents those who are poor as somehow anomalous to the wider society in which they live. Although McKay does not use the term flawed consumer, this ideological assumption can be linked to blaming the poor for their own poverty—they are just spending their money wrongly—and does not seek to address wider social concerns, such as why people may spend money on taboo or negatively-stereotyped items such as televisions (see above), cheap frozen food, and cigarettes.[7]

Acknowledging that poverty is more than just economic circumstance, Jo (2013: 519) focuses on how shame in poverty is both externally influenced and internally experienced and sheds light on the

[7] See Paterson et al. (2017) for a discussion of how such items are used as indexical markers deployed to negatively evaluate members of the working classes.

explicit role of the wider society'. She argues that the relationship between poverty and shame is constructed 'from the dominant discourse'—i.e. through language and cultural norms which are 'collectively assembled by multiple institutions which are governed by those with power and influence' (Jo 2013: 522). Such an interpretation of how discourses of poverty are utilised supports her claim that poverty 'cannot be fully interpreted outside of the specific social context in which it occurs' (Jo 2013: 519). It is clear then, that poverty is more than a statistical measure of income or consumer expenditure. Fukuda-Parr (2006: 7) explicitly notes that poverty relates to 'public policy' and 'is now widely considered to be a multidimensional problem' which is manifest in 'a complex set of deprivations'. She argues that twenty-first century definitions of poverty 'have refocused the concept of poverty as a human condition that reflects failures in many dimensions of human life' which include not only long-held indexes of poverty such as homelessness, unemployment, and poor health, but also include 'powerlessness and victimisation, and social injustice' (Fukuda-Parr 2006: 7). However, whilst including such elements within a definition of poverty serve to illustrate its multidimensionality, Fukuda-Parr does not give any examples of how, or indeed if (relative) poverty could actually be measured.

1.4 Summary

One of the aims of this book is to compare the more traditional (quantitative) calculations of poverty with the discursive construction of poverty in the UK press. To this end, we compare government-endorsed statistics, such as census data and unemployment figures, to the location and representations of poverty present in our two corpora (see Chapter 4). Each type of data presents a form of reality—it expresses a discourse of poverty in geographical space—but neither the statistics nor the discursive representation capture the full complexity of poverty. Lorenzo-Dus and Marsh argue that poverty 'defies easy definition', includes a multitude of factors and is a 'social, political and/or security issue' with links to 'social exclusion and discrimination, economic migration, and terrorism and (inter)national insecurity' (2012: 275). They note that poverty 'is (re)produced through discourse practices, most of which are enacted by groups with direct access to social, cultural and political power' (Lorenzo-Dus and Marsh 2012: 275).[8] We interrogate just how these different statistical and discursive depictions of poverty correlate (or diverge) with an aim of uncovering the ideologies expressed in discourses of poverty.

As poverty is multifaceted, we do not wish to provide a formal definition. Rather, we take a data-led approach to our corpora and analysis, with the aim of investigating how the two newspapers conceptualise poverty and how they locate it in space, in order to compare these media representations of poverty with statistical datasets. In accepting that poverty can be realised in different ways, we take a holistic approach to understanding it and conceptualise it as a multifaceted social phenomenon. For example, we note Galbraith's (1958) claim that poverty occurs when people's 'income, even if adequate for survival, falls markedly behind their community' (cited in Lansley and Mack 2015: 14), but we emphasise that an absence of adequate finances is not whole story; ideologies of poverty stretch beyond mere economics. Indeed, Galbraith notes that it is community norms which determine 'the necessary minimum for decency' (cited in Lansley and Mack 2015: 14), and this leads to the conclusion that to conceptualise someone as being in poverty is, at least in part, to make a social judgement. Galbraith goes even further by suggesting that, because of such social judgements, people in poverty are 'degraded' insofar as they are conceptualised as living beyond 'the grades or categories which the community regards as acceptable' (cited in Lansley and Mack 2015: 14). These social judgements are expressed in public policy, in media depictions of the poor, and, most importantly for the present work, through language.

[8]Furthermore, Lorenzo-Dus and Marsh (2012: 277) note that discourse analysis undertaken in South America has shown that there is 'a tendency in political and media elite discourses to quantify poverty, typically through statistics that deprive those being thus defied of their individual identity' alongside the 'construction of "the poor" as passive, indolent and immoral'.

The prevalent themes discussed in Sect. 1.3 demonstrate some of the most prominent attitudes to those experiencing poverty. There is also a growing body of research which considers how the mass media (and the public who engage with it) evaluate the poor and the working classes in twenty-first century Britain. For example, in their analysis of public responses to the television programme *Benefits Street*, Paterson et al. (2017) found that members of the public drew on stereotypes of working class identities and accepted the media's (implicit) negative evaluation of particular activities and cultural norms, such as the consumption of alcohol/tobacco. The use of similar stereotypes was also found in van der Bom et al.'s (2018) analysis of audience response to the second series of *Benefits Street*. They found that the poor were homogenised, insofar as they were understood to look the same, talk the same, and value the same practices (some of which were deviant behaviours associated with crime and low morals). These findings correlate well with Biressi's (2011) consideration of what we would term poverty porn programming, and Skeggs and Wood's (2011) collection focusing on how social class is depicted on reality television.

Similarly, Bennett (2012) analysed *chavspeak*—the language associated with working class identities in texts such as 'chav dictionaries', and guides on how to speak chav. He concludes that by characterising chavs (and arguably all working-class people) linguistically 'language ideologies concerning the incorrectness of the non-standard and the inarticulacy of the poor are implicated in broader social ideological trends, discourses about not only the kinds of language that people use, but the kinds of people that exist in British society' (2012: 21). This homogenising notion that the poor constitute a particular kind of person taps into neoliberalism—insofar as people are considered to be responsible for their own fate—and related characterisations of the deserving and undeserving poor (Katz 2013). Although the deserving/undeserving poor distinction is considered by some to be somewhat old fashioned, it does seem able to account for certain media representations of poverty, especially when benefits receipt is the primary focus of media texts.

Combined, this body of research points towards an understanding of poverty that draws upon Bourdieu's (1986, reprinted 2010) notions of social, economic, and cultural capital, insofar as poverty relates to people's economic resources (how much money they have, where that money comes from, and how they spend that money), their social resources (whether they are employed, if they have access to education, adequate health care, etc.), and cultural resources (their hobbies, consumer habits, and local network norms). Whilst there is evaluation of the poor in the mass media along these lines—van der Bom et al. (2018) found that the clothing people wore on the second series of *Benefits Street* was a primary site for critical evaluation, and there were related links to flawed consumerism—there appears to be less acceptance of the macro-structural constraints on these forms of capital, such as low wages, changes to government benefits (such as the Welfare Reform Bill), the geographical location of available jobs, access to adequate transport links, etc.

Our investigation of media discourses on a large scale, using our two multi-million word corpora, focuses on the nuances of how different aspects of poverty are deployed in relation to geography. In the two chapters which follow, we introduce readers unfamiliar to corpus linguistics, critical discourse analysis, and GIS to the fundamentals of our chosen methods. For those who are already familiar with one or more of these methods and their related techniques, Chapters 2 and 3 may not be necessary. We pick up our analysis of discourses of poverty and place in Chapter 4, which demonstrates how the combination of linguistics and geography—in the form of GTA—can illuminate an as-yet-untapped aspect of poverty discourses by comparing the locations of poverty expressed by statistical measures with those referenced in media texts.

References

Bauman, Z. 2004. *Work, Consumerism and the New Poor.* Buckingham: Open University Press.

Bennett, J. 2012. 'And What Comes Out May Be a Kind of Screeching': The Stylisation of Chavspeak in Contemporary Britain. *Journal of Sociolinguistics* 16 (1): 5–27.

Biressi, A. 2011. 'The Virtuous Circle': Social Entrepreneurship and Welfare Programming in the UK. In H. Wood & B. Skeggs (eds.). *Reality Television and Class.* London: British Film Institute/Palgrave Macmillan, pp. 144–155.

Block, D. 2013. *Social Class in Applied Linguistics.* London: Routledge.

Bourdieu, P. 1986/2010. The Forms of Capital. In I. Szeman & T. Kaposy (eds.). *Cultural Theory: An Anthology.* Oxford: Wiley Blackwell, pp. 81–93.

Chambers, R. 2006. What is Poverty? Who Asks? Who Answers? Poverty in Focus. International Poverty Centre: United Nations Development Programme. http://www.ipc-undp.org/pub/IPCPovertyInFocus9.pdf. Accessed 23/9/2015.

Dorling, D., R. Mitchell, M. Shaw, S. Orford, & G. Davey Smith. 2000. The Ghost of Christmas Past: Health Effects of Poverty in London in 1896 and 1991. *British Medical Journal* 321: 1547–1551.

Fukuda-Parr, S. 2006. The Human Poverty Index: A Multidimensional Measure. *Poverty in Focus.* International Poverty Centre: United Nations Development Programme. Online. http://www.ipc-undp.org/pub/IPCPovertyInFocus9.pdf. Accessed 11/11/2015.

Galbraith, J. K. 1958. *The Affluent Society.* London: Penguin.

Gordon, D. 2006. The Concept and Measurement of Poverty. In C. Pantazis, D. Gordon, & R. Levitas (eds.). *Poverty and Social Exclusion in Britain.* Bristol: Policy Press, pp. 29–70.

Gordon, D. 2011. Consultation Response: Social Mobility and the Child Poverty Review. *Policy Response Series* 2, PSE 2011, pp. 4–5. http://www.poverty.ac.uk/pse-research/pse-uk/policy-response.

Jo, Y. N. 2013. Psycho-social Dimensions of Poverty: When Poverty Becomes Shameful. *Critical Social Policy* 33 (3): 514–531.

Katz, M. B. 2013. *The Undeserving Poor* (second edition). Oxford: Oxford University Press.

Kress, G. 1994. Text and Grammar as Interpretation. In U. Meinhof & K. Richardson (eds). *Text, Discourse and Context: Representations of Poverty in Britain.* London: Longman, pp. 24–47.

Lansley, S., & J. Mack. 2015. *Breadline Britain: The Rise of Mass Poverty.* London: Oneworld.

Lee, P. 1999. Where are the Deprived? Measuring Deprivation in Cities and Regions. In D. Dorling & S. Simpson (eds.). *Statistics in Society.* London: Arnold, pp. 172–180.

Lister, R. 2004. *Poverty.* Cambridge: Polity Press.

Lorenzo-Dus, N., & S. Marsh. 2012. Bridging the Gap: Interdisciplinary Insights into the Securitization of Poverty. *Discourse and Society* 23 (3): 274–296.

Mack, J., & S. Lansley. 1985. How Poor is too Poor? Defining Poverty. In J. Mack & S. Lansley (eds.). *Poor Britain.* London: George Allen & Unwin.

McKay, S. 2004. Poverty or Preference: What Do 'Consensual Deprivation Indicators' Really Measure? *Fiscal Studies* 25 (2): 201–223.
Meinhof, U. H., & K. Richardson (eds). 1994. *Text, Discourse and Context: Representations of Poverty in Britain*. London: Longman.
Misturelli, F., & C. Heffernan. 2008. What is Poverty? A Diachronic Exploration of the Discourse on Poverty from the 1970s to the 2000s. *The European Journal of Development Research* 20 (4): 666–684.
Morgan, O., & A. Baker. 2006. Measuring Deprivation in England and Wales Using 2001 Carstairs Scores. *Health Statistics Quarterly* 31: 28–33.
Morris, R., & V. Carstairs. 1991. Which Deprivation? A Comparison of Selected Deprivation Indexes. *Journal of Public Health Medicine* 13(4): 318–325.
Noble, M., G. Wright, G. Smith, & C. Dibben. 2006. Measuring Multiple Deprivation at the Small-Area Level. *Environment and Planning A* 38: 169–185.
OED. 2017. poverty, n. OED Online. www.oed.com/view/Entry/149126. Accessed 02/11/2017.
Pantazis, C., D. Gordon, & P. Townsend. 2006. The Necessities of Life. In C. Pantazis, D. Gordon, & R. Levitas (eds.). *Poverty and Social Exclusion in Britain*. Bristol: Policy Press, pp. 89–122.
Paterson, L. L., L. Coffey-Glover, & D. Peplow. 2016. Negotiating Stance Within Discourses of Class: Reactions to *Benefits Street*. *Discourse & Society* 27 (2): 195–214.
Paterson, L. L., D. Peplow, & K. Grainger. 2017. Does Money Talk Equal Class Talk? Audience Responses to Poverty Porn in Relation to Money and Debt. In A. Mooney & E. Sifaki (eds.). *The Language of Money and Debt: An Interdisciplinary Approach*. Basingstoke: Palgrave, pp. 205–232.
Skeggs, B., & H. Wood (eds.). 2011. *Reality Television and Class*. London: British Film Institute/Palgrave Macmillan.
Townsend, P., P. Phillimore, & A. Beattie. 1988. *Health and Deprivation: Inequality and the North*. London: Routledge.
UN. 1995. *The Copenhagen Declaration and Programme of Action. World Summit for Social Development, 6–12 March 1995*. New York: United Nations.
van der Bom, I., L. L. Paterson, K. Grainger, & D. Peplow. 2018. 'It's Not the Fact They Claim Benefits but Their Useless, Lazy, Drug Taking Lifestyles We Despise': Analysing Audience Responses to Benefits Street Using Live Tweets. *Discourse, Context & Media* 21: 36–45.

2
Corpus Linguistics, Critical Discourse Analysis, and Poverty

The purpose of this chapter and the one that follows is to introduce readers unfamiliar with linguistic and/or geography-based approaches to poverty to the tools that we have chosen to use. The chapter begins with an overview of corpus linguistics, what it is (the systematic, computationally-aided analysis of large bodies of texts using specialist software) and what assumptions corpus analysis makes about language. Section 2.1 also describes some of the tools associated with corpus analysis, with illustrative examples. Section 2.2 introduces and defines what we mean when we use the term *discourse* and, leading on from this, we introduce the core principles of critical discourse analysis (CDA) in Sect 2.3. The final section of this chapter considers the benefits of combining corpus linguistics and CDA for the analysis of social phenomena, before leading into a consideration of the geographical aspects of our analysis of poverty in Chapter 3.

L. L Paterson and I. N Gregory, *Representations of Poverty and Place*,
https://doi.org/10.1007/978-3-319-93503-4_2

2.1 Introducing Corpus Linguistics

Corpus linguistics centres on the systematic computational analysis of large bodies of electronically held texts—known as corpora—which are taken to be representative of a particular text type, genre, or language variety. The term *corpus linguistics* can be used to refer to a method of analysis, but also represents a methodology which assumes particular characteristics about language. The most basic definition of a corpus is that it is 'simply a collection of texts' (McCarthy and Carter 2004: 147), which have particular characteristics in common. For example, texts could be all of the same type, publication date, mode (spoken/written/signed), topic, or language variety. Tognini-Bonelli (2001: 2) stipulates that to define a dataset as a corpus it must have been created with the express purpose of being 'used for linguistic analysis'. Thus, a random selection of texts, collected somewhat haphazardly, cannot constitute a corpus. This book utilises two corpora of UK newspaper texts, each of which comprises written British English in the form of news articles from national sources. The two sources we have chosen to analyse are the *Guardian* and the *Daily Mail* and our two corpora total almost four hundred million words. For details of corpus construction, see Chapter 4.

The method of corpus linguistics relates to the systematic application of particular corpus tools, such as frequency counts, collocation, and concordance analysis, many of which are explained below. In a methodological sense, corpus linguistics works with some basic assumptions about language. The ethos behind corpus linguistics is that, by utilising the processing power of computers and specialist corpus software, the researcher can work with many more texts than would be feasible if undertaking a manual analysis. Providing that a corpus can be said to be representative of its designated text type or language variety, analysing many texts simultaneously allows the researcher to spot patterns that occur beyond the scope of manual analysis. The empirical basis of corpus linguistics is founded upon the idea that a corpus will be able to indicate linguistic norms for a more generalisable whole. Biber et al. (1994: 171) argue that this empirical foundation is what 'allows us to test assumptions [or hypotheses] about language use against patterns found in naturally occurring discourse'. Especially where assumptions about language and corpus data are found to be in conflict, it is imperative that any claims made about the results of corpus analyses be applicable to more than just the corpus itself. The analysis of large bodies of texts can provide robust indications that linguistic patterns—in this case relating to the discussion of UK poverty—repeat across a large dataset and represent the systematic characterisation and evaluation of a particular social issue across wider society.

Showing that a linguistic feature or specific use of language is generalisable is a key goal of using corpora for language analysis, and Stubbs (2001: 168) notes that multiple occurrences of a phenomenon in a corpus show 'that meanings [and/or usage] are not personal and idiosyncratic' but rather, representative of wider language use. This supports Kennedy's (1998: 4) stance that not only do corpora provide means for 'identifying the elements and structural patterns which make up the systems we use in a language', they also aid in 'mapping out our use of these systems'. Thus, a corpus analysis of the language surrounding the term *poverty* may indicate trends in how this phenomenon is conceptualised in UK media discourse. For example, the terms *child* and *fuel* are the top two L1 collocates—words occurring immediately to the left of *poverty*—in our *Daily Mail* corpus. This finding suggests that these two particular aspects of poverty—*child poverty* and *fuel poverty*—are considered to be more important than *international poverty* (which occurs 166th in the L1 collocate list). Similarly, in the *Guardian* corpus, the top L1 collocates of *poverty* are also *child* and *fuel* (with *international* occurring in 151st place), suggesting that the key elements of how poverty is represented in the mass media may be similar across our chosen sources.

This simple example begins to illustrate that corpora can be used at all levels of linguistic analysis, from the word (or even morpheme—the smallest contrastive unit of meaning) upwards. Indeed, some of the simplest calculations that corpus software can perform is to count the frequencies of each word that occurs in a given corpus. Such counts can be used, along with other corpus tools (explained below), to compile dictionaries of the language under investigation (Longman and

Macmillan produce dictionaries this way). Corpus linguistics can also be used interdisciplinarily to address social issues; the ESRC Centre for Corpus Approaches to Social Science (CASS) specialises in stretching the boundaries of corpus linguistics (http://cass.lancs.ac.uk/).

However, corpus linguistics (as a method and methodology) is not without criticism. One popular opposition is the claim that corpus analysis provides (only) quantitative data. Such criticism is underpinned by the notion that counting linguistic features is no match for their close analysis: showing that a phrase occurs twenty times cannot tell you how that phrase is used. Relatedly, those opposing corpus data may argue that examples taken from a corpus are decontextualised and thus the implications of the use of particular linguistic features go unanalysed. However, there is simply no reason why corpus analysis cannot also provide qualitative data. Research combining corpus linguistics with discourse analysis—of which this book is an example—represents a method of analytical triangulation which is continuing to grow in popularity (Sect 2.4). McCarthy and Carter (2004: 148) claim that 'linguists have begun to see the value' of using corpora to see if 'local insights' based on individual texts can be generalised across texts 'from similar contexts'. Additionally, Mautner (2007: 54) notes that the 'awareness' of using corpora to generate qualitative data 'has been increasing, over the past ten years or so' and now corpora may be used 'for uncovering relationships between language and the social'.

Having established the core concepts of corpus linguistics, understanding the ethos underpinning such analyses is only the first step. Corpus analysis is performed with specialist software and a suite of tools designed to aid the researcher in searching large bodies of texts. We have used corpus-software CQPweb (Hardie 2012), but there are other pieces of software available (both commercial and free-to-use).

One of the most basic calculations corpus software can perform is the generation of **frequency lists**. In its essence a frequency list is an alphabetical list of each word in the corpus with information about how many times that word occurs. (Note the term 'word' is used here for simplicity, a frequency list can also give information about punctuation, numbers, and other characters.) They can also contain information about how many texts in a corpus the word appears in (the word's

distribution across the corpus). However, whilst calculating frequency may appear simple, consideration must be given to complex issues such as what constitutes a word. Decisions have to be made about whether to treat contractions, such as *don't* and *haven't*, as one word or two. Similar questions arise in relation to compound nouns, such as *hair brush*, *hair-brush*, and *hairbrush*, which may occur in similar, but different forms across a corpus, and differences in spelling also need to be considered, especially if a corpus contains different language varieties. As frequency lists are used as the basis for other corpus calculations (keywords, dispersion plots, etc.) the choices made when generating them have the capacity to influence results further on in the analysis.[1]

Using frequency lists as a basis, **keywords** can be generated. A positive keyword (usually known just as a 'keyword') is a word that is statistically more likely to occur in the corpus under analysis than in comparable general language. A negative keyword is a word which occurs statistically less frequency in the corpus than would be expected based on its occurrence in general language. To generate a list of keywords, the frequency list of a corpus is compared to the frequency list of a reference corpus. A reference corpus is designed to be representative of a particular language variety. Keyword lists are useful for determining which topics are dominant in your corpus. Here we modify the concept of keywords to facilitate co-text analysis as explained in Chapter 4.

To measure the relationship between words, corpus linguists can used **collocation**. Collocations occur 'when a word regularly appears near another word, and the relationship is statistically significant in some way' (Baker 2006: 95–96). They are important because the meaning of a word is influenced by the other words around it and any repeated and/or consistent collocations may be significant. For example, in the *Guardian* corpus, the top twenty collocates of *poverty* include items such as *relative* and *absolute*, which indicate that poverty is a measurable concept, alongside *child* and *fuel* (as discussed above), and *unemployment*

[1]Furthermore, frequency lists can also be lemmatised, which means that all forms of a word (e.g. *swim, swam, swum, swimming*) are treated as part of one whole, rather than as separate items in the corpus.

and *in-work*, which suggest that employment and poverty are linked concepts in UK media texts. Similarly, for the *Daily Mail*, collocates such as *abject, relative, rate*, and *grinding* also suggest that poverty can be measured, but there is less indication that the *Daily Mail* presents poverty as directly linked to working people.

In order to calculate the statistical value of a collocation Baker et al. (2008: 279) note that three pieces of information are needed: 'the frequency of the node [the target word that you're investigating], the frequency of the collocates, and the frequency of the collocation'.[2] Decisions must be made about how close two words need to be to each other in discourse to constitute a pattern. There is a stronger link between words that are immediate collocates—words occurring side-by-side—than if the two words are only loosely collocated, such as they occur in the same paragraph. Collocates tend to be grouped semantically or grammatically to facilitate further analysis. However, it is important not only to spot the patterns in collocates, but also to note collocates which do not appear to fit with the others.

Moving towards more qualitative data, **concordance lines** are alphabetically ordered lists of all occurrences of a given search term in a corpus within their immediate co-text (i.e. circa ten words either side). Concordance lists are extremely useful in corpus analysis as all instances of a search term can be sorted in terms of their surrounding text, which makes it easier to see repeated patterns. Figure 2.1 shows a sample of concordance lines for the search term *and poverty* in the 2015 section of the *Guardian* corpus.

Analysing what repeated concepts are linked to poverty through the use of the coordinating conjunction *and* gives an indication as to how poverty is presented in a wider context. For example, in the ten concordance lines given here, there are five references to food (*food banks, food blogger, food, dietary*, and *hunger*), and five references to money (*benefits, income, tax, minimum wage*), but the two concepts do not seem to

[2]Collocations can be measured using different statistical calculations, such as log-likelihood and mutual information (a calculation based on how often a word occurs and how often that word occurs with the target node). For more information on corpus statistics, see Brezina (2018).

prominent in the coming months and years . Yes , food **banks**	and poverty	pay are terrible blights , but they affect only a relatively small
all knowledge of the claims against her . Frances Perraudin Food **blogger**	and poverty	campaigner Jack Monroe has joined the Green party , less than a
intersecting instead with multiple risk factors that increase in line with **deprivation**	and poverty	. Paediatric health experts point out infant deaths can be avoided through
last nine years . The report by the Fabian Commission on **Food**	and Poverty	said : " While health and dietary breakthroughs in schools during the
the benefit cap] is certain to be an increase in **homelessness**	and poverty	. " Shelter , the housing charity , said the benefit cap
government 's benefit cap plans threaten at least 100,000 households with **homelessness**	and poverty	, research finds . The cap , introduced by the coalition in
children across the world who are not in school because of **hunger**	and poverty	. " In many ways , I feel we are just beginning
analyses official statistics to examine key trends in living standards , **inequality**	and poverty	. It found that while income inequality barely changed across social groups
for a decent rise in the minimum wage . Levels of **inequality**	and poverty	will also by determined by decisions on tax and social security .
gone into reverse , potentially leading to extremist , nationalism , **intolerance**	and poverty	for the vast majority , would we be too embarrassed to mention

Fig. 2.1 Sample concordances for *and poverty* in the *Guardian* (2015)

overlap (notwithstanding the term *food banks*) as they do not occur in the same concordance lines. The separation of *poverty and food* from *poverty and money* could be an element of media representations of poverty worthy of analysis. Indeed, to support or refute such findings, more concordance lines would need to be analysed. To perform discourse analysis on concordance lines, one must look for overarching patterns, but complement this with a focus on individual examples to see how these patters come about. Once all patterns in the data have been established, analysis of those concordance lines that do not fit a pattern should take place, with an aim of investigating why they might not include particular keywords or support particular discourses (see Baker 2006: 92).

The final corpus tool to be discussed here is a suite of resources known as **taggers**. The purpose of a tagger is to add an additional level of information to texts in a corpus. For example, part-of-speech (POS) taggers assign each word in a corpus a grammatical tag (such as singular noun, personal pronoun, verb, etc.). Taggers can also work above the level of the word, marking boundaries between sentences or other grammatical units. Furthermore, semantic taggers can assign elements of a text into pre-defined categories relating to semantic fields, grouping together like terms. Such taggers are particularly useful when analysing discourse and/or when focusing on key themes. For example, Paterson et al. (2017) used the USAS semantic tagger provided by Wmatrix (Rayson 2008) to analyse the semantic field of money and commerce in focus group transcripts. They used the corpus software to group together references to money that basic corpus query searches would have missed (for example, their results included 'down and outs', and 'well to do' as well as the expected 'poor' and 'banker').

Whilst the selection of corpus tools will depend somewhat on the research at hand, this overview acts to initiate those who have little-to-no experience of corpus linguistics with some of the tools that researchers performing corpus analyses have at their disposal. However, corpus methods of analysis are only one part of our approach to discourses of poverty. The following section includes a definition of how we use the term *discourse* and provides a brief overview of CDA—an interdisciplinary field of study which interrogates the relationship between language and societal power.

2.2 Defining Discourse

The term *discourse* is used to mean many things both in everyday life and within linguistics. Baker and McEnery (2015: 4) go so far as to suggest that the term 'can be an excluding shibboleth which does little to make academic research accessible or relevant to people who do not work or study in the social sciences'. Discourse can refer simply to a stretch of text that is either spoken or written; in this sense it is being used as a more formal term for *text* but the two may be used interchangeably. In this book we make the distinction between *discourse* and *text*; the term *text* is used to denote examples of written British English that take the form of newspaper articles from the *Daily Mail* and the *Guardian*. *Text* is thus used here as a neutral label for stretches of language, words, sentences, paragraphs, headlines, etc. which constitute a definable whole. In this instance, a text from the *Guardian* constitutes a piece of written language with a headline, sometimes a byline, a lead-in paragraph, and a body text. In contrast, we use *discourse*, as discussed towards the end of this section, to describe how language encodes, reflects, (re)produces, and challenges social norms.

The term discourse can also be used to refer to linked ideas or overarching concepts, sometimes represented by labels such as educational discourse, political discourse, religious discourse, and academic discourse. Each of these terms refers to a fairly stable (but somewhat malleable) structuring of ideas and topics around a central theme. Used in this sense, a discourse of religion, for example, is likely to include terms such as *holy, priest, church, synagogue, Muslim, Sabbath, god*, etc. Educational discourses are likely to express idea that all children should attend school, study core subjects, such as maths, English, and science, and are also likely to promote the positive aspects of education. The dominance of such educational discourses are likely to lead to mass social agreement and the acceptance of the UK (or other) school system as the common sense status quo. The establishment and deployment of such discourses can act as a window on the social context surrounding a text and can allow text authors to invoke particular (political) evaluations of a given topic.

However, such discourses are not fixed. For example, one realisation of poverty discourse could relate to starvation, homelessness, poor sanitation, disease, and death, whist other poverty discourses could include associations with government benefits, unemployment, laziness, flawed consumerism, etc. The type of discourse evoked will depend on the context, and, as such, discourses are impossible to document in their entirety. This interpretation of *discourse* is important for the present study as it begins to show the importance of how people use language to represent particular events, conditions, people, etc. If a particular poverty discourse can become entrenched within a given society then the unequal distribution of resources that can lead to poverty can come to be seen as common sense, and those who the discourse benefits/impedes may become invisible. Thus, the use of particular discourses, and their endorsement at the institutional level (government, schools, the mass media) can become powerful in terms of Gramsci's *hegemony* (Wodak and Meyer 2009: 8)—or oppression by consent. From a CDA perspective (see Sect 2.3), if the status quo is not systematically challenged, and is accepted as common sense, the social systems implicated in the (re) production of poverty shall remain undisturbed and be replicated by members of society, who are complicit in the reproduction of such poverty discourses.

Altheide (2000: 287) argues that 'when symbols are pervasive they both reflect and contribute to frames and discourse for subsequent meaning configuration'. Thus the representation of particular narratives of poverty and their location in particular places by the mass media may impact on future depictions of the poor and have wider social and political ramifications, such as being used to influence/justify changes in government policy. For example, there is evidence that once a place is poor, it will remain so; Gregory (2009) showed that places in the UK that were poor 100 years ago still tend to be poor today, and Dorling et al. (2000) showed that between 1889 and 1991 there was very little change to the relative poverty rates of different London boroughs. As a result of their association with poverty, poor places may gain bad reputations as areas where opportunity is limited, and this may impact upon the economic profile of an area or the social evaluations of people who live there (see McKenzie 2015 for an ethnographic approach to life in poor communities).

Altheide takes the position that '[t]heoretical boundaries are breached when mass media content and forms are part of our every-day lives and contribute to social definitions of self, others, and social issues' (2000: 289). This observation sits well with Breit's (2010: 621) claims that discourses 'mediate the relationship between concrete linguistic aspects of texts (e.g. use of certain vocabularies or formulation) and the implication of texts in wider societal or political contexts'. Of course, language itself is not intrinsically powerful. It only becomes powerful when people start to use it.

Language can be used to reinforce existing power in relationships, but can also be used to alter and challenge those relationships. It can also tell us something about the relationships between people—who is attributed with linguistic power based on their social status, for example. Power is a social phenomenon, not a linguistic one. Certain linguistic structures can gain social significance, but nevertheless, they are only powerful under the right circumstances: the words 'I sentence you to four years in prison' only carry weight if spoken by a recognised judge; a toddler repeating the same words does not have the same effect (this is known as illocutionary force). Relatedly, *discourse*, in the sense that we are using it, and in the sense that it is generally (although not always) accepted to mean within CDA (see below), refers to the way that language is used to reflect, shape, and encode societal norms and values. Particularly, one aspect of CDA is a focus on how the norms and values of the powerful are presented through the use of particular linguistic structures as common sense (cf. Fairclough 2001). To illustrate how linguistic structures can influence the representation or characterisation of a particular event, we can draw on our corpora.

1. The rise in poverty rates is largely due to stagnating wages and benefit cuts (G news: society, Nov 2012).

Example (1) includes three occurrences of nominalisation—a linguistic device where a verb is turned into a noun—which serve to disguise the processes that are expressed in the sentence. For example, 'the rise in poverty rates' includes the notion that 'poverty rates are rising', a proposition which is accepted without question. Similarly, 'stagnating wages' and 'benefit cuts' presuppose that 'wages are stagnating' and 'benefits are being cut (by the government)'. None of these three processes—rising, stagnating and cutting—are actions in the sentence; they are backgrounded and placed in noun phrases. Such nominalisations make it difficult to challenge the claims embedded within a sentence; it is hard to argue that 'poverty rates are not rising' because the notion that 'poverty rates are rising' is taken to be common sense, expressed as 'the rise in poverty rates'. The sentence is not making the claim that 'poverty rates are rising' but rather it is assuming agreement that poverty rates are rising and making a claim about the causes of such a phenomenon. Similarly, (1) is not arguing that 'wages are stagnating' or 'benefits are being cut', but it takes these processes for granted and reports that their end state 'stagnating wages' and 'benefit cuts' are the reason for 'the rise in poverty rates'. It is difficult (although not impossible) given the use of nominalisations in this sentence to argue that 'poverty is not rising', 'wages are not stagnating' and 'benefits are not being cut'. Thus, the author of this text is establishing the status quo of their argument by using a particular linguistic feature. Nominalisations are just one of a huge number of linguistic devices that can be used to encode one's interpretation of a given topic within language, and their analysis is just one tool at the disposal of the discourse analyst. By being more aware of the power of language we can begin to recognise and question the societal and political ramifications of language usage.[3] The aim of the next section is to introduce readers to an interdisciplinary approach to language analysis known as CDA which aims to foreground the social values that are encoded linguistically within texts.

[3]On a macro scale it might be that particular language varieties are deemed as socially more appropriate, or acceptable, or beautiful, and so on. For example, double negatives such as 'I didn't hear nothing' have traditionally been rejected as 'bad English'. These judgements do not make the language variety under scrutiny intrinsically good or bad, but the social values attached to certain language varieties are powerful.

2.3 Critical Discourse Analysis

The analysis of discourse, in its most basic form, refers to the close linguistic analysis of structures above sentence level. Discourse analysis focuses on how elements of a text work together to construct a (coherent) whole. Whilst discourse analysis includes analysis of grammatical forms, such as adjectives, noun phrases, clauses, etc., it recognises that the meanings held within a text are socially constituted and cumulative, insofar as meaning is created across (and beyond) a whole text. Taking the word *poverty* as an example, written on a page, the use of a combination of seven letters to represent three syllables, this linguistic signifier means nothing without readers drawing upon their own existing knowledge of society. *Poverty* can conjure up images of dying children, famine, war-torn countries, homelessness, council estates, begging, destitution, etc., but the exact interpretation of this term each reader has will influence their response to the topic. However, human beings do not arrive at interpretations of words in isolation.

Critical discourse analysis acknowledges that texts are read within specific (temporal, geographical, political) contexts, and external influences can affect how a text is produced and distributed. Just as the close linguistic analysis of one feature or one occurrence of a particular word is incomplete, discourses also are not restricted to a particular (single) text. They are cumulative, built up over time and across modes and outputs. For example, the association between benefit recipients and welfare fraud is overrepresented in the mass media with extreme cases being foregrounded (see Lundström 2013). An example from the *Daily Mail* corpus, (2) demonstrates how benefit fraud is sensationalised.

2. Beggars belief: Scrounger, 34, who lay in doorways PRETENDING to be homeless caught living at home with his MOTHER in her 230,000 village house (DM news, May 2014).

In this case the benefits claimant is labelled a 'scrounger' and is not referred to by name. The newspaper's negative evaluation of this person is evidenced through the use of capitalisation and the listing of the value of the mother's house: not only is the homeless person living in a house, but a relatively expensive one in a presumably-enviable village location. Whilst this is just a single example, Lansley and Mack (2015: 142) note that the use of *scrounger* in UK newspapers was four times higher in 2010 than it had been between 1993 and 2003 (although the gap between these dates could hide fluctuations in usage). The repetition of this term, and others like it, are evidence of scrounger discourse, where benefits claimants are portrayed as (unjustly) receiving high welfare payments and spending them frivolously (see van der Bom et al. 2018).

What makes discourse analysis critical is its explicit focus on language and power; it is underpinned by the perspective that language is a social phenomenon which reflects, (re)constructs, and rejects social (power) norms. Wodak (1999: 186) argues that language 'is not an isolated phenomenon' but rather it is 'deeply social, intertwined with social processes and interaction'. As Fairclough (2001: 21) explains:

> in seeing language as discourse and as social practice, one is committing oneself not just to analysing texts, nor just to analysing processes of production and interpretation, but to analysing the relationship between texts, processes, and their social conditions, both the immediate conditions of the situational context and the more remote conditions of institutional and social structures.

The term *critical discourse analysis* does not refer to a single, formulaic method of research or to a unified theory of society and social construction: 'CDA has never been and has never attempted to be or to provide one single or specific theory. Neither is one specific methodology characteristic of research in CDA' (Wodak and Meyer 2009: 5). What unites practitioners of CDA is their focus on the relationship between language (as evidenced through close textual analysis) and wider social issues. According to Scheuer (2003: 143) analyses will discuss texts 'on a macrosocial level, often with reference to global political movements' and will generally discuss ideology. Ideology is another term with multiple overlapping definitions. For Fairclough this term relates to the relative acceptance of ideas presented as common sense. He argues that ideologies (note the plural) 'are closely linked to language, because using language is the commonest form of social behaviour, and the form of social behaviour where we rely most on "common-sense" assumptions' (Fairclough 2001: 2). Others may look to alternative definitions of ideology, such as the notion of symbolic violence (cf. Bourdieu and Wacquant 2004). The common core underpinning such interpretations of ideology (or indeed hegemony) is the notion that the oppressed are unconsciously complicit in their oppression. As Fairclough (2001: 3) argues, ideology 'is the primary means of manufacturing consent'.

Breit (2010: 621) notes that 'discourse is intrinsically linked with its social and material context; it is socially constituted as well as socially constituting, thus contributing to (re)constructing specific identities, social relations, and systems of knowledge'. Focusing on discourses of corruption, he argues that how journalists (and the social structures surrounding them, editors, newspaper owners, etc.) choose to frame a particular issue allows them to 'to reduce the complexities, ambiguities, and contradictions that often characterize activities related to corruption' (2010: 621). Clearly these choices stretch far beyond discourses of corruption, and we can see their effect on discourses of poverty, with the use of scrounger discourses and the choice of the mass media to focus on extreme cases of poverty (or indeed benefit fraud) in order to maintain a particular caricature of the poor who can be homogenised and negatively evaluated (see Skeggs and Wood 2011). For example, Lansley and Mack (2015: 141) report on the Turn2Us charity's finding that, over 50% of tabloid articles about benefits printed between 1995 and 2011 included 'negative vocabulary'. The systematic repetition of particular characterisations of social groups can influence wider public opinion and become part of the dominant discourses of poverty, class, the deserving and undeserving poor, etc., discourses that can then be utilised in texts as if they are common sense.

In his conceptualisation of discourse Fairclough (2001: 18–19) argues that language is an intrinsic part of society (not something which is external) which constitutes a socially-conditioned social process which is influenced 'by other non-linguistic parts of society'. The representations of any social phenomena put forward by powerful institutions, such as the mainstream mass media, have the potential to influence public (and governmental) opinion. Fairclough (2001: 38–39) suggests that power can be realised in discourse when 'powerful participants' are '*controlling and constraining the contributions/of non-powerful participants*' (original italics). In face-to-face interaction this can take the form of interruptions or topic shifts, but on an institutional level within media texts, we can ask questions about who gets to talk, how their arguments are reported, and how people and actions are evaluated. As Fairclough (2001: 43) notes, '[i]n the British media, the balance of sources and perspectives and ideology is overwhelmingly in favour of existing power-holders'. Indeed, in our corpora, it is rare to find direct quotations from those experiencing poverty, and even when such quotations are included in newspaper texts, they are framed by the rest of the articles in which they appear. Thus, the newspapers hold the power over how poverty is represented and evaluated.

2.4 Corpus-Based CDA and the Interrogation of Poverty

The combination of corpus linguistics with CDA is not a new method of analysis, but one which has been evolving since the end of the twentieth century, as corpus tools developed and became more widely available due to advances in computing. As discourses are cumulative, it follows that analysing large bodies of texts would be beneficial for the critical discourse analyst. However, corpus linguistics is not usually focused on the kind of close reading typical of CDA, nor does it automatically address the social and political context surrounding the texts held within a corpus. Despite these apparent differences in focus and scale, the two methodologies can be successfully combined to produce robust triangulated analyses of the linguistic representation, rejection, and (re)construction of social phenomena. Whilst the methods of analysis associated with corpora and CDA tend to be conceptualised as quantitative and qualitative respectively, this is erroneous. As discussed above, corpora can be used to inform qualitative analysis (specifically through close reading of concordances and an in the analysis of repeated syntactic patterns) and CDA benefits from quantification, insofar as demonstrating the existence of a linguistic pattern, as opposed to an isolated construction in a single text, contributes to arguments about how ideologies are indexed and presented.[4]

Discussing the benefit of using corpus linguistic methods to inform CDA Hardt-Mautner (1995: 8) notes that the analysis of concordance lines 'provide[s] new ways of kick-starting the analysis because it enables researchers to pursue even the most tentative leads'. She argues that using concordance programmes within CDA means that a researcher can 'describe syntactic and semantic properties of key lexical items exhaustively rather than selectively' and as a result they can 'look at a large number of occurrences rather than generalise in an undisciplined fashion on the basis of a few purposely selected examples' (1995: 23–24). This arguably makes any claims made about the data under analysis more robust. As Kennedy (1998: 9) notes, corpus linguistics is not just about how many times certain constructions occur, nor is it concerned 'only with what is said or written, where, when and by whom', but rather it is also concerned with 'how particular forms are used'. As such, corpus linguistics can be informed by a CDA approach which focuses on the social function(s) of the use of particular linguistic constructions, thus answering the question 'why' particular forms are used within a particular context. The basic premise that analyses using corpus linguistics tools tend not to focus on wider social factors involved in text construction is directly addressed and critiqued when combined with the ethos of CDA.

Richardson (2006: 29) argues that CDA involves analysis and criticism of just how social power and social norms are represented 'both explicitly and implicitly' within texts. Linking to corpus analysis, Baker (2006: 19) is careful to note that just because a particular pattern can be found in a corpus does not mean that the pattern is representative of 'mainstream ways of thinking'. Taking a CDA-influenced perspective he notes that 'a sign of true power is in not having to refer to something, because everybody is aware of it' and argues that sometimes what is not written or spoken is actually more important than what is (Baker 2006: 19). Indeed, Baker et al. (2008: 282)

---

[4]Baker and McEnery (2015) provide a clear introduction to corpus-based approaches to discourse analysis. Their collection of edited papers is of interest to readers who wish to know more about corpus-based (critical) discourse analysis, including its many associated methods, and the topics that scholars have analysed with this mixed method.

also note Kress and van Leeuwen's (2001) claim that critical analyses must take 'into account absences as well as presences in the data', arguing that a major concern with corpus analysis is that it 'tends to focus on what has been explicitly written' (2008: 297). This criticism is a sound one, as corpus software is not designed to look for the absence of data, and this must be taken into consideration when using corpus data to inform CDA. Nevertheless, combinatory analyses are possible. In Paterson's (forthcoming) analysis of discussions of UK poverty in Below the Line newspaper comments, members of the public debated child poverty using references to the responsibilities and failings of (single) mothers. In contrast, references to (single) fathers were rare, and when (single) fathers were mentioned, their mentions were either rejected or presented as isolated cases. Thus the absence of (single) fatherhood in debates about UK child poverty serve to gender the debate and frame child poverty as a problem directly associated with poor motherhood. The quantification of references to mothers and fathers—produced using corpus analysis—demonstrates a pattern across texts, but this pattern is only understood through close analysis of the occurrences of such terms and their subsequent relation to wider social norms which situate women as primarily responsible for child rearing.

The systematic analysis of the gendering of poverty debates and the use of corpus linguistics to bring such social practices to light correlates well with CDA's political focus. Wodak (2001: 9) notes that the critical element of CDA refers to 'taking a political stance explicitly' whilst also having distance from the data and being able to embed the data within society and social norms. Thus, to combine corpus linguistics, which provides a certain distance from the data, with CDA, one has to begin corpus work acknowledging the political purpose of a particular analysis. It is important for researchers to acknowledge their own position in relation to their object of analysis. In the present case, both authors are from middle-class, white British backgrounds and have no first-hand experience with poverty. As such we cannot present an insider's view. Our knowledge of poverty comes from observing those in poverty, either first hand or through social networks, or mediated through other channels, such as second-hand accounts of poverty presented in the mass media. It is on these media-controlled accounts that we focus our analysis.

2.5 Summary

This chapter has served to introduce readers to the theoretical underpinnings and applications of corpus linguistics and CDA. The benefits of corpus linguistics include the ability to process large amounts of data—much more than could be easily facilitated using manual analysis alone—and can lead to the identification of patterns of language use across large datasets. For the present study, using a corpus-based approach helped to identify the use of place-names across a total of almost four hundred million words. The way that textual data is presented in corpora, and the ability to generate concordances lines, is also particularly well suited to geotagging place-names (see Chapter 3) and manipulating textual data so that it can be used in GIS. Our focus on CDA is complementary to our use of corpora, as it facilitates a consideration of textual (and statistical) representations of poverty within their wider social context. Thus, not only can we plot the references to place-names included in media texts, and thus compare them to statistical measures of poverty, we can also take a more qualitative look at exactly how ideologies of UK poverty are encoded within texts.

However, whilst the final section of this chapter discussed how corpus linguistics and CDA can be used in combination, there was no real consideration of geography. This is because, traditionally, corpus linguists have not explored the geographies within texts that they have analysed. Whilst there may be some consideration about where a text is from when compiling a corpus—for example, if the aim is to construct a corpus of British English or Australian English—there tends to be little-to-no consideration of the places mentioned within texts. In Chapter 3 therefore, we switch our focus to explore the basics of the ways in which Geographical information systems (GIS) represent and analyse features in geographical space. This provides the underpinning that allows Chapter 4 to bring together corpus-based and GIS approaches to create GTA, the major methodological advance that allows us to explore the geographical representations of poverty in the remainder of the book.

References

Altheide, D. L. 2000. Tracking Discourse and Qualitative Document Analysis. *Poetics* 27 (4): 287–299.

Baker, P. 2006. *Using Corpora in Discourse Analysis*. London: Continuum.

Baker, P., C. Gabrielatos, M. KhosraviNik, M. Kryzanowski, T. McEnery, & R. Wodak. 2008. A Useful Methodological Synergy? Combining Critical Discourse Analysis and Corpus Linguistics to Examine Discourses of Refugees and Asylum Seekers in the UK Press. *Discourse and Society* 19 (3): 273–306.

Baker, P., & T. McEnery (eds.). 2015. *Corpora and Discourse Studies*. Basingstoke: Palgrave.

Biber, D., S. Conrad, & R. Reppen. 1994. Corpus-Based Approaches to Issues in Applied Linguistics. *Applied Linguistics* 15 (2): 169–189.

Bourdieu, P., & L. Wacquant. 2004. Symbolic Violence. In N. Scheper-Hughes & P. Bourgois (eds.). *Violence in War and Peace: An Anthology*. Oxford: Blackwell, pp. 272–274.

Breit, E. 2010. On the (Re)Construction of Corruption in the Media: A Critical Discursive Approach. *Journal of Business Ethics* 92 (4): 619–635.

Brezina, V. 2018. *Statistics in Corpus Linguistics: A Practical Guide*. Cambridge: Cambridge University Press.

Dorling, D., R. Mitchell, M. Shaw, S. Orford, & G. Davey Smith. 2000. The Ghost of Christmas Past: Health Effects of Poverty in London in 1896 and 1991. *British Medical Journal* 321: 1547–1551.

Fairclough, N. 2001. *Language and Power* (second edition). London: Longman.

Gregory, I. N. 2009. Comparisons Between Geographies of Mortality and Deprivation from the 1900s and 2001: Spatial Analysis of Census and Mortality Statistics. *British Medical Journal* 339: b3454, 676–679.

Hardie, A. 2012. CQPweb—Combining Power, Flexibility and Usability in a Corpus Analysis Tool. *International Journal of Corpus Linguistics* 17: 380–409.

Hardt-Mautner, G. 1995. Only Connect. Critical Discourse Analysis and Corpus Linguistics. *UCREL Technical Papers* 6. http://ucrel.lancs.ac.uk/papers/techpaper/vol6.pdf. Accessed 18/10/2009.

Kennedy, G. D. 1998. *An Introduction to Corpus Linguistics*. London: Longman.

Kress, G., & T. van Leeuwen. 2001. *Multimodal Discourse: The Modes and Media of Contemporary Communication*. London: Arnold.

Lansley, S., & J. Mack. 2015. *Breadline Britain: The Rise of Mass Poverty.* London: Oneworld.
Lundström, R. 2013. Framing Fraud: Discourse on Benefit Cheating in Sweden and the UK. *European Journal of Communication* 28 (6): 630–645.
Mautner, G. 2007. Mining Large Corpora for Social Information: The Case of Elderly. *Language in Society* 36 (1): 51–72.
McCarthy, M., & R. Carter. 2004. Focus-on Issue: Corpus Linguistics (Part I)—Introduction. *Journal of Pragmatics* 36 (2): 147–148.
McKenzie, L. 2015. *Getting By: Estates, Class and Culture in Austerity Britain.* London: Polity Press.
Paterson, L. L. Forthcoming. Electronic Supplement Analysis of Multiple Texts: Exploring Discourses of UK poverty in Below the Line Comments.
Paterson, L. L., D. Peplow, & K. Grainger. 2017. Does Money Talk Equal Class Talk? Audience Responses to Poverty Porn in Relation to Money and Debt. In A. Mooney & E. Sifaki (eds.). *The Language of Money and Debt: An Interdisciplinary Approach.* Basingstoke: Palgrave, pp. 205–232.
Rayson, P. 2008. From Keywords to Semantic Domains. *International Journal of Corpus Linguistics* 13 (4): 519–549.
Richardson, J. E. 2006. *Analysing Newspapers: An Approach from Critical Discourse Analysis.* Basingstoke: Palgrave Macmillan.
Scheuer, J. 2003. Habitus as the Principle for Social Practice: A Proposal for Critical Discourse Analysis. *Language in Society* 32 (2): 143–175.
Skeggs, B., & H. Wood (eds.). 2011. *Reality Television and Class.* London: British Film Institute/Palgrave Macmillan.
Stubbs, M. 2001. Texts, Corpora, and Problems of Interpretation: A Response to Widdowson. *Applied Linguistics* 22 (2): 149–172.
Tognini-Bonelli, E. 2001. *Corpus Linguistics at Work.* Amsterdam: John Benjamins.
van der Bom, I., L. L. Paterson, K. Grainger, & D. Peplow. 2018. 'It's Not the Fact They Claim Benefits but Their Useless, Lazy, Drug Taking Lifestyles We Despise': Analysing Audience Responses to Benefits Street Using Live Tweets. *Discourse, Context & Media* 21: 36–45.
Wodak, R. 1999. Critical Discourse Analysis at the End of the 20th Century. *Research on Language and Social Interaction* 32 (1–2): 185–193.
Wodak, R. 2001. What CDA Is About—A Summary of Its History, Important Concepts and Its Development. In R. Wodak & M. Meyer (eds.). *Methods of Critical Discourse Analysis.* London: Sage, pp. 1–13.
Wodak, R., & M. Meyer. 2009. Critical Discourse Analysis: History, Agenda, Theory and Methodology. In R. Wodak & M. Meyer (eds.). *Methods of Critical Discourse Analysis* (second edition). London: Sage, pp. 1–33.

3

Geographical Information Systems and Textual Sources

At its core the geographical information systems (GIS) data model consists of a table of data in which each row is linked to a spatial location in the form of a point, line, polygon or pixel. While this is a highly effective way of representing some types of data it has traditionally been thought to be incompatible with others, particularly unstructured textual data such as corpora. Solutions to this do exist, although, as currently available, they rely on converting from an unstructured text to a table of attribute data with combined spatial data. While this is not a perfect solution, it does allow texts to be explored and analysed geographically. This, in turn, allows us to conduct the geographical analyses of text that form the main theme of this book.

'Humans are spatial beings' who 'exist and interact in natural and human environments that occupy space over time' (Siebert 2000: 538). One of the major developments in IT in recent years has been the exponential rise in the availability of digital corpora. As described in the previous chapter, this has led to the development of corpus linguistics as an analytic approach that makes use of the availability of

L. L Paterson and I. N Gregory, *Representations of Poverty and Place*,
https://doi.org/10.1007/978-3-319-93503-4_3

this type of source. Space and geography have, however, largely been neglected by corpus linguistics. This is at least in part because the tools and approaches used in corpus linguistics are not well suited to exploring location. Since the 1990s geographers have increasingly used GIS to represent, analyse, and visualise data that can be mapped. A continuing criticism of GIS, however, is that it is primarily suited for use with quantitative sources, usually structured in tabular form. In their traditional form GIS are thus not well suited to the analysis of textual sources.

To date, developments within the fields of GIS and corpus linguistics have occurred in parallel with little overlap: GIS has largely not made use of textual sources while corpus analysis has largely ignored geography. Bringing the two together, to allow texts to be analysed within a GIS framework, requires two developments: firstly the identification of place-names within the text, and secondly the linking of place-names to coordinates to allow the place-name to be mapped. This can be achieved using a technique called *geoparsing* which uses techniques from Natural Language Processing (NLP) to identify candidate place-names within the text, and matches these to a gazetteer[1] to allocate them to a coordinate (Grover et al. 2010). This allows the place-names within the corpus to be mapped and facilitates analysis of the geographies within texts (Gregory et al. 2015). Once places have been mapped, Geographical Text Analysis (GTA)—described in detail in Chapter 4—can be used to analyse the text in more sophisticated ways. This chapter introduces GIS and its constituent fields. Section 3.1 introduces the technology as it has been developed to handle quantitative data and the limited extent to which the qualitative have also been incorporated. Section 3.2 explores geoparsing, how it works, and why gazetteers are so fundamental to it. Section 3.3 explores some of the more conceptual issues that problematise representing space in this way.

[1]A gazetteer is a directory or index of place-names and their corresponding coordinates. It may also contain additional information about a place including, alternative spellings, population statistics, and notes on physical features.

3.1 An Introduction to GIS

Geographical information systems are frequently thought of as a type of computer mapping system. This over-simplifies what a GIS is able to do. In many ways a GIS is a type of database which allows users to query, visualise, and analyse data that are spatially referenced, in other words, data that have a location associated with them. This is achieved because every item of data, represented as a row in a database table, is linked to a location on the map (see, for example, DeMers 2008; Heywood et al. 2011; Lo and Yeung 2006). While this data model is relatively crude, GIS-based approaches have been applied to a wide range of topics across the Earth and social sciences. GIS has become a fundamental tool for many geographers and has led to the development of a field called geographical information science (GISc) which explores how to use geographical information effectively and appropriately (Goodchild 1992). The adoption and acceptance of GIS within geography and beyond has been far from uncontroversial (see the essays in Pickles 1995 and the response by Openshaw 1997). In its early stages a wide range of criticisms were made particularly about the quantitative nature of GIS and the perception that the field was driven by technical developments which were adopted uncritically. Responses to these criticisms led to the development of the sub-field of *critical GIS* in which a more sensitive approach to using the technology is adopted (Schuurman 2004). GIS has also started to move away from its quantitative origins with the development of *qualitative GIS* which has been used to study issues such as the geographies of fear of crime or prejudice (Cope and Elwood 2009).

The first stage in understanding what GIS is and the potential it offers to researchers across disciplines is to stand back from it and understand what geographical information is. In theory any information that refers to a location on the Earth's surface is geographical information. In practice, however, information really only becomes geographical information when the researcher is interested in how different locations are different from each other. One of the most obvious examples of geographical information in the social sciences is census data.

(a)

(b)

ID	Name	Population	Unemployment
1	Newton	4235	862
2	Sutton	1729	209
3	Wood Side	7621	1012
4	Castlehill	6980	562

Fig. 3.1 Using a combination of **a** spatial data and **b** attribute data to represent some hypothetical census data

To take the census, the study area (usually a country) is subdivided into precisely defined areas such as counties, districts, or output areas (OAs). The number of people, and sub-divisions such as their sex, age, occupational status, ethnicity, and so on, are then counted for each area with these counts being recorded in a table where there is a row for every area and the columns provide information on the population structure, such as total population, numbers of people in each occupation, etc. Thus, the census combines information about location (in the form of the areas used to count the data) that say *where* the data refer to, with tabular information that says *what* is at each location.

In GIS parlance, the tabular data is referred to as **attribute data**. Each row of attribute data is linked to a geographical representation of its location which is called the **spatial data**. With census data, the spatial data will be representations of the zones used to collect and categorise the data. This structure is shown in Fig. 3.1 which represents the spatial and attribute data for some hypothetical census statistics.

Spatial data can be represented in a number of different ways. The simplest form of spatial data is a point, in which a location is represented using a single coordinate pair (x, y) as shown in Fig. 3.2a. Points can be used to represent a wide variety of features including individual addresses or the locations of buildings, such as hospitals or supermarkets. Depending on scale, points can also be used to represent larger features such as towns and cities. Linear features such as roads, railways, or rivers are represented using lines which, as Fig. 3.2b shows, are created by joining together two or more points. Areas or zones, such as census districts or lakes, are represented using polygons. As Fig. 3.2c shows,

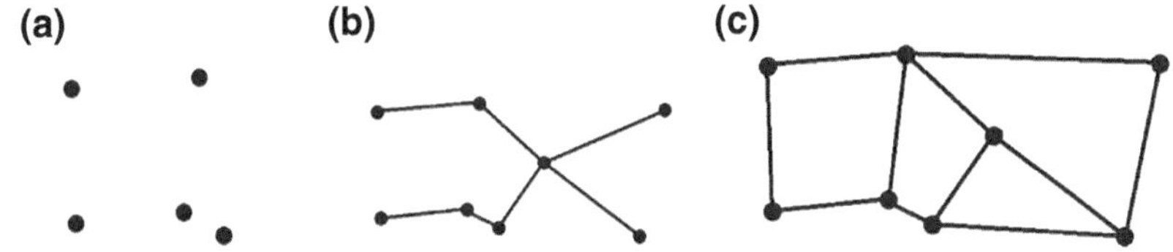

Fig. 3.2 Vector data representing **a** points, **b** lines and **c** polygons. Each point, line segment, and polygon is linked to its own attribute data, as shown in Fig. 3.1

a polygon is created from one or more lines that completely enclose an area. Points, lines and polygons are thus all created from coordinate pairs with every point, line segment, or polygon having its own attribute data. In GIS parlance, points, lines and polygons are termed **vector data**. Vector data are good at representing discrete features such as buildings, towns, roads, rivers, lakes and administrative areas.

An alternative type of spatial data are **raster data**. Rather than sub-divide the study area into separate features, raster data attempt to represent continuously varying features such as height or the spread of pollution. It does this by sub-dividing the study area into small regular pixels, usually squares, with each pixel having its own value, as shown in Fig. 3.3. Typically raster data will be represented graphically with high values being shaded in darker colours. The pattern that the pixels create will be of interest in describing the way that the height of the terrain varies or a pollution incident has spread. Raster data are less common in examples from human geography but, as we will see, are frequently used to simplify point data by representing the density of points across a study area.

Data on different themes are stored in GIS **layers**. Each layer consists of one type of data and contains both spatial and attribute data. A layer's spatial data will normally be **georeferenced**. This means that the coordinates that it uses are in a real-world coordinate system which can either use a map projection, such as British National Grid, or be in latitude and longitude.

The data model described above, in which spatial and attribute data are linked together is at the core of GIS. It allows the researcher to ask

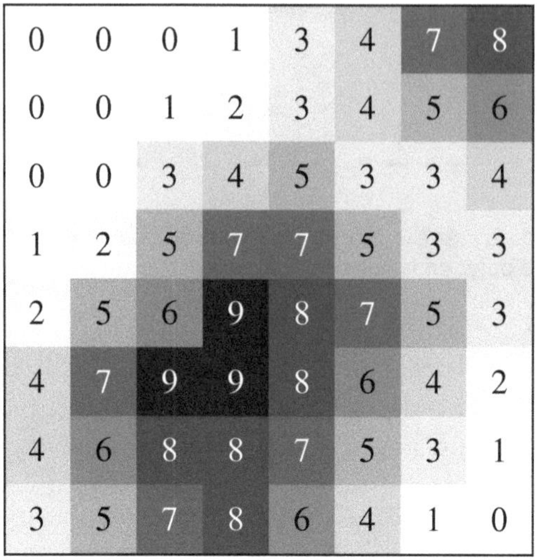

Fig. 3.3 An example of raster data. Each cell is of known size with the numeric value representing an attribute such as height or density

questions of the attribute data and map the results, or to select locations on the map and query their attribute data. The first of these would enable a question such as 'where are places with unemployment rates above 10% found?', the second would ask 'what percentage of people at this place are unemployed?'.

While this is a very simple structure, it opens up much potential for understanding geographical phenomena. Four major opportunities can be identified: structuring of data, data integration, visualisation, and spatial analysis (Gregory et al. 2003). Structuring simply refers to the fact that the data model allows us to know more about the way the data are related to each other. For example, we know what is at a particular location, what is at neighbouring locations, and so on. As all of the data within a GIS database have been georeferenced to real-world location, theoretically location can be used to integrate any data within GIS. Thus, for example, if we have data on the addresses of individual shops as points, census data representing the population for polygons, and data on the transport network as lines, all of which have been taken from different sources, these can be brought together to explore, for example, how shop locations compare to background populations, taking into account likely transport routes. From a visualisation perspective, GIS is obviously well suited to creating and exploring maps. Higher-tech visualisations can also be produced using GIS, including animations to show change over time and virtual worlds to attempt to recreate landscapes digitally.

Spatial analysis (also known as spatial statistics) is a form of analysis that explicitly includes location. This can be interpreted informally as simply any analysis in which location is included. However, there is also a field of statistics called spatial analysis in which the coordinate data are made an explicit part of a statistical analysis. An important feature of statistical spatial analysis is that the results of the analysis will change if the features under study are moved. There are clear analogies between mapping and statistical spatial analysis on one hand and, for example, scatter plots and regression analysis in conventional statistics. Scatter plots may suggest a relationship but techniques such as regression are needed to confirm the pattern really exists and to quantify it. In the same way, a map may suggest a pattern or relationship, while spatial statistics are used to confirm this and to quantify its extent.

Spatial analysis techniques vary from relatively simple techniques which attempt to identify whether a series of points cluster or not, to techniques that attempt to quantify how the relationship between two or more variables varies over the study area (Fotheringham et al. 2000; Lloyd 2011). One important feature of spatial analysis is that there are two potential types. On the one hand there are conventional statistical summaries, known as *global* or *whole map* statistics. These say, for example, that the points within a dataset tend to cluster across the study area or that there is a relationship between two variables across the study area. There is also the potential to create *local* statistics which can say, for example, that the data cluster in these areas but not in others, or that a relationship between two variables is different in different parts of the study area (Fotheringham 1997). Local statistics are usually represented using maps.

GIS is well suited to analysing quantitative data which can be allocated to clearly defined locations. GIS has been used extensively to analyse census data and in many other types of demographic analysis

(Reibel 2007). Epidemiological studies of health and disease patterns have been a rich seam for GIS (Cromley and McLafferty 2012; Rushton 2003). Events such as crimes or road traffic accidents have also been extensively analysed using GIS as precise locations are available as part of the recording of these events (Chainey and Ratcliffe 2005). A significant criticism of GIS is, however, that its analyses tend to be data led. If the required data are available with both spatial and attribute components then GIS is well suited to analysing it. If not, it cannot be incorporated into a GIS database and is thus likely to be excluded from the analysis. This criticism is valid and suggests that if GIS is to spread beyond its strongholds in quantitative social science and the Earth sciences it needs to be able to handle a wider range of sources.

One way in which this has been done is through the development of the field of *qualitative GIS* (Cope and Elwood 2009). While a traditional GIS analysis of crime, for example, would analyse the types of crime recorded at specific locations, a qualitative GIS analysis might explore fear of crime by asking participants where they felt safe and unsafe. Their responses are then georeferenced, perhaps by asking the participants to mark the relevant locations on maps, and can be analysed. One of the best examples of this type of work is Mei Po-Kwan's analysis of fear of crime among Muslim women in Columbus, Ohio after the September 11th attacks (Kwan 2008).

Although qualitative GIS broadens the scope for GIS analysis it requires the same basic technology. Attribute data are likely to be nominal, ordinal, or interval data in tabular form albeit trying to quantify something intangible such as perception. Spatial locations will still be represented by points, lines, polygons, or pixels but these become somewhat problematic due to the precise nature of these features. While it is sensible to represent a census district using precise polygon boundaries, representing the places where people feel unsafe is likely to be more difficult. In some cases, such as 'the other side of the tracks' or in clearly defined neighbourhoods it is possible for a person to put precise boundaries to areas they regard as unsafe. It is more likely, however, that they can say where they definitely feel unsafe and definitely feel safe but that a boundary placed between them would be highly arbitrary. GIS is thus not good at handling this type of situation due to the imprecise nature of the spatial data.

3.2 Geoparsing: The Link Between Texts and GIS

Converting a text into a GIS layer requires three stages: first the place-names need to be identified, second a coordinate or other spatial representation needs to be found for the place-names, and third, a way of appropriately converting the required co-text into tabular form needs to be found. The first two stages of this are referred to as **geoparsing**, a process by which place-names are identified in a text or corpus in the **geotagging** stage and then allocated to a coordinate in the **georesolution** stage (Grover et al. 2010). Geotagging is a NLP task that makes use of the fact that place-names are proper nouns. The use of Named Entity Recognition (NER) algorithms to identify proper nouns is a well-established part of the NLP toolkit. Once the proper nouns have been identified, further rules can be used to produce a list of candidate place-names and separate these from other proper nouns such as people's names.

The georesolution phase then involves matching the candidate place-names with one or more gazetteers which will provide coordinates for the place-names. In its simplest form a gazetteer is a database table that lists place-names and their associated real-world coordinates. Frequently gazetteers will host a range of other information also associated with the place-name such as variant spellings, information about the administrative hierarchy, such as which district, county or state the place is found in, and what type of feature it is, such as a settlement, mountain, forest, and so on (Southall et al. 2011; Berman et al. 2016). There are a number of publically available gazetteers, perhaps the most widely used of which is Geonames (Geonames, n.d.). This is freely available with global coverage and is increasingly updated using crowd-sourcing. The Getty Thesaurus of Geographical Names (TGN) is another widely used general purpose gazetteer (Getty Research Institute, n.d.).

Other gazetteers have more specific purposes, for example, the Ordnance Survey's 1:50,000 gazetteer gives the 1 km grid square in which place-names appear on its 1:50,000 maps (Ordnance Survey 2014), while the Pleiades gazetteer was specifically created to incorporate place-names from the Ancient World (Pleiades, n.d.; Simon et al. 2016).

The accuracy of the coordinate information will also be crucially affected by the gazetteer. Some gazetteers are very clear about what their coordinates refer to. The OS 1:50,000 gazetteer, for example, gives the coordinates of the centroids of the 1 km grid squares of place-names that are included on the 1:50,000 series maps. This makes it relatively easy to understand: place-names are included if they are included on that series of maps and their coordinates show where the place-name is located on the map, which is not necessarily exactly where the place actually is. It also means that the coordinates form a regular grid of locations that are one kilometre apart in both *x* and *y*. Thus, assuming the place can be represented by a precise point location and that the location of the place-name on the map accurately and sensibly represents the location of the place, the OS gazetteer is likely to locate the place to within 500 metres in *x* and *y* of where it should be. With other gazetteers, such as Geonames, it is harder to know exactly what the point provided represents.

In theory, a geoparser will provide a coordinate for every place-name within a text. In reality this process is complex and error prone. The main reason for this is that place-names are far from simple and unambiguous and therefore are difficult for computers to handle in a fully automated manner. The first major set of problems lies at the geotagging stage. It is often difficult to determine whether a proper noun refers to a place, person, or other feature. For example, 'Lancaster' is a town in the north-west of England. However 'Stuart Lancaster' is a person (a recent England rugby coach), the 'Duke of Lancaster' may be a person or may be a public house, and the 'Lancaster' was a well-known Second World War aeroplane. Rule-based systems, such as assuming that a word is not a place-name if it is preceded by a title such as 'Mr', 'Ms', or 'Duke of', or by a first name taken from a lexicon, or followed by a word such as 'bomber' or 'aeroplane' may help to resolve this but will not be fool-proof and will require manual checking. A second problem is that place-names frequently consist of more than one word making them both harder to geotag and to disambiguate. 'Oxford', 'Oxford Street' and 'Oxford Road' are entirely different places, as are 'York' and 'New York'.

Another source of ambiguity is that place-names may refer to more than one place. Many place-names that originated in Europe are also found in North America including obvious ones such as Boston (Massachusetts), London (Ontario), and Paris (Texas), and less obvious ones such as 'Lancaster' which is also found in Pennsylvania, New Hampshire, and California. Resolving to the correct continent may not be a major problem, however, similar ambiguities occur at more local levels. Within Britain there are several different places called, for example 'Newport', 'Newcastle', 'Wellington', 'Barrow', 'Bradford', and 'Whitchurch'. The place-name Kensington was a source of ambiguity in reports concerning poverty, as it referred to both the Royal borough of Kensington and Chelsea in London—which tends to be associated with affluence—and the inner city area of Kensington, Liverpool, which is associated with high poverty and unemployment rates. Sometimes full names may be used to disambiguate place-names, for example, 'Newcastle upon Tyne' or 'Newcastle under Lyme' but these are not used universally and are often left to the reader to determine.

Spelling variations represent a further set of problems. 'Saint Helen's' can be spelled in six different ways depending on whether and how 'Saint' is abbreviated ('Saint', 'St.' or 'St') and whether 'Helens' is given an apostrophe. 'Newcastle', 'Newcastle on Tyne', 'Newcastle-upon-Tyne' and so on represent a further set of complexities. In addition to these genuine variations, there can also be variations caused by spelling errors or data capture issues particularly where sources have been digitised using optical character recognition (OCR) technology (Tanner et al. 2009). Finally, there are also issues around what does and does not constitute a place-name. Ultimately this is a decision for the researcher. In most cases, people geoparsing a text will be most interested in the names and locations of features such as settlements. A decision needs to be taken about whether to include, for example, street names or the names of local features such as pubs, hotels, and other buildings.

At the other extreme it may be sensible to exclude high-level features such as countries, British counties, and US states, or at least to not represent them as points. Beyond this, there may be further decisions that a researcher needs to make. For example, we had to consider 'Westminster' as a special case. We chose to keep those instances where Westminster referred to an identifiable geographical area, and remove those where it was used metonymously to refer to the UK parliament and/or the government.

Automated solutions can be found to help to resolve some of these problems. Disambiguation can be assisted by using the locations of place-names that occur nearby in the text and selecting the option that is nearest to these. Spelling variations can be handled by having common variants in the gazetteer or through the use of fuzzy matching techniques. While these technical solutions may help, in reality place-names are so complex that fully geoparsing a large corpus in an entirely automated manner is likely to leave a situation where the result is has a considerable number of errors and where the researcher will be unaware of what the implication of these errors is likely to be. Thus geoparsing must be complemented by at least some manual analysis in order to ensure (and increase) the accuracy of the results.

A way of achieving this, which we use in the present study, is termed **concordance geoparsing** (Rupp et al. 2014; Gregory et al. 2015). Rather than geoparse the entire corpus, this works on the assumption that only relatively small parts need to be geoparsed at one time. The user selects a search term and extracts a relatively wide set of co-text around this, such as 50 words left and right. This co-text, which comes in the form of concordance lines (see Sect. 2.1), is then geoparsed. The results of the geoparsing can then be explored using both the concordance lines and by mapping the results. Where errors or ambiguities are spotted these can be corrected and, importantly, the corrections written to a file that means that when a new search-term is geoparsed these corrections can be applied automatically. In many cases, corrections are likely to allow the gazetteer to be improved or updated. In other cases, they may only be resolved as flagging, for example an ambiguous place-name as needing manual intervention. Concordance

Trial re-tests of claimants in <enamex long="-2.23" lat="53.8" st_name="Burnley">Burnley</enamex> and <enamex long="-2.1" lat="57.13" st_name="Aberdeen">Aberdeen</enamex> found 68.6 per cent either did not have a valid claim and were unable to prove they were too ill to take a job

Fig. 3.4 A fragment of geoparsed newspaper text taken from the *Daily Mail*

geoparsing allows users to geoparse in an iterative manner in ways that means that they understand the issues around how place-names are used in the corpus and can correct them as appropriate. It also enables gazetteers to be improved and enhanced. Concordance geoparsing is not mutually exclusive from geoparsing a whole corpus. It can be used in the first instance to gain an understanding of place-names in the corpus and to build up corrections that can be applied when the whole corpus is geoparsed.

Whatever form of geoparsing is used, the result will be that geotags are added to either the entire corpus or to concordance lines derived from it. These geotags are likely to be in XML format. They will identify place-names and provide other information as attributes. This attribute information will include the coordinates, and may also include additional information such as a standardised version of the place-name and perhaps other information derived from the gazetteer. An example of a geoparsed fragment of newspaper text is shown in Fig. 3.4. The place-names are identified using an XML tag, 'enamex' whose name, by convention, is surrounded by angle brackets (< >). The original spelling of the place-name is enclosed within the tag in the form *<enamex> place-name </enamex>* where the second tag, whose name starts with a slash, indicates the end of the place-name. The first tag also includes the attribute information which, in this case, includes latitude (lat), longitude (long), and a standardised version of the place-name's spelling (st_name).

The final stage in the process is to convert from this text format to the tabular format required by GIS. Technically this is reasonably straight-forward. A program identifies each geotag and converts it into a row in a table. Each row represents a place-name instance from the corpus. At a minimum it will include the place-name and a latitude and longitude or x and y figures for it. A range of other information is also likely to be desirable including: standardised versions of the place-name, any other information from the geotag, information on where in the corpus the instance has been extracted from, such as a file-name and word number, and perhaps the search-term used, if concordance geoparsing. Finally some co-text around the place-name is likely to also be included to provide some context about what is being said about the place. However, this is likely to be fairly limited as most database formats limit text fields to a maximum of 255 characters.

Effectively, therefore, geoparsing starts with an unstructured text and converts it into a table in which each row represents a place-name. Converting this into a GIS layer is straight-forward, most types of GIS software can easily convert coordinate data in a table into spatial data, so that a table can be converted into a point layer. Fundamentally, this manipulation of text into a new format that stresses its geography does mean the free-flowing nature of the text has been lost. However, the geoparsing process puts us in a position where the text can be explored, visualised, and analysed geographically in ways that were previously impossible, opening the potential for new forms of analysis.

3.3 Realities of Place and Space

As described above, GIS represents features as points or other graphic objects on a Euclidean plane and geoparsing allows us to georeference and map a text. One key issue, however, is the exact relationship between 'place' as a construct and place-names and extracted and georeferenced from a text. This issue concerns the notion of place as a conceptual/psychological reality, but also depends on what language users actually mean when they use a place-name. Whilst references to a geographical space do occur in our corpora, place-names can also be used as a metaphor/hyponym for the people living within particular geographical boundaries. Thus, the locations mentioned in the corpus, even though they can be assigned global coordinates, cannot simply be taken to depict a particular area of landmass. It is the critical investigation of what these terms mean, how they are used, and how they are evaluated, which interrogates the ideological function of place-names in media texts.

The location of the production of texts and the places they refer to can index powerful strategies. For example, in 2011 South Sudan was formally recognised as a country, but its conceptual realisation as a separate entity in global politics would not have been possible if institutionally-produced texts rejected its new, independent identity by refusing to use the signifier 'South Sudan' when referring to a particular geographical location/ideological entity. Similarly, the renaming of a geographical area has ramifications for its assumed identity and implied ownership. The history of Heraklion, Crete is a good example of this. The city's current name is rooted in Greek mythology, but at several points in history it has been given names that reflected its Byzantine (Kastro), Arab (Rabdh el Khandaq/Chandax) and Venetian (Candia) rule. Thus we can see how linguistic choices can be socially/politically powerful in references to place.

Whilst name changes can illustrate the power of linguistic choice, critical discourse analysts must question the most foundational concepts within their research. Thus, we must ask what is meant by *place* as an integral part of investigating how references to place are used within wider discourse frameworks. Cresswell (2004: 1) notes that 'no-one quite knows what they are talking about' given that *place* is 'not a specialized piece of academic terminology' and as such, does not have a singular definition.[2] He argues that '[w]riting about and researching place involves a multi-faceted understanding of the coming together of the physical world (both "natural" and "cultural"), the processes of meaning production and the practices of power that mark relations between social groups' (Cresswell 2004: 122). However, Porter et al. (2015: 33) note that further work within Historical GIS may shed light on how people use the term *place* and 'could usefully examine what "place" meant' to the authors of texts, questioning whether place-names were

[2]See Cresswell (2004) for an overview of different approaches within human geography to notions of 'place'. He notes that geographers and philosophers such as Sack (1997) and Malpas (1999) argue that society and geography are connected through 'place', but 'the realm of the 'social' has no particular privilege in discussions of place' (2004: 31). 'Malpas and Sack are arguing that humans cannot construct anything without being first in place – that *place is primary to the construction of meaning in society*' (Cresswell 2004: 32).

'primarily a reference to an environment or shorthand for the "type" of people who lived there'. Cresswell (2004: 103) acknowledges the power of place within wider society. Suggesting that places can help to create notions of 'in' and 'out' or 'us' and 'them'.

Questions of naming highlight potential ambiguities in noun use and problematize the concept and processes of naming more generally. They also illustrate the homogenising function of using place-names in discourse. An international news report about 'Wales', for example, could construct the entire country as a uniform and tangible whole. In turn, its population, unless specified elsewhere in the text, are all assumed to hold the same social values, economic status, and/or political beliefs. This feature of language is especially pertinent when place-names are used in their possessive forms, e.g. 'London's property owners', 'Bradford's youth'. This effect is extended even further when abstract concepts are used and geographical locations are personified, e.g. 'Yorkshire's fear', 'Ireland's joy'.

As an example, Dreier (2005) writes about the asymmetrical distribution of news stories across different neighbourhoods and cities in the US, noting that particular urban (poor) areas tend to be frozen out of media reports unless they are related to something sensational or breaking news. Whilst fundamentally his analysis relies on considerations of social and physical space and place, he does not systematically look at the geography of the places that he mentions. Such an analysis would support his work significantly, potentially providing robust evidence for his arguments. One flaw of Dreier's paper is that he does not consult any primary data, but instead draws together anecdotes from the wider literature (and elsewhere). However, his work does show the gap in the literature where a combination of CDA and GIS could provide evidence to support or challenge hypotheses related to how often and in what capacity particular geographical locations are referred to in the news media.

Issues of scale and representation may also be important. It is possible that the geographical area referred to in a text remains constant, whilst the lexemes used to refer to it change. For example, a newspaper headline could include a reference to Nottingham, but within the lead paragraph, there could be references to a smaller, more specific location, such as West Brigford, and, further still, a later reference to an even more specific location like Lady Bay. Here, the term 'Nottingham' is being used to refer to a very small area of landmass that constitutes part of a suburb of the city. Thus, it is likely that, when using GIS, any characteristics associated with Lady Bay could be mapped to, and thus associated with, the whole of Nottingham. This argument is particularly salient when considering ethnographic work undertaken in the St Ann's area of Nottingham by McKenzie (2015) which references the contrasts between St Ann's and more affluent parts of the city, such as West Brigford; plotting references to Nottingham (meaning St. Ann's) in the same way as references to Nottingham (meaning West Brigford) in the same location on a map will not give an accurate picture of how the two terms were used. This problem can also be turned on its head, insofar as the lexemes used in a text may remain constant, but refer to different geographical locations, e.g. references to events located in Soho and Kensington could both be referred to using the term 'London'. Close analysis of the surrounding co-text within which place-names are used will highlight if there are repeated patterns of reference like this that our analysis must address.

Concordance analysis can help with most of these issues as the co-text of a search term or place-name provides more information about how exactly place-names are used. Close reading of concordances can show which characteristics are associated with a particular geographical area and we can perform a version of keyword analysis to determine how the co-text surrounding place-names differs (see Chapter 4). In order to address issues concerning the different scale of place-name mentions (county, city, borough, district, etc.) we can tailor our analysis to the different levels, aggregate place-names mentioned to defined geographical areas (such as a local authority district) and also use density smoothing (see Chapter 4) to even out the effects of different types of place-names.

3.4 Summary

GIS is based around a crude but effective data model in which a table of data is provided with locational information using spatial data—points, lines, polygons, or pixels. This model allows the researcher to ask questions of the database including *where* are these features located? and *what* is at this location? This provides a highly effective framework for understanding the geographies of the features under study. In particular, it allows the researcher to structure the data, integrate it with other data using location, visualise it through maps and other representations, and to analyse it in ways that explicitly include location.

A major limitation of this data model is that it requires a tabular structure in which each feature in the database is a separate record linked to one, and only one, spatial reference. Despite this, it is still possible to represent corpora within GIS. This requires the use of geoparsing in which each place-name is identified and provided with a spatial reference. This is then used to convert the text to a table with each place-name forming a separate row. Once a text has been geoparsed it can quickly be converted into GIS layer for subsequent analysis. As we will see in Chapter 4, this analysis can start with simple dot maps but, to be effective it needs to draw on a combination of techniques from spatial analysis to focus on geography, corpus linguistics to focus on text, critical discourse analysis to focus on the ideologies associated with what is being said about place, and close reading of appropriate parts of the text. By drawing these together, the remainder of the book will explore newspaper discourses about poverty and place in the UK.

References

Berman, M. L., R. Mostern, & H. Southall. 2016. Introduction. In M. L. Berman, R. Mostern, & H. Southall (eds.). *Placing Names: Enriching and Integrating Gazetteers*. Bloomington: Indiana University Press, pp. 1–11.

Chainey, S., & J. Ratcliffe. 2005. *GIS and Crime Mapping*. Chichester: Wiley.

Cope, M., & S. Elwood (eds.). 2009. *Qualitative GIS: A Mixed Methods Approach*. London: Sage.

Cresswell, T. 2004. *Place: A Short Introduction*. London: Blackwell.

Cromley, E. K., & S. L. McLafferty. 2012. *GIS and Public Health*. London: Guilford.

DeMers, M. 2008. *Fundamentals of Geographical Information Systems* (fourth edition). Chichester: Wiley.

Dreier, P. 2005. How the Media Compound Urban Problems. *Journal of Urban Affairs* 27 (2): 193–201.
Fotheringham, A. S. 1997. Trends in Quantitative Methods I: Stressing the Local. *Progress in Human Geography* 21: 88–96.
Fotheringham, A. S., C. Brusdon, & M. Charlton M. 2000. *Quantitative Geography: Perspectives on Spatial Data Analysis.* London: Sage.
Goodchild, M. F. 1992. Geographical Information Science. *International Journal of Geographical Information Systems* 6: 31–45.
Gregory, I. N., C. Donaldson, P. Murrieta-Flores, & P. Rayson. 2015. Geoparsing, GIS and Textual Analysis: Current Developments in Spatial Humanities Research. *International Journal of Humanities and Arts Computing* 9: 1–14.
Gregory, I. N., K. Kemp, & R. Mostern. 2003. Geographical Information and Historical Research: Current Progress and Future Directions. *History and Computing* 13: 7–22.
Grover, C., R. Tobin, K. Byrne, M. Woollard, J. Reid, S. Dunn, & J. Ball. 2010. Use of the Edinburgh Geoparser for Georeferencing Digitized Historical Collections. *Philosophical Transactions of the Royal Society A* 368: 3875–3889.
Heywood, I., S. Cornelius, & S. Carver. 2011. *An Introduction to Geographical Information Systems* (fourth edition). Pearson: Harlow.
Kwan, M.-P. 2008. From Oral Histories to Visual Narratives: Re-presenting the Post-September 11 Experiences of the Muslim Women in the United States. *Social and Cultural Geography* 9 (6): 653–669.
Lo, C. P., & A. K. W. Yeung. 2007. *Concepts and Techniques of Geographical Information Systems* (second edition). Toronto: Pearson.
Lloyd, C. D. 2011. *Local Models for Spatial Analysis* (second edition). Boca Raton, FL: CRC Press.
Malpas, J. E. 1999. *Place and Experience: A Philosophical Topography.* Cambridge, MA: MIT Press.
McKenzie, L. 2015. *Getting By: Estates, Class and Culture in Austerity Britain.* London: Polity Press.
Openshaw, S. 1997. The Truth about Ground Truth. *Transactions in GIS* 2: 2–24.
Ordnance Survey. 2014. The National Grid FAQs. https://www.ordnancesurvey.co.uk/support/the-national-grid.html. Accessed 19/2/2016.
Pickles, J. (ed.). 1995. *Ground Truth: The Social Implications of Geographic Information Systems.* New York: Guilford Press.
Pleiades. n.d. Pleiades. https://pleiades.stoa.org. Accessed 11/7/2017.

Porter, C., P. Atkinson, & I. N. Gregory. 2015. Geographical Text Analysis: A New Key to Nineteenth-Century Mortality. *Health and Place* 36: 25–34.
Reibel, M. 2007. Geographic Information Systems and Spatial Data Processing in Demography: A Review. *Population Research Policy Review* 26: 601–618.
Rupp, C. J., P. Rayson, I. N. Gregory, A. Hardie, A. Joulain, & D. Hartmann. 2014. Dealing with Heterogeneous Big Data When Geoparsing Historical Corpora. *Proceedings of the 2014 IEEE Conference on Big Data*, pp. 80–83.
Rushton, G. 2003. Public Health, GIS, and Spatial Analytic Tools. *Annual Review of Public Health* 24: 43–56.
Sack, R. 1997. *Homo Geographics*. Baltimore: Johns Hopkins University Press.
Schuurman, N. 2006. Formalization Matters: Critical GIS and Ontology Research. *Annals of the Association of American Geographers* 96 (4): 726–739.
Siebert, L. J. 2000. Using GIS to Document, Visualize, and Interpret Tokyo's Spatial History. *Social Science History* 24 (3): 537–574.
Simon, R., L. Isaksen, E. Barker, & P. de Soto Canamares. 2016. The Pleiades Gazetteer and the Pelagios Project. In M. L. Berman, R. Mostern, & H. Southall (eds.). 2016. *Placing Names: Enriching and Integrating Gazetteers*. Indiana University Press: Bloomington, pp. 97–109.
Southall, H. R., R. Mostern, & M. L. Berman. 2011. On Historical Gazetteers. *International Journal of Humanities and Arts Computing* 5: 127–145.
Tanner, S., T. Munoz, & P. H. Ros. 2009. Measuring Mass Text Digitization Quality and Usefulness: Lessons Learned from Assessing the OCR Accuracy of the British Library's 19th Century Online Newspaper Archive. *DLib Magazine* 15 (7/8).

4

Conducting GTA Using Poverty as a Search Term

Chapter 3 introduced geographical information systems (GIS) as a special form of database designed for use with spatially referenced data. It also explored geoparsing, the process by which the geographical components of a text can be incorporated into the data models required by GIS. This involves identifying the place-names in the text and allocating them to coordinates. In this way an unstructured text is converted into a GIS point layer with attribute data in tabular form which enables textual sources to be analysed within a GIS environment. To analyse a geoparsed text, we can combine techniques from different fields to determine where the text is talking about—using methods from spatial analysis—and what it is saying about these places—using techniques from corpus linguistics. The method resulting from the combination of approaches is termed *Geographical text analysis* (GTA) (Gregory and Donaldson 2016; Murrieta-Flores et al. 2015; Porter et al. 2015).

The aim of this chapter is primarily to describe GTA as a set of techniques. It demonstrates how GTA works and provides an initial exploration of the ways that the media represent poverty and place. Section 4.1 discusses how corpora suitable for analysing media discourses of poverty were created. The rest of the chapter is concerned with an exemplar

L. L Paterson and I. N Gregory, *Representations of Poverty and Place*,
https://doi.org/10.1007/978-3-319-93503-4_4

GTA using the single corpus query: <*poverty*>.[1] This query was designed to return all hits of *poverty* as well as terms such as *anti-poverty*, *poverty-stricken*, etc. Using <*poverty*> as an example, a variety of approaches to GTA are explored. First, density smoothing is used to identify the major geographical patterns associated with poverty within the text. Spatial segregation analysis is then used to explore the differences in the geographies of the two newspapers. These techniques explore the basic geographies that the texts associate with the search-term. We then move to using variations on corpus linguistics techniques to identify the discourses that different newspapers associate with different places. The patterns found for <*poverty*> are then compared with other data, namely quantitative data on poverty and the background geographies from the two newspapers, to identify possible reasons for the patterns found. The findings of this chapter are preliminary because it attempts to represent a complex, multi-faceted issue such as poverty using a single search-term. This simplicity of approach also leads to problems of small numbers once we start exploring instances in different places. Nevertheless, the chapter provides some initial findings that we return to in later chapters.

4.1 Constructing the Corpus

Our analysis of the representation of poverty and place is restricted to UK national newspapers due to their strong pedigree as news sources with large audiences. We chose to focus on two contrasting news sources—the *Guardian* and the *Daily Mail*—over a time span of five years (2010–2015). This period coincides with a change of government in the UK, with the Coalition government of Conservative and Liberal Democrat MPs coming to power to replace Labour in 2010. In 2015 there was further change when the Conservative party won an overall

[1] The corpus queries we used are given in angled brackets. The asterisks are known as wildcards in corpus query syntax and are used to denote that the query term can be prefixed/followed by zero or more characters. So the query <book*>, for example, would return hits for *book, books, bookend, booked*, etc.

majority. Throughout our period Conservative MP David Cameron was Prime Minister and his governments introduced fiscal policies within an overarching discourse of austerity. Policies, such as Welfare Reform—an overhaul of the UK benefits system—have impacted upon the lives of the poor. Other changes to the benefits system, including the introduction of a benefits cap and the removal of the Spare Room Subsidy (also known as the bedroom tax), decreased the amount of money that people can receive.

Our first source, the *Daily Mail* is a right-leaning tabloid newspaper which has consistently endorsed the Conservative party and its austerity-based policies. Specifically, we have sourced articles from the newspapers' online entity *Mail Online*. The *Daily Mail*'s circulation figures were 1,657,867 in May 2015 (Turvill 2015), with its website traffic measured at 14,383,578 average daily browsers in February 2016 (Jackson 2016), making it the most popular newspaper in Britain. Our second source, the *Guardian,* is a left-leaning broadsheet that respectively endorsed the Liberal Democrat and Labour parties in the 2010 and 2015 UK general elections. The newspaper tends to stand in opposition to government cuts to welfare budgets and related services. Its circulation figures for May 2015 were 178,758 copies per day (Turvill 2015) although this figure does not include website traffic,[2] which was measured at 8,872,392 average daily visitors in February 2016 by the Audit Bureau of Circulation (Jackson 2016), making it the second most-visited daily UK newspaper.

To include as much media coverage of poverty as possible, our corpora include all texts that fit the following criteria: (i) texts appearing in the online versions of the *Daily Mail*/*Mail on Sunday* OR the *Guardian*/the *Observer*, (ii) texts published between January 2010 and July 2015 (inclusive), and (iii) texts categorised by the two sources as 'news' or 'comment' (articles categorised as 'sport', 'travel', etc. were not included). As there were no restrictions on corpus size, and to ensure maximum potential coverage of poverty, we have chosen to use whole texts. The texts used represent a broad genre of online newspaper articles published under the

[2]The *Guardian* does not make a branding distinction between its print and online content.

masthead of established news institutions. It is worth noting that we took the newspapers' own classification of articles without question, and thus there could be some slight discrepancy between sources. If an article was categorised as an example of a 'debate' text by the *Daily Mail* then we accepted this. Whether on close inspection different readers would agree with such a classification is beyond the scope of the present study. The two newspapers differ in their classification systems; the *Guardian* texts had more subdivisions (news: politics, news: society, news: news, and commentisfree) than the *Daily Mail* texts (news, debate). Whilst such differences are just one way in which the corpora differ, here the *Guardian* news categories have been conflated and commentisfree has been taken as comparable to the *Daily Mail*'s debate section. As such, the corpora are taken to be comparable insofar as they represent the same text type, from UK national publications, across the same time period.

The *Daily Mail* corpus contains 342,154 articles in comparison with the *Guardian*'s 64,976 texts, meaning that the *Daily Mail* produces an average of 168.47 online texts per day in the tested categories compared with the *Guardian*'s 31.9. Whilst this discrepancy may seem initially surprising due to the comparable size of the two newspaper institutions, the *Daily Mail* articles include the recycling of material (where a phrase/sentence from one article is repurposed for a slightly different article) and we have controlled for this in our close analysis. The total word count for each corpus (324,692,331 and 56,403,306 respectively) indicates that articles from the *Daily Mail* also tend to be longer (with averages of 948.97 and 868.06 words per article). However, the *Daily Mail* website includes content that is produced in partnership with other newspapers, particularly the Chinese news source the *People's Daily*. Removing this type of article from the corpus (as it is not comparable with the content of the *Guardian* corpus), as well as removing articles relating to the arts (as this is a separate section in the *Guardian* which was not included in the corpus) leads to the following figures for the *Daily Mail*: 341,431 texts, 324,239,704 words (averages 168.11 per day and 949.65 words long) as shown in Table 4.1. Whilst we cannot claim that the corpora are representative of the *Daily Mail* and *Guardian* per se (they do not include sports articles, reviews, etc.) we can claim that both the *Daily Mail* and *Guardian* corpora are representative of news and debate journalism in both sources.

Table 4.1 Breakdown of *Daily Mail* and *Guardian* corpora

	Total		News		Comment	
	No. of words	No. of texts	No. of words	No. of texts	No. of words	No. of texts
Daily Mail	324,239,704	341,431	308,113,484	326,774	16,126,220	14,657
Guardian	56,403,306	64,976	36,530,430	43,508	19,872,876	21,468

The texts were mined from the two newspapers' websites. All boilerplate information (surrounding images, advertisements, html links, etc.) were removed and the articles were saved in a text file format. The articles were grouped by month and XML tagged for their source publication, month of publication, and article type (news or debate). They were also marked up using two types of linguistic tagging. Firstly parts of speech (POS) tags were assigned to each word in the texts and then semantic tags were added using the USAS tagger (Rayson et al. 2004). When the tagging had been completed, the texts were uploaded into the corpus software CQPweb (Hardie 2012) to facilitate the first stage of GTA.[3] We used the whole of each corpus to generate our corpus queries (see Chapter 5), but our GTA of poverty and its related discourses focuses on the news sections of our corpora only. We chose to focus on those texts which represented the institutional voice of each newspaper, as opposed to those in the comment/debate sections which were likely to include more individual/personal opinions about poverty.

4.2 Establishing the Geographies of Poverty in the Two Newspapers

Exploring the two newspapers' representations of poverty and place starts with a simple linguistic query on the use of the word 'poverty'. Searching for <*poverty*> returned 8004 instances in the *Guardian* and 9737 instances in the Daily Mail. The *Daily Mail* corpus is larger

[3]Our thanks go to Andrew Hardie for his invaluable help with this part of the process.

than the *Guardian* (see Sect. 4.1) so these figures were normalised to facilitate comparison. Thus, with 141.9 instances of <*poverty*> per million words (pmw), the *Guardian* seems significantly more interested in poverty than the *Daily Mail* which only has 30.0 instances pmw. Concordance geoparsing (see Sect. 3.2) was then used to convert these instances and their co-text into a format suitable for GTA.

As discussed in Chapter 3, place-names are complex and ambiguous. One particular issue is the importance of scale. Where place-names refer to towns and villages they can sensibly be represented within a GIS using a point. Larger areas, however, are more problematic. For example, if a city such as London is represented using a point, then how does this point relate to place-names within the city, such as Westminster or Islington. Similar issues exist with names of countries, counties, and other high-level administrative units. We chose to exclude generic references to poverty in the UK, England, Wales, Scotland, and Northern Ireland due to their lack of geographical specificity. Below this, high level administrative areas including county names and 'London' were flagged as being 'high-level units' so that these could be handled differently when required in subsequent analysis. Smaller cities and lower-level administrative areas including districts and parliamentary constituencies were not flagged as it was felt that within this analysis these can realistically be represented using a point. This choice is somewhat arbitrary and its implications will be returned to below.

The resulting geo-parsed data can be used to identify **place-name co-occurrences** (PNCs) which are defined as the occurrence of a place-name within 10 tokens either side of the search-term. PNCs are the basic unit of analysis within GTA. They consist of the search-term, the place-name, and the co-text that surrounds them, and can be represented using a point representing the location referred to by the place-name. Thus (1), below, forms a PNC between poverty and Blackpool because the two words are within 10 word tokens of each other. More than one PNC can be created by a single instance of the search-term. Example (2) generates two PNCs, one for Birmingham and one for Liverpool.

1. Mike Barry, once a debt adviser with Citizens Advice, and now operations director of the town's credit union, is dismayed—both by

Blackpool's worsening **poverty** and by the rise of the corporate moneylenders[4] (G news: news, July 2013).

2. More than 20% of children experience severe **poverty** in Birmingham and Liverpool (G news: society, Feb 2011).

The number of PNCs provides an indication of how closely the search-term is associated with place. In this case, neither of the two newspapers associates <*poverty*> with place particularly strongly. The *Guardian* contains 245 <*poverty*> PNCs, while the *Daily Mail* has 237. This means that only 3.06% and 2.43% of instances of the raw tokens of <*poverty*> found in each corpus respectively result in a PNC.

The resulting PNCs can be mapped as point data. However, patterns from dot maps are difficult for the human eye to perceive. For this reason a technique called **density smoothing** can be used to make the patterns within the data more understandable. Effectively, density smoothing converts the point pattern into a raster surface in which each raster cell's value measures how many points are near to that cell using a formula by which points nearer to the cell are given a higher weighting than those further away (Lloyd 2011).[5]

Density smoothed maps of <*poverty*> in the two corpora are shown in Fig. 4.1. These maps must be interpreted with caution because place-names flagged as high-level units have been included. The densities have been classed using z-scores. A z-score measures how far from the mean each value lies, a z-score of 0.0 is the mean of the dataset, 1.0 is one standard deviation above the mean, −2.0 is two standard deviations below the mean and so on. The higher class intervals on the map use z-scores of 1.96 and 2.58 respectively which are the absolute values that

[4] Bold text indicates the search-term, underlined text is the place-name.

[5] Key to this is the concept of a *bandwidth* which measures how quickly the weighting declines with distance. If the bandwidth is too low only areas very close to points will be identified and the density smoothing will not improve on the point pattern, if it is too high, the variations across the study area will be smoothed out. Bandwidths can be justified using measures based on the *standard distance* of the dataset, a measure similar to the standard deviation. In this case we use the formula proposed by Fotheringham et al. (2000: 149) $h_{opt} = \left[\frac{2}{3n}\right]^{1/4} \sigma$ where h_{opt} is the optimal bandwidth, σ is the standard distance, and n is the number of points in the dataset.

less than 5% and 1% of the observations should exceed assuming a two-tailed normal distribution. These thresholds therefore provide an indication of spatial clustering although they should not be taken as formal measures of statistical significance.

Figure 4.1 shows that the *Guardian*'s coverage of <*poverty*> is strongly concentrated on London, the only part of the country that has z-scores above 2.58. Perhaps more surprisingly, the second most concentrated cluster is centred on York which is the only other place with values above the 1.96 threshold. Working from north to south, there are weaker clusters centred on Glasgow, the north-east of England, Liverpool, and the M62 corridor,[6] Birmingham, the south-east outside of London, and Torbay in Devon (see Fig. 4.1 in the book introduction for the locations of these places). The association of major urban centres with poverty is not surprising, but the major cluster at York and the lesser cluster at Torbay are somewhat unexpected. In the density smoothed map of the *Daily Mail*'s PNCs, the pattern appears even more London-centric than the *Guardian*'s as nowhere beyond London crosses the 1.96 threshold. 48.9% of the *Daily Mail*'s PNCs lie within the London cluster compared to 37.1% in the *Guardian*. Beyond London, there are no obvious clusters in York or Torbay. Much of the remainder of the *Daily Mail* map looks similar to the *Guardian*'s. There are clusters in Glasgow, north-east England, the M62 area (although this is more concentrated on Manchester and spreads less to the east than in the *Guardian*), Birmingham, and the south-east beyond London. Two clusters that appear in the *Daily Mail* but not the *Guardian* are Belfast and Margate, in Kent.

Comparing map patterns by eye is difficult and highly subjective so, instead, spatial analysis can be used to conduct a more formal test as to whether and where two patterns differ. This involves using a technique called spatial segregation analysis (Rowlingson 2015; Diggle et al. 2005)[7] that compares two datasets to identify places that have significantly more points from one dataset than the other. The results of using spatial segregation analysis to compare <*poverty*> from the two

[6] The M62 motorway runs east-west across the north of England from Hull to Liverpool.

[7] We are very grateful to Barry Rowlingson for this assistance with this.

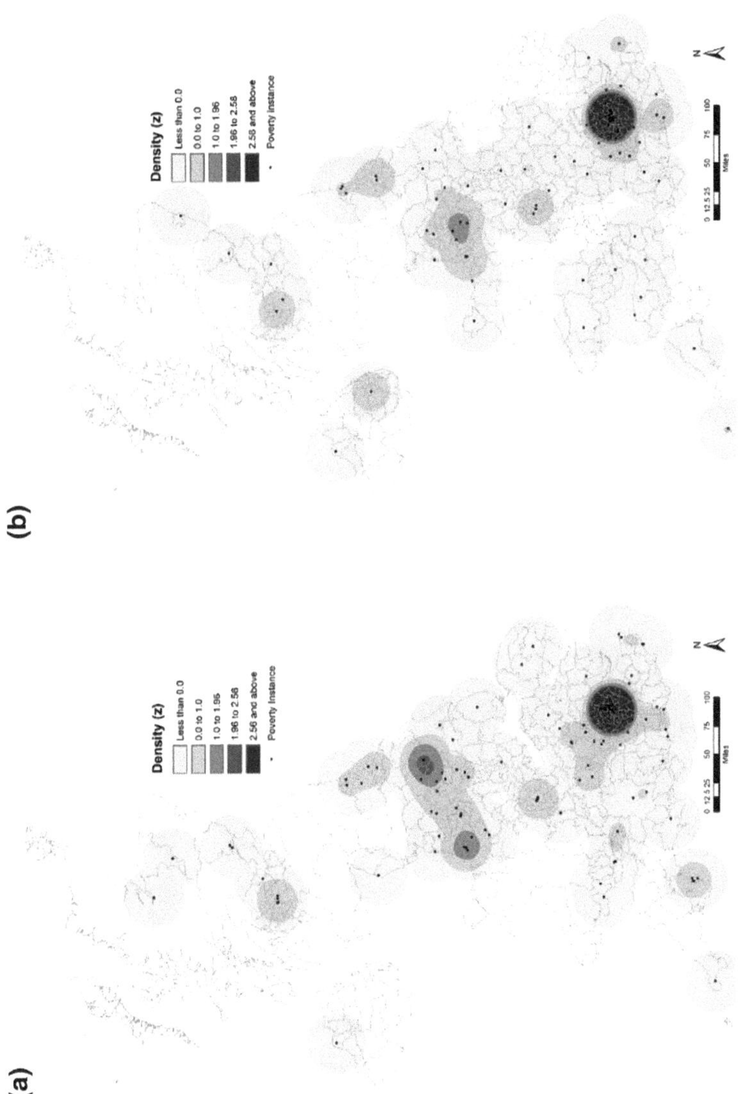

Fig. 4.1 Density smoothed maps of <*poverty*> PNCs: **a** *Guardian* **b** *Daily Mail*

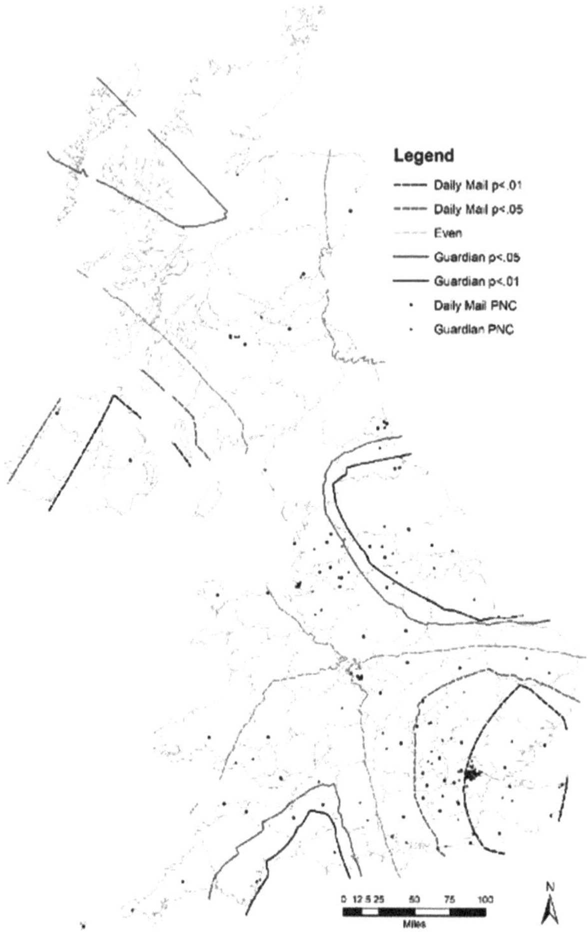

Fig. 4.2 Statistical comparison of the PNCs from the *Daily Mail* and the *Guardian*

newspapers are shown in Fig. 4.2. A global test[8] on this pattern gives a value of $p = 0.01$ suggesting that the two patterns do vary significantly from each other by location. The local statistics, shown in Fig. 4.2,

[8]Spatial analysts distinguish between global and local statistics. A global statistic, usually expressed as a single summary statistic such as a *p*-value or r^2, gives the average pattern or relationship across the study area. Local statistics, by contrast, express the relationship at multiple

confirm that the *Daily Mail*'s coverage of poverty concentrates more heavily on London than the *Guardian*'s. This is particularly true to the east of London. The *Daily Mail* is also prevalent in Northern Ireland because of the cluster in Belfast, a place that has no *Guardian* PNCs for <*poverty*>. The *Guardian* associates poverty far more with parts of eastern England, particularly east Yorkshire, than the *Daily Mail*. This is only partly caused by the York cluster; the *Guardian* also seems to concentrate more than the *Daily Mail* on other parts of Yorkshire, as well as further north to Middlesbrough and south into Lincolnshire. The *Guardian* also concentrates on Devon more than the *Daily Mail*, an emphasis that can be explained by its Torbay cluster. Having established where each newspaper talks about poverty, the next step is to interrogate what each newspaper is saying about poverty in these locations.

4.3 Geographical Variations in Discourses of Poverty

The basic finding from our spatial analysis is that, when the newspapers mention poverty within the scope of place, they both strongly associate <*poverty*> with London. Nearly a half of the *Daily Mail* PNCs and over a third of the *Guardian*'s refer to London or places within it. Beyond London, both newspapers largely concentrate on the major urban centres. Spatial analysis, and the maps that it creates, are excellent tools for identifying and describing spatial patterns. However, they are very limited in their ability to explain why these patterns exist. To understand the patterns and the differences between them, we must move away from mapping and spatial analysis, and back into the corpora from which the patterns emerged.

The easiest point of interest to address using the corpora is to question what it is about the unexpected places, such as York and Torbay

locations across the study area and, as a consequence, are usually shown in map form. They show what the pattern or relationship is at each location (Fotheringham 1997). As an example, a global statistic might suggest that across the country there is a positive relationship between unemployment and crime. Local statistics, however, might show that this relationship is strong in some areas, weaker in others, and is not present or even negative in others.

from the *Guardian* and Margate from the *Daily Mail*, that leads to their association with poverty. The obvious first approach to this is to closely read the concordances that create the PNCs. The *Guardian*'s York cluster is formed by seventeen PNCs all of which refer to York itself and all of which are in the society section of the newspaper. Significantly, eleven occur in a single article, which focuses on York's attempts to make itself a poverty-free city. There are also implications within the concordances that, although York is a relatively wealthy place, it contains a significant amount of hidden poverty, as shown in (3–4).

3. York embodies a specifically middle-England kind of **poverty** (G news: society, July 2014).
4. If work was guaranteed to drag you out of poverty, York should not have a **poverty** problem (G news: society, July 2014).

The *Guardian*'s relatively high concentration on east Yorkshire is only partly driven by its emphasis on York, which accounts for seventeen of its forty PNCs in this area (by contrast the *Daily Mail* has twelve). The *Guardian* also talks about poverty in Bradford, particularly in relation to race, and seems to have a range of stories across this region (5). The *Daily Mail*'s concentration on Belfast is largely explained by its name appearing in several lists of areas with high child poverty or other deprivation indicators, such as (6). These types of list rarely appear in the *Guardian*.

5. Research published last month by the Joseph Rowntree Foundation suggests that Bradford's real problem—**poverty**—has been overlooked (G news: society, Aug 2011).
6. CONSTITUENCIES WITH THE WORST LEVELS OF CHILD **POVERTY** 47 per cent Manchester Central 43 per cent Belfast West 43 per cent Glasgow North East 42 (DM news, Feb 2013).
7. Top of the 'at-risk' list are the 'English Riviera' towns of Torquay, Paignton and Brixham. The groups experiencing **poverty** vary from region to region. In Torbay (G news: society, June 2012).

The Torbay cluster in the *Guardian* and the Margate cluster in the *Daily Mail* are both perhaps a little misleading. Torbay is created from only seven PNCs of which four are repeated occurrences of (7). From the *Daily Mail*, the Margate cluster is created from three PNCs, all of which are associated with celebrities. One refers to Tracy Emin who 'grew up in **poverty** in Margate' while the other two refer to Mary Portas' efforts to reform retailing in the town which, it was claimed, was ignoring the town's problems with poverty. The fact that these clusters are created from so few PNCs is indicative of the relatively low z-scores that they are given in Fig. 4.1.

Exploring the concordances themselves allows us to identify what is driving patterns with relatively small numbers of instances. Analysing larger amounts of text requires the use of corpus linguistic techniques. Keyness is a corpus linguistics measure that allows one corpus or sub-corpus to be compared with another to identify which words are found significantly more/less frequently in one than in the other. These words are known as keywords (Baker 2006, see also Sect. 2.1). A variation of keyness, **contrastive concordance analysis**, can be used to compare two sets of PNCs. The word frequencies within one set of PNCs is compared with another set to discover which **PNC keywords** have statistically significant log likelihood scores. These can be used to compare how a single newspaper represents poverty in different places, or to compare the two newspapers' representation of poverty in particular places. An obvious question generated by the maps is the extent to which each newspaper discusses poverty in London differently from poverty in the rest of the country.

Table 4.2 identifies the PNC keywords for <*poverty*> in London when compared to elsewhere in the country. Starting with keywords in London, exploring the co-text reveals that *outer* is a keyword because there is a perception that poverty is spreading from the parts of inner London, that have traditionally been associated with poverty, into areas in outer London. This also leads to a number of instances of *now* as in they '*now* live in *outer* London'.[9] Other than this, it is difficult to discern any major trends about what is being said about London due to small numbers and sometimes the multiple occurrences of phrases

[9] Italics indicate PNC keywords.

Table 4.2 PNC keywords in the *Guardian* comparing the co-text of <*poverty*> in London with the rest of the UK[a]

Place	Sig.	Keywords
London	<.01	outer, wealth, notoriously, mixed, most, compared, now
London	<.05	regions, only, because, alongside, number, than, disparity, rate, wide, reveal, where
Rest of UK	<.01	region, hidden
Rest of UK	<.05	life, constituency, last, five, says, happy, she, crime

[a]PNC keywords are found within 10 words of the search-term, are statistically significant using log-likelihood at the level shown by 'Sig.', have a minimum frequency of 3 and are presented in reverse order of log-likelihood score. Place-names have been excluded.

including lists of place-names. An example of this is that *notoriously*, *mixed*, *wealth*, and *most* all come from (8), which gives 5 PNCs: Kensington and Chelsea, London, Enfield, Brent, and Waltham Forest, which account for almost all of the observed occurrences of these PNC keywords.

8. Other good performers among poorer parts of the country are the London boroughs of Kensington and Chelsea (where **poverty** and *wealth* are *most notoriously mixed*), Enfield, Brent, and Waltham Forest (G news: society, June 2013).

The PNC keywords for outside London show some slightly more interesting patterns. *Hidden* comes in part from the discourse about York which frequently refers to 'hidden poverty'. There are also a number of instances of hidden poverty being found in counties, mainly in the south-east of England. These continue to develop what was found in York, namely that the *Guardian*'s take on poverty outside London is associated with hidden poverty in relatively wealthy places. *Constituency* follows this theme, the most commonly cited being David Cameron's Witney constituency, which is again used to highlight poverty in relatively affluent, or *leafy* places. The PNC keyword *crime* makes direct links between crime and poverty, and *she* tends to refer either to individual women who have risen from poverty in a particular place, or who are talking about it in relation to places outside London. The findings for *region*, which is distorted by the phrase 'region to region', *happy*

Table 4.3 PNC keywords in the *Daily Mail* comparing the co-text of <*poverty*> in London with the rest of the UK

Place	Sig.	Keywords
London	<.01	two, one, rate, reached, country, protest, he, Victorian, years
London	<.05	slum, caf, says, reason, cereals, imported, walked, Keely, poorest, improved, great, compared, depression, Facebook, home, become, during, high, rose, class, byword, nostalgia, despite, situation, capital, broadly, miles, men, walk, show
Rest of UK	<.01	too, risks, lowest, people, left, care, we
Rest of UK	<.05	level, making, road, citing, wherever, small, fuel, herself, find, families, local, her, poorer, five, here, taking, miss, ignoring

which comes from a single quote that occurs in multiple PNCs, *five* which refers to one in five people in an area living in poverty, and *says*, which is used to preface a quote, are less illuminating.

Trying to sub-divide the poverty PNCs into more detailed classes than simply London and the rest of the UK rapidly runs into small number problems. One interesting finding is that when the non-London urban clusters of Liverpool, the M62, Yorkshire (excluding York), Glasgow and Birmingham are compared with the rest, *life* is significant at the $p < 0.01$ level and *fuel* at the $p < 0.05$ level. *Life* either discusses the link between poverty and low life expectancy or people being condemned to a life in poverty, and 6 of the 7 instances of this are found in these urban areas, while *fuel* refers to fuel poverty. This suggests that the issues of low life expectancy, life-long poverty, and fuel poverty are primarily associated with major urban areas in contrast to the hidden poverty in more rural areas.

Table 4.3 shows the *Daily Mail*'s PNC keywords comparing London with the rest of the UK. Analysing the *Daily Mail*'s concordance lines shows that that the newspaper often repeats sentences or paragraphs several times in different articles. An example of this is a story repeated in several texts which contrasts the poverty in the borough with an expensive café in Tower Hamlets that sells breakfast cereal for £2.50 or £3.20 a bowl (depending on the article). Within these stories, example (9) occurs 6 times and (10) occurs 4 times.

9. Tower Hamlets has the highest *rate* of child **poverty** in the *country*—it *reached* 49 per cent this year (DM news, Dec 2012).
10. In Tower Hamlets, where *one* in *two* children live in **poverty** (DM news, Dec 2014).

These two examples[10] do much to explain the high instances of *two*, *one*, *rate*, *reached*, and *country*. This story is also responsible for a number of PNC keywords that are significant at the $p < 0.05$ level namely *caf*, *says*, *reason*, *cereals*, *imported*, *Keely*, *Facebook*, and *nostalgia*.

A number of more reliable themes also emerge from the *Daily Mail*'s keywords about poverty in London: London is associated with poverty because of men who were born into poverty in London and rose out of it. This explains the occurrences of *he*, *become*, and *rose*. Historical stories about poverty are also frequently related to the city. Again, the phenomenon of repeated phrasing is apparent, with 6 references to the Jarrow marches which, although used in different contexts, are realised similarly to (11) and lead to *protest*, *men*, *walk*, and *walked* appearing as PNC keywords.

11. when 200 *men walked* to London to *protest* about unemployment and **poverty** (DM news, July 2010).

History also emerges in other ways. *Victorian* and *slum* occur because of discussion of London slums, particularly those in the East End in the Victorian era, and the phrase '*during* the *Great Depression*' puts all of these words (except 'the') onto the list of PNC keywords.

The *Daily Mail* includes some positive stories about modern poverty in London. For example, there are reports about pupils who have achieved good educational results despite living in areas with high levels of poverty, which account for many instances of *high* and *despite*. The *Daily Mail* also contrasts poverty in London, particularly East End

[10]These two examples also demonstrate the limitations of using PNC keywords for non-lemmatised data. Clearly (9) and (10) both refer to child poverty, but one refers to 'children' and the other 'child'. Combined it is likely that the lemma CHILD would be a PNC keyword, but separately they do not meet significance thresholds.

places such as Limehouse and Poplar, with affluence elsewhere. This leads to *compared* being a PNC keyword. The *Daily Mail* also compares poverty in London with the affluence of David Cameron's Witney constituency. This contrasts with the *Guardian*'s perspective, where poverty in Witney is seen as a problem, albeit a hidden one. *Improved*, *situation*, and *broadly* largely come from one PNC, as in (12).

12. 42 per cent of children were below the poverty line in the constituency of Bethnal Green and Bow while 41 per cent were living in **poverty** in Poplar and Limehouse. The *situation* has *broadly improved* since 2011 (DM news, Feb 2013).

Again, this story is putting a more positive slant on the situation. By contrast, *capital* occurs in part because of London is described as the '**poverty** *capital* of Europe'. Finally, *home* is always used in relation to an individual's home rather than in relation to homelessness, while *class* is usually used in relation to 'the top of the class' rather than social class.

Outside of London there are again issues of repeated text. Example (13) leads to four PNCs which, between them, account for most instances of *care*, *we*, *wherever*, *find*, and *citing*. Only one instance of *care* refers to children being taken into care. Similarly, a list of Local Authorities occurring with '*Lowest* Level of Child Poverty' gives nine PNCs which accounts for most instances of *too, risks, lowest, level*, and *local*.

13. Mr. Miliband said people *care* about inequality '*wherever we find* it', *citing* child **poverty** in Glasgow and Liverpool, unemployment in Motherwell and Newcastle and (DM news, Sept 2014).

Three of the PNC keywords, *herself*, *her*, and *Miss*, refer typically to stories about women who were born into poverty but raised themselves out of it, or who had come into a large sum of money. These PNC keywords are indicative of a trend in the *Daily Mail* to focus on individual stories (see Chapter 6). There are also reports about women who either left someone in poverty while spending money on themselves, or conversely, where someone else had left a woman in poverty. Another story associated with women refers specifically to Mary Portas, who is represented as '*ignoring* **poverty** in Margate and *making* it too trendy', and contributes to the PNC keyness of *making* and *ignoring*. *People* is similar to the feminine-marked terms discussed above as it typically refers to either people who have risen from poverty or been left in it. In cases where people have risen from poverty the article usually implies agency, while in cases where people have been left in poverty it implies powerlessness.

In contrast to the occurrences of positive slants on poverty we see associated with London, there does not appear to be a positive slant on stories located elsewhere. For example, *fuel* and *families* draw attention to fuel poverty and families in poverty outside London. *Small* and *poorer* have only three instances each and thus wider trends are not identifiable. As with the *Guardian*, attempting to compare urban areas away from London with the remaining places quickly runs into small number problems. The only PNC keywords that are significant at $p < 0.01$, have a frequency of five or over, and are not parts of place-names or numbers, are *we* and *have*. Comparing London as depicted in the *Guardian* and the *Daily Mail*, the latter seems far more interested in child poverty in London than the *Guardian*. The *Daily Mail* has 37 PNCs with the word 'child' in their co-text compared to only 11 in the *Guardian*. This is at least in part caused by the *Daily Mail* listing places with high rates of child poverty, and areas of London feature heavily in these lists. *Combat* for the *Daily Mail* also comes from this, as it is associated with ways to combat child poverty (although this is largely based on multiple PNCs from one instance of *combat*).

In general, there are two main themes that emerge from the two newspapers' discussions of poverty in different places: (i) those associated with aggregate poverty where poverty is treated as an issue for society, and (ii) poverty associated with individual people and, often, their rise from it (which is frequently linked to gender as well as place). No strong theme emerges from the *Guardian*'s discussions about aggregate poverty in London other than poverty's spread from inner to outer London. The *Daily Mail*, by contrast, has much more to say. It has a somewhat mixed message that, on the one hand, points to improvements in poverty in London, while also describing London as the 'poverty capital of Europe' and comparing poverty in inner-city London with the wealth in other parts of the country, especially David

Cameron's Witney constituency. Outside London, both newspapers have fairly similar themes on aggregate poverty. Both talk about fuel poverty, but the *Guardian* talks about the links between poverty, crime, and low life expectancy, while the *Daily Mail* talks about families in poverty in a more personalised way. The one theme not found in the *Daily Mail* is the *Guardian*'s discussion of hidden poverty in typically more wealthy areas. It is worth stressing, however, that this analysis is limited by relatively small numbers of fewer than 250 PNCs in both cases, especially as some PNCs are caused by having multiple place-names near to the search-term or the same story being reproduced several times. Nevertheless, this analysis does much to shed light on the different discussions of and perspectives on poverty that create the patterns identified by the spatial analysis.

4.4 Comparing Representations of Poverty with Quantitative Measures

So far we have shown that both newspapers' coverage of poverty is heavily skewed towards London—the *Daily Mail* more than the *Guardian*—and then tends to concentrate on other major cities, although there are exceptions to this such as York, Torbay, and Margate. This poses the question of to what extent this is justified. In other words, are the newspapers actively concentrating on areas that have high levels of deprivation? As described in Chapter 1, deprivation can be measured quantitatively using indicators such as Carstairs scores which, in this case, can be derived from 2011 census data by summing the z-scores from four variables: overcrowded housing, low-skilled work, unemployment, and lack of a car. Scores of 0.0 indicate average levels of deprivation, higher values indicate higher levels of deprivation, with values above 4.0 indicating that on average each of the four measures is one standard deviation above the mean (Morgan and Baker 2006).

Carstairs scores for local authority districts in the UK in 2011 are shown in Fig. 4.3. Conceptually, comparing these to PNCs for <*poverty*> is simple as both datasets are available in geo-referenced form—the PNCs are geo-referenced using points, while the Carstairs scores are

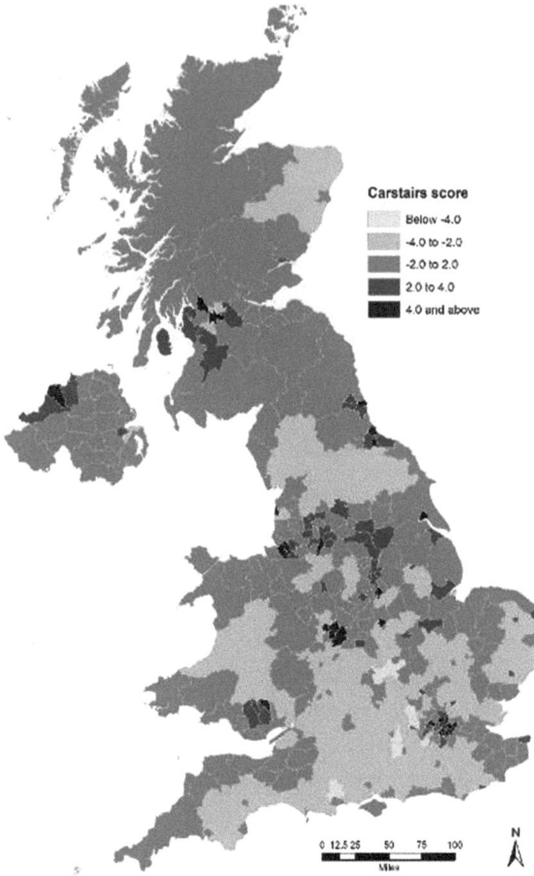

Fig. 4.3 Carstairs scores for the UK from the 2011 census. Polygons show local authority districts

for local authority districts. If all of the PNCs referred to local authority districts or sub-divisions of them then comparing the two would be simple. However, the place-names in the PNCs refer to a range of features including settlements such as cities, towns and villages, and a range of administrative units including London boroughs, districts, parliamentary constituencies, and counties. One solution to this could be to ignore higher-level units which, as described above, are already flagged as such, and compare the remainder with Carstairs scores at local authority district level. An alternative is to aggregate the Carstairs scores to county level and compare these with all PNCs. This is more reliable but the Carstairs scores will be averaged out across large areas with potentially highly variable rates of poverty, particularly in London which includes some of the wealthiest and most deprived parts of the UK. This is part of what geographers refer to as the modifiable areal unit problem (Openshaw 1984; Wong 2009) where relationships between two datasets will vary according to both the scale at which the relationship is measured, and on the arrangement of the aggregated units. It is considered good practice to analyse data at the lowest possible level of aggregation to avoid these issues, and/or to repeat the analysis at more than one scale.

Using Carstairs scores at local authority district level, and thus ignoring PNCs classed as referring to high-level units, Table 4.4 compares the number of districts with different levels of deprivation with the number of PNCs referring to them in the two newspapers. In general, this shows that the two newspapers do concentrate their coverage of poverty on areas that have higher levels of deprivation. The *Daily Mail* seems to do this somewhat more than the *Guardian*: 86% of the *Daily Mail*'s PNCs are in districts with above average deprivation (a Carstairs score of above 0.0) compared to 75% of the *Guardian*'s, with similar differences at higher levels of deprivation.

Table 4.5 explores the extremes of this in more detail by looking at the ten districts with the most PNCs for each corpus. Five places—Tower Hamlets, Liverpool, Glasgow, Islington and Middlesbrough—are on both lists and also have high levels of deprivation. Beyond this, the *Daily Mail* seems to concentrate more than the *Guardian* on areas with

Table 4.4 The occurrences of PNCs from the two newspapers in local authority districts with differing levels of deprivation

Carstairs scores	*Guardian*		*Daily Mail*	
	Count	%	Count	%
Above 0.0	133	76.4	145	86.3
Above 2.0	105	60.3	128	76.2
Above 4.0	75	43.1	97	57.7
All	174	100.0	168	100.0

Table 4.5 Local authority districts with the most PNCs from the *Guardian* and the *Daily Mail*

Top 10 *Guardian* Districts				Top 10 *Daily Mail* Districts				Top 10 Carstairs Districts			
District	*G* PNCs	*DM* PNCs	Carstairs	District	*G* PNCs	*DM* PNCs	Carstairs	District	Carstairs	*G* PNCs	*DM* PNCs
York	17	0	−0.77	Tower Hamlets	14	35	6.53	Newham	7.50	0	3
Tower Hamlets	14	35	6.53	Manchester	3	13	4.20	Hackney	7.27	2	6
Liverpool	12	10	5.07	Liverpool	12	10	5.07	Kingston upon Hull	6.73	2	0
Glasgow City	9	6	4.71	Glasgow City	9	7	3.20	Tower Hamlets	6.53	14	35
Torbay	6	0	1.03	Belfast	0	6	4.71	Barking & Dagenham	6.15	2	0
Birmingham	6	1	4.90	Hackney	2	6	7.27	Sandwell	5.90	0	2
Lambeth	5	3	5.13	City of London, Westminster	0	5	3.40	Southwark	5.85	1	3
Bradford	5	2	3.17	Middlesbrough	4	4	5.73	Middlesbrough	5.73	4	4
Islington	4	4	4.88	Islington	4	4	4.88	Wolverhampton	5.73	0	0
Kensington & Chelsea	4	1	2.08	Lambeth	5	3	5.13	Leicester	5.72	0	1
West Oxfordshire	4	0	−3.25	Thanet	2	3	2.47				
Middlesbrough	4	4	5.73	Southwark	1	3	5.85				
				Newham	0	3	6.53				
				Stockton-On-Tees	0	3	4.21				

high levels of deprivation. The lowest Carstairs score in the *Daily Mail*'s list is Thanet in north Kent with a Carstairs score of 2.47, while the rest are all over 3.0. By contrast, the *Guardian* has two places—York and West Oxfordshire—that have below average deprivation and a further two—Torbay and Kensington and Chelsea—which have Carstairs scores that are lower than Thanet. The *Guardian* thus appears to have an interest in poverty in some places that are relatively affluent. This is not present in the *Daily Mail*.

Looking at the areas with the highest Carstairs scores (Table 4.5) the *Daily Mail* seems to concentrate on high deprivation areas more than the *Guardian*, with twice as many of its PNCs referring to places in these areas. In both cases, Tower Hamlets dominates the list with over half of all of the PNCs for these ten districts, although the cereal café story contributes significantly to the *Daily Mail's* interest in this area. There are three other east London districts with very high levels of deprivation: Newham, Hackney, and Barking and Dagenham. In comparison to Tower Hamlets these districts attract very little attention with only 6 and 9 PNCs in the *Guardian* and the *Daily Mail* respectively. Away from London, it is noticeable that the districts with high levels of deprivation are not big cities but are instead Kingston upon Hull, Sandwell and Wolverhampton (both in the Black Country), Middlesbrough, and Leicester. This may in part be a result of the modifiable areal unit problem. Deprived areas in major cities may be aggregated with wealthier areas thus averaging their Carstairs scores, while smaller places are more homogeneous. Nevertheless, with the exception of Middlesbrough, poverty in these places is largely ignored by both newspapers. If the list is broadened to cover all thirty districts with Carstairs scores over 4.0 we find that, within our scope of ten words either side, the *Guardian* never mentions poverty in relation to 9 of these while the *Daily Mail* does not mention it in 12. Neither newspaper associates <*poverty*> with Blaenau Gwent (south Wales), Knowsley (Liverpool), Greenwich (London), West Dunbartonshire (outside Glasgow), Wolverhampton or Walsall (both in the Black Country).

Table 4.6 uses Spearman's rank correlation coefficients to compare deprivation and numbers of PNCs for local authority districts. Overall, the *Guardian*'s PNCs correlate slightly more strongly with Carstairs

Table 4.6 Spearman's rank correlation coefficients comparing district-level Carstairs scores & PNCs

	N	*Guardian*	*Daily Mail*
All	404	.316**	.231**
Carstairs <= 0.0	217	−.016	−0.14*
Carstairs > 0.0	187	.321**	.333**
Carstairs > 2.0	88	.362**	.294**
Carstairs > 4.0	30	.155	.288
Daily Mail instances > 0	66	.594**	.568**
Guardian instances > 0	73	.296*	.522**
Daily Mail and *Guardian* instances > 0	27	.398*	.532**

**significant at $p < 0.01$, *significant at $p < 0.05$

scores than the *Daily Mail*'s but both are statistically significant. Perhaps unsurprisingly given what we have already seen, the significance disappears if only districts with very high levels of deprivation (above 4.0), or below average deprivation, are considered. Excluding districts for which the *Daily Mail* has no PNCs raises its correlations noticeably; however, excluding areas for which the *Guardian* has no PNCs reduces its coefficients. This is because the *Daily Mail* concentrates its attention on areas with relatively high deprivation while the *Guardian*'s PNCs are more dispersed across the range of poverty values.

In summary, these analyses seem to show that the two newspapers generally do concentrate their coverage of <*poverty*> on areas that can be shown quantitatively to have high levels of deprivation. The *Daily Mail* does this more than the *Guardian*, which also draws attention to poverty in some more affluent places. Within this, however, there are some clear exceptions, particularly with districts with high deprivation being largely ignored by either or both newspapers.

4.5 Comparing Representations of Poverty with the Newspapers' Background Geography

Rather than focusing on deprived areas, an alternative interpretation of the spatial analysis of <*poverty*> is that newspapers simply talk about some places more than others. If newspapers show geographical favouritism in the places that they represent overall—either as a result of conscious editorial decisions or unconscious biases—then the geographies they associate with poverty, or indeed any other theme, will follow this more general use of place-names. We therefore need to be able to identify whether our results for <*poverty*> are more than just an indication of how newspapers refer to place more generally. In many ways this question is similar to one that has an established history in spatial analysis, namely do certain types of events tend to cluster against a geographically variable background population. A classic example of this is whether diseases such as childhood cancers cluster in particular places, the challenge being that any map of these diseases is likely largely to represent the background population distribution and it will thus be difficult to identify clusters of disease cases from background population clusters in towns and cities. A range of statistical approaches have been developed to identify such clusters (see, for example, Openshaw et al. 1987; Besag and Newell 1991; Fotheringham and Zhan 1996; and Kulldorf 1997). In our case we are using Kulldorf's (1997) spatial scan statistic, a technique that considers every point location for which a background population is recorded. It tests whether there are statistically significantly more or fewer events near to each location under the null hypothesis that events are distributed at random among the background population. 'Near' is defined using circles of increasing radii around the points that make up the background population. The most statistically significant locations are recorded.

Rather than diseases in a population, in GTA the question becomes whether the distribution of PNCs simply reflects the background geography of place-names in the corpus as a whole or whether there are hotspots—places where more instances of PNCs are found than expected from the background—or coldspots—where there are fewer than expected. The 'events' are the locations of PNCs of the search-term, in this case <*poverty*>. The background population is more difficult to define. Ideally, the entire corpus would be geoparsed and the locations of all place-names within it would provide the background geography (Donaldson et al. 2017). Here, however, this is not practical due to the difficulties in geoparsing corpora of this size. An alternative approach is to test the search-term PNCs against a sample of other PNCs that might be thought to provide a realistic background geography. This is similar to testing for clusters of a disease by comparing the pattern of disease events with patterns from diseases that are not thought to exhibit clustering.

To generate a background population we decided to geoparse a random sample of 5% of all the occurrences of *the* in our corpora. *The* is the most common word in the English language and is likely to have regular distribution across a corpus. 153,000 instances of *the* in the *Guardian* included 9206 PNCs (located within the UK, using the same criteria as were used for <*poverty*>), and 782,000 instances of *the* in the *Daily Mail* gave 46,596 PNCs (normalised frequencies of 252.01 and 151.23 per million words, respectively). The normalised frequencies seem to suggest that the *Daily Mail* tends to refer to UK place-names much less than the *Guardian* does, and this should be kept in mind throughout the analysis of poverty (and when using this method for comparing different corpora). The locations for *the* PNCs, shown in Fig. 4.4, provide what can be taken to be the background geography of place-names within the two corpora. Kulldorf's scan statistic can then be used to identify which places have more/fewer PNCs than the background geography would have us expect. In this way we are able to establish how the geography of the search-term varies from the background geography of the corpus as a whole. This method can be replicated for any English language corpus to provide a background population of the place-names mentioned.

Figure 4.5 shows the results of the Kulldorf analysis. The three major hotspots in the *Guardian* are east London, east Yorkshire, and Torbay. Thus the *Guardian*'s coverage of <*poverty*> in these areas is not an artefact of general place-name distribution. The only other two statistically significant hotspots are High Wycombe (west of London) and Preston in north-west England. These can be disregarded as they are generated by 2 and 1 PNCs respectively, albeit in areas that do not co-occur with *the* in the 5% sample. The coldspots stretch from the Thames Estuary to Suffolk, and from the English border counties through southern Scotland to Fife. These are centred on rural areas, but Newcastle-upon-Tyne is in the southern part of the Border coldspot, and the Thames Gateway area lies in the southern

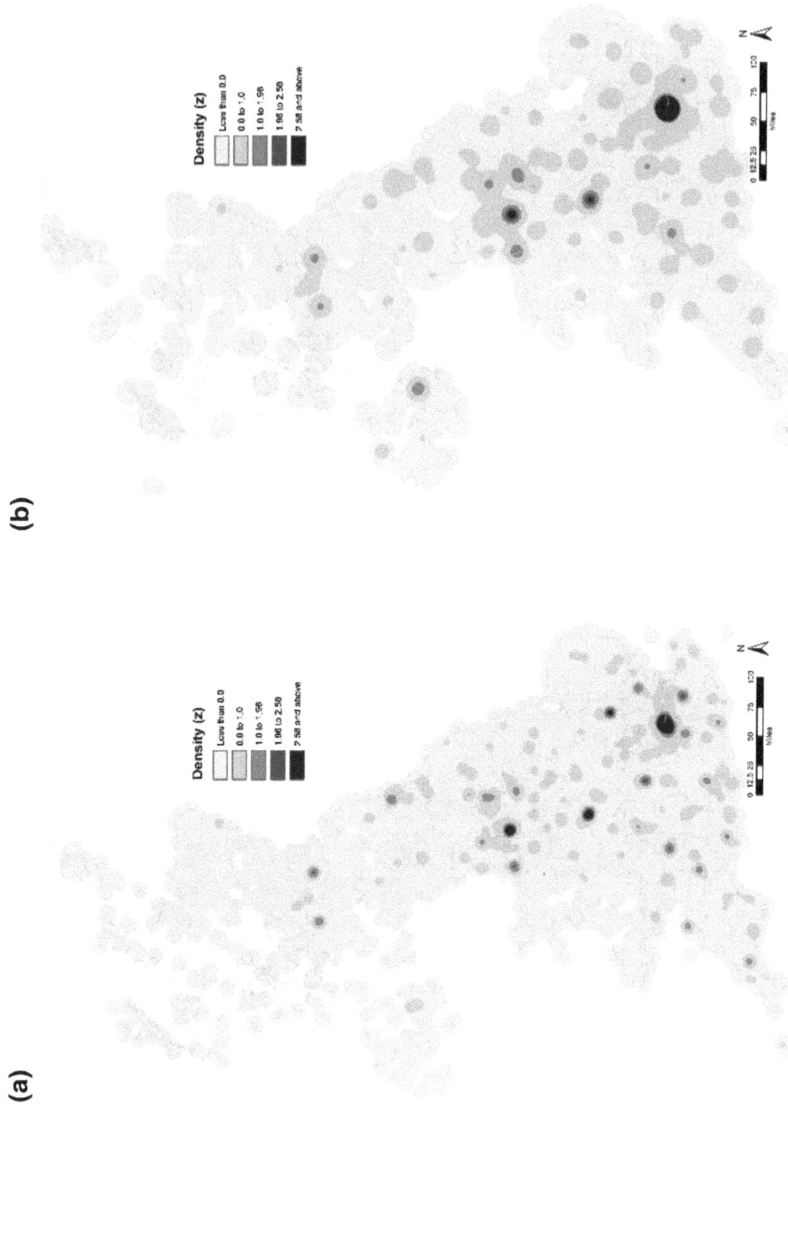

Fig. 4.4 Density smoothed maps of *the* PNCs. Note that for legibility individual instances have not been shown as points: **a** *Guardian* **b** *Daily Mail*

Fig. 4.5 Kulldorf analysis of <*poverty*> using a 5% sample of *the* as the background population. Points identified are those from the background population that are at risk of being in a hot or cold spot: **a** *Guardian* **b** *Daily Mail*

part of the East Anglian coldspot. The absence of Belfast and other previously identified areas is perhaps explained by the fact that the *Guardian* apparently does not tend to refer to these areas. The Kulldorf results for the *Daily Mail* show two major hotspots—London and Liverpool—and a further two minor hotspots at Wokingham (west of London) and York that are a result of only one PNC. As with the *Guardian*, much of East Anglia is a coldspot, although this stretches further north through Lincolnshire and into eastern Yorkshire. South-west London and Surrey form a second coldspot with Birmingham and much of the West Country forming a third. This coldspot is perhaps similar to the Border one from the *Guardian* in that it is largely rural but has a large urban centre on its fringe, in this case Birmingham. This coldspot also contains Bristol.

These results reveal further insights into the places that the two newspapers associate with <*poverty*>. Although Fig. 4.1 showed that both newspapers' coverage of <*poverty*> is very London-centric, Fig. 4.5 suggests that this is can largely be explained by the newspaper's coverage of place being London-centric. The exception to this is East London which stands out in both newspapers as being more closely associated with poverty than this London-centric coverage would lead us to expect. This does correspond with the highest Carstairs scores being found in districts in East London. Elsewhere, the surprising finding is that, with the exception of Liverpool in the *Daily Mail*, urban centres with high levels of deprivation, such as Glasgow, Manchester, and Birmingham, do not receive more attention than would be expected. Neither do smaller high deprivation areas such as Middlesbrough, Hull, Leicester, or south Wales. The *Guardian* associates places such as York and Torbay with poverty in ways that would not be expected either from the newspaper's background geography or the places' levels of deprivation. Rural areas, particularly in East Anglia, tend to be under-represented by both papers. These areas typically do not have high levels of deprivation as measured by Carstairs scores, but equally are not particularly wealthy.

4.6 Summary

This chapter has shown how GTA enables us to identify and explore the geographies that the two newspapers associate with a particular theme. Focusing on the single search-term <*poverty*>, it has explored a range of techniques that allow us to identify the areas that the two newspapers associate with this search-term, compare these two geographies to see whether and where they are different, and explore the language in PNCs. It also compared data extracted from texts to statistical sources. Both newspapers concentrate their coverage of <*poverty*> on London in general and smaller areas like Tower Hamlets in particular. This is especially true for the *Daily Mail.* Outside London, the other major urban centres are also associated with poverty, particularly Liverpool and Glasgow, although both newspapers tend not to focus on Birmingham and the West Midlands, while the *Guardian* also does not consider Belfast or, to a lesser extent, Manchester. The PNC keywords suggest a broadly similar discourse about aggregate poverty in the major cities outside London, with issues such as fuel poverty and links with crime and low life expectancy being raised. However, the *Daily Mail* tends to talk about this in relation to individuals and families while the *Guardian* does so in a more aggregate way. Within London, the *Daily Mail* carries stories that emphasise improvements and relative success stories, such as areas that have good exam results despite high levels of poverty, but it also describes London several times as the 'poverty capital of Europe'. The *Daily Mail* also draws attention to historical poverty in London. Neither of these themes is really apparent in the *Guardian.* Away from the urban centres, the *Guardian* focuses on 'hidden' poverty in more affluent areas, including Witney, the south-east more generally, and York. These stories are far less common in the *Daily Mail.*

Even this initial analysis has shown how the two newspapers are both similar and different in their approaches to poverty and place. There are some initial indications in the PNC co-text of the different ideological stances of the two newspapers. Individualisation is important in the *Daily Mail*, for example, which could be seen to endorse a neoliberal attitude towards poverty and its causes. Similarly, a focus on historical poverty could be used to endorse the position that poverty no longer exists in the UK. To determine whether these initial trends are representative of wider discourses of poverty, it is important to test more search terms and Chapter 5 details how we set out to do this.

Comparing the pattern of PNCs with Carstairs scores and the background geographies from the newspapers shows that the two newspapers broadly focus on areas with high levels of poverty when these are in big cities (with notable exceptions, such as Birmingham, Belfast and, to a lesser extent, Manchester). They are also patchy in their coverage of London, particularly the East End, where Tower Hamlets gets most of the attention and nearby districts with similarly high levels of deprivation such as Hackney, Newham, and Dagenham and Redbridge, receive far less. Outside London, areas of high deprivation away from big cities are generally under-represented. Due to its stories about hidden poverty, the *Guardian* concentrates on rural areas in the south-east in particular. However, these areas receive less attention related to poverty than they do overall in the newspaper suggesting that these stories perhaps reflect an interest in these areas and the people within them. The Kulldorf analysis reinforces this by suggesting that both newspapers concentrate their coverage of poverty on east London in particular, over and above what would be expected from their background geographies.

As noted above, these findings must be treated with caution because they are based on a single search-term and rapidly run into small number problems. This is particularly true when lists of place-names cause multiple PNCs from one instance of a search term and is exacerbated by the *Daily Mail*'s habit of reproducing exact phrasings several times in different texts. Nevertheless, they do demonstrate the potential for using GTA to understand the discourses around poverty and place. Fundamentally, the preceding analysis constitutes proof of concept of large-scale concordance geoparsing and GTA. It also reveals that there are some clear geographies and biases in the way that this topic is presented in the two newspapers. But discourses of poverty are not restricted to the geographical profile of a single term. In the next chapter we document how GTA can be scaled up to incorporate multiple search terms centred on a single theme.

References

Baker, P. 2006. *Using Corpora in Discourse Analysis*. London: Continuum.

Besag J., & J. Newell. 1991. The Detection of Clusters in Rare Diseases. *Journal of the Royal Statistical Society Series A* 154: 143–155.

Diggle, P., P. Zheng, & P. Durr. 2005. Nonparametric Estimation of Spatial Segregation in a Multivariate Point Process: Bovine Tuberculosis in Cornwall, UK. *Journal of the Royal Statistical Society Series A* 54: 645–658.

Donaldson, C., I. N. Gregory, & J. E. Taylor. 2017. Locating the Beautiful, Picturesque, Sublime and Majestic: Spatially Analysing the Application of Aesthetic Terminology in Descriptions of the English Lake District. *Journal of Historical Geography* 56: 43–60.

Fotheringham, A. S. 1997. Trends in Quantitative Methods I: Stressing the Local. *Progress in Human Geography* 21: 88–96.

Fotheringham, A. S., C. Brusdon, & M. Charlton. 2000. *Quantitative Geography: Perspectives on Spatial Data Analysis*. London: Sage.

Fotheringham, A. S., & F. Zhan. 1996. A Comparison of Three Exploratory Methods for Cluster Detection in Spatial Point Patterns. *Geographical Analysis* 28: 200–218.

Gregory, I. N., & C. Donaldson. 2016. Geographical Text Analysis: Digital Cartographies of Lake District literature. In D. Cooper, C. Donaldson, & P. Murrieta-Flores (eds.). *Literary Mapping in the Digital Age*. Abingdon: Routledge, pp. 67–87.

Hardie, A. 2012. CQPweb—Combining Power, Flexibility and Usability in a Corpus Analysis Tool. *International Journal of Corpus Linguistics* 17: 380–409.

Jackson, J. 2016. Independent, Mirror, Express and Star Suffer Sharp Fall in Traffic. *Guardian* 17/3/2016. https://www.theguardian.com/media/2016/mar/17/independent-mirror-express-and-star-suffer-sharp-fall-in-traffic. Accessed 12/5/2017.

Kulldorf, M. 1997. A Spatial Scan Statistic. *Communications in Statistics: Theory and Methods* 26: 1481–1496.

Lloyd, C. D. 2011. *Local Models for Spatial Analysis* (second edition). Boca Raton, FL: CRC Press.

Morgan, O., & A. Baker. 2006. Measuring Deprivation in England and Wales Using 2001 Carstairs Scores. *Health Statistics Quarterly* 31: 28–33.

Murrieta-Flores, P., A. Baron, I. N. Gregory, A. Hardie, & P. Rayson. 2015. Automatically Analysing Large Texts in a GIS Environment: The Registrar

General's Reports and Cholera in the Nineteenth Century. *Transactions in GIS* 19: 296–320.
Openshaw, S. 1984. *The Modifiable Areal Unit Problem. Concepts and Techniques in Modern Geography 38.* Norwich: Geo Books.
Openshaw, S., M. Charlton, C. Wymer, & A. Craft. 1987. A Mark 1 Geographic Analysis Machine for the Automated Analysis of Point Data Sets. *International Journal of Geographical Information Systems* 1: 335–358.
Porter, C., P. Atkinson, & I. N. Gregory. 2015. Geographical Text Analysis: A New Key to Nineteenth-Century Mortality. *Health and Place* 36: 25–34.
Rayson P., D. Archer, S. Piao, & T. McEnery. 2004. The UCREL Semantic Analysis System. *Proceedings of the Beyond Named Entity Recognition Semantic Labelling for NLP Tasks Workshop*, Lisbon, Portugal, pp. 7–12.
Rowlingson, B. 2015. *Spatial Segregation Analysis.* Personal Communication.
Turvill, W. 2015. National Newspaper Circulations, May 2015: Mail on Sunday Overtakes Sun on Sunday, Times Remains Only Growing Title. http://www.pressgazette.co.uk/national-newspaper-circulations-may-2015-mail-sunday-overtakes-sun-sunday-times-remains-biggest-growing/. Accessed 15/1/2016.
Wong, D. 2009. The Modifiable Areal Unit Problem. In A. S. Fotheringham & P. A. Rogerson (eds.). *The Sage Handbook of Spatial Analysis.* London: Sage, pp. 105–124.

5
How to Use GTA in Discourse Analysis

Whilst the GTA of <*poverty*> in the previous chapter provided a way into our corpus data and demonstrated that there are patterns in how the *Guardian* and the *Daily Mail* refer to poverty in geographical space, the linguistic aspect of the analysis so far has been restricted to the results of one search term. Interrogation of a single term is insufficient for illuminating wider elements of the relationship between poverty and place. Whilst the PNC keywords for <*poverty*> suggested some potential ideological links between poverty and place, the analysis, so far, has remained largely at the lexical level. One of the biggest problems we face is that it is possible to talk about *poverty* without ever using that specific term. For example, a text may refer to 'the poor in Newcastle', 'deprived areas of Birmingham' or use more evaluative lexis, such as 'scroungers queue outside Burnley benefits office'. All of these (albeit fictional) examples tap into a wider discourse of poverty and place. Thus, the analysis in the preceding chapter neatly demonstrates how GTA can be used to analyse the geographical associations of a particular search term, but it cannot tell us anything conclusive about the wider discourses associated with poverty, and the ideologies they index.

L. L Paterson and I. N Gregory, *Representations of Poverty and Place*,
https://doi.org/10.1007/978-3-319-93503-4_5

In this chapter, we document how we selected additional search terms (Sect. 5.1), detail the processes for using GTA across multiple search terms and large corpora, and discuss some of the decisions that we had to make in terms of where the boundaries surrounding discourses of poverty lie (Sect. 5.2). We consider the interconnectedness of discourses and note some of the other social issues, such as crime rates and the accessibility of the UK housing market, which were closely linked to discourses of poverty and place.

5.1 Selecting Search Terms

In order to establish what terms were being used to talk about and talk around poverty in our corpora, we used collocation analysis (see Sect. 2.1) to find terms which were suitable for geoparsing. We began by generating a list of collocate lemmas[1] for <*poverty*> in both the *Daily Mail* and the *Guardian* corpora. This was the first step in the process of selecting suitable search terms and generating corpus queries. Collocates had to occur within ten words either side of the node, have a minimum frequency of 5, and a minimum collocation frequency of 5. Ten words either side is quite a wide span for determining collocates, but we chose this distance to parallel the span used when calculating PNCs. Furthermore, we wanted to include not only those terms which are close collocates of <*poverty*> but also those words which may occur slightly further away in a text but were pivotal to expressing ideas about poverty. However, we were mindful that the broader the span, the higher the potential number of collocates. In order to centre our analysis on lemmas which had a strong association with poverty, as indicated by a high collocation value, we chose to focus on the top 100 collocates of <*poverty*> in each corpus (Table 5.1), all of which had log-likelihood

[1]A lemma refers to all forms of a word: e.g. the lemma BEG includes *beg, begging, beggar, begged, begs*, etc.

Table 5.1 Top 100 collocates for<*poverty*>

Daily Mail	Both	*Guardian*
abject, Africa, aid, alleviation, American, census, cent, center, corruption, country, cycle, dependency, economic, education, figure, foundation, 'fuel, global, grow, help, high, labour, law, many, more, nation, pension, per, percent, population, porn', Potok, rural, slum, southern, stricken, struggle, than, tsar, tsar', violence	2020, alleviate, and, below, benefit, charity, child, define, definition, deprivation, Duncan, eradicate, extreme, family, food, Frank, fuel, Garnham, government, grinding, homelessness, household, hunger, in, income, increase, inequality, injustice, into, in-work, level, lift, line, live, low, measure, median, million, mobility, number, of, Oxfam, pensioner, people, poor, poverty, push, rate, reduce, relative, rise, Rowntree, social, tackle, trap, unemployment, wealth, welfare, work	60%, 300,000, absolute, action, Alison, breakdown, by, campaigner, cause, CPAG, credit, cut, disadvantage, educational, eliminate, end, exclusion, fall, field, focus, goal, group, halve, ifs, increasing, living, Milburn, Nicolson, out, parenting, plunge, problem, reduction, rev, root, smith, target, taxpayers, UK, wage, worklessness

values well above the threshold value of 15.13, which made them statistically significant to the level $p < 0.0001$.

Combining collocate lists from the *Daily Mail* and the *Guardian* gave a total of 141 potential search terms (59 terms occurred in both lists). Using Table 5.1, the immediate conclusion that can be drawn about the two newspapers is that they discuss poverty using some similar language (*child, extreme, family, household, government* were common to the top 100 collocates in both corpora). They also draw upon similar themes or semantic fields. For example, 24 of the top 100 collocates in the *Daily Mail* refer to some form of measurement (*grinding, high, level, median, measure*) as do 22 of the *Guardian*'s collocates (*absolute, below, increase, million*). This suggests that both newspapers treat poverty as something which is measurable (*high, increase*) and quantifiable (*million, percent*). Furthermore, both collocate lists include *define* and *definition*, suggesting that there is some dispute over what poverty actually is and how it is defined.

Discounting function words and terms relating to measurement, 31 collocates were unique to the top 100 in the *Daily Mail* and 30 were unique to the *Guardian*'s top 100. Of course, this does not mean that these apparently unique terms never collocate with <*poverty*> in the opposite corpora, indeed many do, but rather the differences in Table 5.1 are indicative of which lemmas, and thus related topics, are given prominence in the co-text of <*poverty*> in each newspaper. For example, three of the collocates unique to the *Guardian* top 100 are proper nouns (*Alison, Milburn,* and *Nicolson*), which indicates that the *Guardian*'s treatment of poverty involves reference to key individuals, such as Alison Garnham, Chief Executive of the Child Poverty Action Group, Alan Milburn, a Labour politician who headed the Social Mobility and Child Poverty Commission, and Rev. Paul Nicolson, a representative of Taxpayers Against Poverty. The *Daily Mail* collocates also include *Garnham* and both sets of collocates include *Frank*, in reference to Labour MP Frank Field, *Oxfam, Rowntree* (as in the Joseph Rowntree Foundation), and *Duncan*, as in Iain Duncan Smith, a Conservative MP who was Secretary of State for the Department of Work and Pensions and who is credited with the introduction of the Universal

Credit benefits system.[2] Taking a closer look at how these individuals are referred to, whilst most are quoted or their policies directly referenced, Nicolson's name only appears in the *Guardian* collocates because he has had 40 letters published. This finding demonstrates that not all collocates are equal when determining their significance in discourses of poverty.

It is also by looking at these unique collocates that we get a sense of how either newspaper connects poverty to place. Of the unique collocates in the *Guardian* top 100 only *UK* makes any reference to location, but the *Daily Mail* collocates include *Africa, American*, and *southern*, which on closer inspection occurs 245 times in the phrase 'the Southern Poverty Law Center'.[3] This institution is based in Montgomery, Alabama and investigating its occurrence in the top 100 collocates tells us that the *Daily Mail* has publish 158 texts referring to it, which, along with *global*, suggests a focus on poverty outside the UK. Secondarily, this suggests that *southern* is probably not a suitable search term for the present analysis.

Indeed, not all of these 141 potential search terms were viable. Numbers like *2020* and function words like *of, in*, and *and* occur too many times in the corpus generally to make geoparsing them worthwhile. For example, *of* occurs 6,794,702 times in the *Daily Mail* corpus but only 6155 (0.09%) of those are within ten words of <*poverty*>, with comparable figures of 1,394,935 and 5158 (0.36%) in the *Guardian*. Thus, geoparsing general items like these would lead to too many potential PNCs that are not related to poverty, which would skew our analysis. Similarly, those collocates which suggest some measurement/scale of poverty—lemmas such as *high, rate, median*, etc.—are likely to be also used to describe other measurable entities. The top five

---

[2]The top *Daily Mail* collocates also include reference to the Labour party, but not the Conservative party (*Conservative* 1638th on the list of collocates and is not significant, and *Tory* is 1265th, LL value 4.039). Whilst occurrences of *labour* also refer to manual labour, etc. as well as the Labour party, the fact that one political party is related to poverty more than the others is worthy of future investigation.

[3]This finding also explains why the American English spelling of *center* occurs in the top 100 collocates as does *Potok*, which is in reference to Mark Potok who works at the Southern Poverty Law Center.

collocates for <high> in the *Guardian* (using the same collocation criteria as above) are *court, street, level, rate*, and *unemployment*, only one of which—unemployment—shows any immediate connection to poverty. Where these measurement terms are used within discourses of poverty and place, they are likely to occur in clusters such as 'high poverty rate' and would be picked up during the geoparsing of <*poverty*>.

Other collocates unsuitable for geoparsing included *child* and *fuel*, both of which were used to premodify *poverty* to draw readers' attention to particular types of poverty or to the impacts of poverty on particular social groups:

1. An end to fuel **poverty** in housing by 2016 (G news: politics, Jan 2010).
2. As we discovered on Monday this week, child **poverty** is now growing (DM news, Jan 2010).

The labels *child poverty* and *fuel poverty* appear relatively fixed. Of the 227 times that *fuel* collocates with <*poverty*> in the *Guardian*, 196 (85%) are occurrences of the phrase *fuel poverty*, and there are similar figures of for the *Daily Mail*: 303 (91.3%) out of 332 collocations are *fuel poverty*. For *child* and *poverty* the figures are 1151 collocations with 527 (34.9%) occurrences of *child poverty* in the *Daily Mail* and 2752 collocations with 1329 (51.7%) *child poverty* in the *Guardian*. The fact that terms such as *fuel poverty* are repeated and seem fixed suggests that most references to people who are unable to afford fuel, or references to children in financial hardship, will be phrased in this way. As such, geoparsing all occurrences of *fuel* and *child* is unlikely to lead to lots of PNCs relating to poverty that do not occur in the phrases *fuel/child poverty*.[4]

A similar pattern occurs with the term 'poverty porn' as it is used to describe a particular type of television programme which present the

[4]A similar argument could be made for *pensioner poverty*. However, we chose to include the query <pension*> as it referred not only to pensioner poverty, but also to the state pension, a type of government benefit.

day-to-day lives of those in receipt of government welfare payments in a pseudo-documentary format for mass audience entertainment (see Paterson et al. 2017). Additionally, lemmas such as *alleviate, eradicate,* and *target* were also used primarily as immediate collocates of *poverty*. However, geoparsing these terms would not likely tell us much about poverty and place, given that we can *alleviate* all sorts of issues (the top R1 collocates for *alleviate* in the *Daily Mail* were *poverty, suffering, pain,* and *pressure*).[5] It would be interesting to geoparse terms like these to see what issues are being *alleviated* or *eradicated* in particular geographical areas, but this is beyond the scope of the present analysis.

Whilst all of the collocates in Table 5.1 would be useful starting point if we were only performing an analysis of poverty, our analysis is complicated by our duel focus on poverty and place. So, for example, the individuals referred to in the *Guardian* top 100 collocates tell us about the types of people whom this particular newspaper refers to when talking about poverty. The prevalence of measurement terms and quantifiers in both corpora demonstrates that the abstract concept of *poverty* is treated as something concrete which can be quantified. The repeated use of the L1 position to premodify poverty (*child poverty, fuel poverty,* etc.) tells us that poverty is seen as something which can be subdivided into discrete categories, whilst the verbs *alleviate, eradicate,* and *tackle* indicate that the newspapers are reporting on or endorsing affirmative action to reduce poverty. Ideologically, this presupposes that:

a. poverty is fundamentally a bad thing,
b. a decrease in poverty would be for the social good,
c. human action can decrease poverty rates, and
d. there are people in positions of power who are acting or should act to decrease poverty.

[5]What this does tell us is that *alleviate* has negative semantic prosody (Stubbs 2001), insofar as we only seem to alleviate things that are bad. *Eradicate* has a similar pattern; its top R1 collocates in the *Daily Mail* include *polio, child, poverty, terrorism,* and *ISIS*. Thus we can argue that poverty is presented as a particularly bad social problem which needs to be addressed.

From our list of collocates, we can begin to conceptualise a discourse or discourses of poverty as drawn upon by the UK media, and we can see which particular lexical items are used when such ideologies are deployed. However, none of these conclusions automatically apply to discourses of poverty AND place.

In order to include only those references to discourses of poverty which relate to places within the UK we had to choose terms to geoparse which we thought would be most fruitful. Thus, we eliminated proper nouns (with the exception of Iain Duncan Smith), function words, quantifiers and measurement terms, collocates which predominantly premodified *poverty* (i.e. *fuel, child*, etc.), words for social groups (*people, group, population*), and general terms like *push* and *live*. This left us with 24 potential search terms which appeared to be key terms in discourses of poverty: *benefit, charity, credit, cut, deprivation, Duncan, exclusion, food, homeless, household, hunger, income, inequality, mobility, parenting, pension, poor, poverty, social, taxpayers, unemployment, wage, welfare, worklessness*. But even with this relatively small number, as is shown in Sect. 5.2, some search terms were more associated with poverty and place than others.

To these 24 collocates we added 11 terms relating to money and employment, including *cost, earn, expense, penniless, price, salary, spend*, and *redundant*. We complemented *homeless* with *beg* and, as *food* was too general, we chose to narrow this term to focus on a *food banks* and also included *starve* in relation to *hunger*. The term *social* too was too broad (its top collocates in the *Guardian* are *care, mobility, worker, housing*, and *medium*), so we combined it with another potential search term and used the phrase *social exclusion*. We also switched *mobility* for the more general *disability*. Similarly, as geoparsing *parenting* would have been quite broad, we chose to focus on single-parenthood. We also added 17 search terms relating to benefits receipt, which mostly included the names of particular benefits, such as Employment Support Allowance (also known as ESA), as well as related terms such as *austerity, claimant, dole* and *handout*; the latter being included as it is the *Daily Mail*'s preferred term for *benefits*.

From this list of potential search terms we generated 64 different corpus queries (including <*poverty*>), as shown in Table 5.2. We chose

Table 5.2 Search terms in the *Daily Mail* and the *Guardian*

		Daily Mail		*Guardian*	
		No. of hits	Freq. pmw	No. of hits	Freq. pmw
1	*afford*	26,494	85.86	6379	174.62
2	*allowance*	7845	25.42	3318	90.83
3	*austerit*	6217	20.15	2709	74.16
4	{beg}	8490	27.51	391	10.7
5	*benefit*	55,297	179.21	19,611	536.84
6	*charit*	45,018	145.89	11,841	323.4
7	*claim*	301,829	978.17	26,897	736.29
8	*communit*	72,368	234.53	17,829	488.06
9	*cost*	117,875	382.01	18,336	501.94
10	credit*	28,766	93.22	5309	145.33
11	cut*	112,251	363.78	28,920	791.67
12	*depriv*	4381	14.2	1948	53.55
13	*disab*	20,457	66.3	4227	115.71
14	DLA	327	1.06	265	7.25
15	dole*	2616	8.48	261	7.14
16	Duncan Smith*	3604	11.68	1919	52.53
17	earn*	37,803	122.51	5126	140.32
18	*employ*	87,550	283.73	17,042	466.52
19	*entitl*	1699	37.91	2103	57.57
20	*equali*	8049	26.09	4392	120.23
21	ESA*	751	2.43	320	8.76
22	*expens*	34,726	112.54	5383	147.36
23	fit for work	113	0.37	182	4.98
24	(fitness to work|fit-ness-to-work| fit for work)	137	0.07	15	0.41
25	(food bank*|-foodbank*|-food-bank*)	1424	4.61	1347	36.87
26	handout*	2835	9.19	198	5.42
27	hardship*	1754	5.68	430	11.77
28	*home*	482,368	1563.26	40,010	1095.25
29	hous*	304,246	986	33,468	916.17
30	(hunge*|hungr*)	9227	29.9	947	25.92
31	income*	23,655	76.66	7680	210.24
32	IDS*	672	2.18	187	5.12
33	job*	117,232	379.93	22,583	618.2
34	JSA	118	0.38	184	5.04
35	*money*	129,601	420.01	16,662	456.11
36	*paid*	70,692	229.1	9569	261.95
37	pay*	170,672	553.11	24,752	677.57
38	penn*	27,146	87.97	1247	34.14

(continued)

Table 5.2 (continued)

		Daily Mail		*Guardian*	
		No. of hits	Freq. pmw	No. of hits	Freq. pmw
39	pension*	42,851	138.87	9081	248.59
40	personal independence payment	59	0.19	76	2.08
41	PIP	623	2.02	196	5.37
42	poor*	36,648	118.77	9675	264.85
43	<*poverty*>	8689	28.16	5288	144.76
44	price*	82,198	266.39	7428	203.34
45	redundan*	3920	12.7	1484	40.62
46	rehous*	227	0.74	144	3.94
47	rent*	22,241	72.08	4572	125.16
48	*salar*	15,107	48.96	2140	58.58
49	*sanction*	9505	30.8	1934	52.94
50	*scroung*	608	1.97	311	8.51
51	(single father*|single-fat*)	183	0.59	9	0.25
52	(single mother* |single-mot*)	2653	8.60	235	7.32
53	(single parent* |single-par*)	919	3.14	334	9.38
54	social* exclu*	66	0.21	153	4.19
55	*spend*	107,417	348.12	18,357	502.51
56	starv*	6248	20.25	408	11.17
57	struggl*	43,776	141.87	5298	145.03
58	*subsidi*	4649	15.07	1221	33.42
59	*tax*	130,913	424.26	28,920	791.67
60	vulnerable*	14,527	47.08	4794	131.23
61	*wage*	17,340	56.2	5352	146.51
62	*welfare*	17,666	57.25	7726	211.49
63	work*	449,073	1455.35	75,934	2078.65
64	(work capability assessment*|W-CA*|work-capability-assessment)	160	0.52	362	9.91
	Total	3,344,571		535,419	

to make our queries broad by using wildcards; that is we did not merely search for the collocates as listed in Table 5.1, but included all forms of those collocates.[6] For example, the query for the collocate *unemployment*

[6]Corpus query notation used in Table 5.2: * = none or more characters, {} = all forms of a lemma, () = search for all forms within the brackets separated by the pipe (|) symbol.

was <*employ*> which would return hits for *employ, employee, unemployment, unemployed*, etc. Table 5.2 also includes information about the raw number of tokens in the news section of each corpus and the normalised frequencies (hits per million words).

In addition to the terms listed in Table 5.2, we also tested particular items of evaluative lexis, including *chav, feckless, hard working, lazy, lifestyle, luxury, shirker, skiver*, and *useless*, but none of these returned more than five PNCs and many returned none at all. Thus, it can be determined that even if these terms are used within discourses of poverty, they are not talked about in relation to particular places. In some cases these terms were used in the corpora to refer to individuals, and their location was mentioned; however, references to individuals tended to occur as part of wider discourses of crime or benefits fraud, which, for the present analysis at least, were not considered to refer directly to poverty (see Sect. 5.2). Having selected our search terms, run our queries, and downloaded our concordances, the next step was to geoparse the hits for our 63 queries (excluding poverty, see Chapter 4).

5.2 The Boundaries of Discourse

The totals column in Table 5.2 shows that there were over 3.3 million hits for these search terms in the news sections of the *Daily Mail* corpus and over half a million in the *Guardian* corpus. However, the *Guardian* corpus is smaller than the *Daily Mail* corpus, and not all of the hits in Table 5.2 will relate directly to poverty. To address the first issue, normalising to hits per million words shows that the *Daily Mail* uses the search terms on average 10,315.12 times pmw whilst the *Guardian* uses them 9,492.69 times pmw, which makes their use across corpora more comparable. The second issue, that not all query hits will be involved in discourses of poverty, is slightly more problematic. In order to ensure that our analysis only included occurrences of our search terms that were used to talk about poverty, erroneous/irrelevant hits had to be removed. One way to do this would be to manually analyse the concordance lines for all 3,879,990 hits listed in Table 5.2, but this was clearly infeasible. We also had the option to take a systematic stratified sample of these almost four million hits but, as is shown below, not all search terms were equally associated with discourses of poverty, and thus taking samples would likely have skewed our results.

To establish which of our search terms were most associated with poverty and place, we decided to geoparse all hits listed in Table 5.2. This had two benefits. It eliminated hits which did not occur within ± 10 words of a place-name—thus greatly decreasing the number of concordance lines for manual analysis—and it also gave us a rough measure of which of our search terms were often associated with place. The raw figures for the geoparsed queries are provided in Table 5.3, which includes information about the number of hits for each query, the number of potential PNCs identified by the geoparser (All PNCs ±10), and the final total of PNCs post manual analysis which were used within discourses of poverty (PNCs post analysis). Information is also provided about the percentage values of final PNCs to total number of original hits, the percentage value of final PNCs compared to the potential PNCs identified by the geoparser, and the normalised frequencies of final PNCs per million words.[7]

The first conclusion that can be drawn from Table 5.3 is that geoparsing all of our query hits significantly decreased the amount of manual analysis needed as there were 503,739 concordance lines containing potential PNCs (434,930 for the *Daily Mail* and 68,809 for the *Guardian*) in comparison to the almost four million total query hits. Whilst still a large number, and geoparsing such large files (e.g. 449,703 concordance lines for <work*> in the *Daily Mail*) did take time, this was the most efficient way to thin our dataset. We chose to manually analyse all 503,739 concordance lines containing PNCs within ± 10

[7]The first column (% of total hits) provides a measure of just how often one of the query hits generated a PNC used within discourses of poverty. The second (% of all PNCs) provides a measure of how often PNCs used within discourses of poverty occurred in the total number of PNCs identified by the geoparser.

Table 5.3 Concordance lines containing PNCs for all search terms

		Daily Mail						*Guardian*					
		No. of hits	All PNCs ±10	PNCs post analysis	% of total hits	% of all PNCs	PNC pmw	No. of hits	All PNCs ±10	PNCs post analysis	% of total hits	% of all PNCs	PNC pmw
1	*afford*	26,494	6927	43	0.16	0.62	0.14	6379	1497	356	5.58	23.78	9.75
2	*allowance*	7845	684	42	0.54	6.14	0.14	3318	204	78	2.35	38.24	2.14
3	*austerit*	6217	1118	8	0.13	0.72	0.03	2709	368	43	1.59	11.68	1.18
4	{beg}	8490	225	40	0.47	17.78	0.13	391	54	18	4.60	33.33	0.49
5	*benefit*	55,297	213	44	0.08	20.66	0.14	19,611	1785	382	1.95	21.40	10.46
6	*charit*	45,018	9881	58	0.13	0.59	0.19	11,841	1728	118	1.00	6.83	3.23
7	*claim*	301,829	25,155	99	0.03	0.39	0.32	26,897	3991	238	0.88	5.96	6.52
8	*communit*	72,368	54,841	44	0.06	0.08	0.14	17,829	1158	58	0.33	5.01	1.59
9	*cost*	117,875	14,310	60	0.05	0.42	0.19	18,336	2165	189	1.03	8.73	5.17
10	credit*	28,766	2989	17	0.06	0.57	0.06	5309	502	58	1.09	11.55	1.59
11	cut*	112,251	958	12	0.01	1.25	0.04	28,920	3200	235	0.81	7.34	6.43
12	*depriv*	4381	855	324	7.40	37.89	1.05	1948	612	383	19.66	62.58	10.48
13	*disab*	20,457	1676	14	0.07	0.84	0.05	4227	339	90	2.13	26.55	2.46
14	DLA	327	21	2	0.61	9.52	0.01	265	7	1	0.38	14.29	0.03
15	dole*	2616	224	20	0.76	8.93	0.06	261	20	11	4.21	55.00	0.30
16	Duncan Smith*	3604	295	15	0.42	5.08	0.05	1919	164	34	1.77	20.73	0.93
17	earn*	37,803	2907	20	0.05	0.69	0.06	5126	587	90	1.76	15.33	2.46
18	*employ*	87,550	561	38	0.04	6.77	0.12	17,042	329	223	1.31	67.78	6.10
19	*entitl*	1699	1070	9	0.53	0.84	0.03	2103	229	6	0.29	2.62	0.16
20	*equali*	8049	968	7	0.09	0.72	0.02	4392	565	87	1.98	15.40	2.38
21	ESA*	751	122	9	1.20	7.38	0.03	320	5	2	0.63	40.00	0.05

(continued)

Table 5.3 (continued)

<table>
<tr><th></th><th></th><th colspan="6">Daily Mail</th><th colspan="6">Guardian</th></tr>
<tr><th></th><th></th><th>No. of hits</th><th>All PNCs ±10</th><th>PNCs post anal-ysis</th><th>% of total hits</th><th>% of all PNCs</th><th>PNC pmw</th><th>No. of hits</th><th>All PNCs ±10</th><th>PNCs post analysis</th><th>% of total hits</th><th>% of all PNCs</th><th>PNC pmw</th></tr>
<tr><td>22</td><td>*expens*</td><td>34,726</td><td>5938</td><td>15</td><td>0.04</td><td>0.25</td><td>0.05</td><td>5383</td><td>668</td><td>69</td><td>1.28</td><td>10.33</td><td>1.89</td></tr>
<tr><td>23</td><td>fit for work</td><td>113</td><td>7</td><td>7</td><td>6.19</td><td>100.00</td><td>0.02</td><td>182</td><td>2</td><td>2</td><td>1.10</td><td>100.00</td><td>0.05</td></tr>
<tr><td>24</td><td>(fitness to work|fitness-to-work)</td><td>24</td><td>5</td><td>2</td><td>8.33</td><td>40.00</td><td>0.01</td><td>15</td><td>0</td><td>0</td><td>0.00</td><td>0.00</td><td>0.00</td></tr>
<tr><td>25</td><td>(food bank* |foodbank* |food-bank*)</td><td>1424</td><td>346</td><td>99</td><td>6.95</td><td>28.61</td><td>0.32</td><td>1347</td><td>284</td><td>128</td><td>9.50</td><td>45.07</td><td>3.50</td></tr>
<tr><td>26</td><td>handout*</td><td>2835</td><td>375</td><td>26</td><td>0.92</td><td>6.93</td><td>0.08</td><td>198</td><td>25</td><td>8</td><td>4.04</td><td>32.00</td><td>0.22</td></tr>
<tr><td>27</td><td>hardship*</td><td>1754</td><td>158</td><td>18</td><td>1.03</td><td>11.39</td><td>0.06</td><td>430</td><td>22</td><td>8</td><td>1.86</td><td>36.36</td><td>0.22</td></tr>
<tr><td>28</td><td>*home*</td><td>482,368</td><td>93,395</td><td>96</td><td>0.02</td><td>0.10</td><td>0.31</td><td>40,010</td><td>9475</td><td>595</td><td>1.49</td><td>6.28</td><td>16.29</td></tr>
<tr><td>29</td><td>hous*</td><td>304,246</td><td>57,913</td><td>88</td><td>0.03</td><td>0.15</td><td>0.29</td><td>33,468</td><td>6723</td><td>291</td><td>0.87</td><td>4.33</td><td>7.97</td></tr>
<tr><td>30</td><td>(hun-ge*|hungr*)</td><td>9227</td><td>810</td><td>14</td><td>0.15</td><td>1.73</td><td>0.05</td><td>947</td><td>163</td><td>8</td><td>0.84</td><td>4.91</td><td>0.22</td></tr>
<tr><td>31</td><td>income*</td><td>23,655</td><td>2096</td><td>36</td><td>0.15</td><td>1.72</td><td>0.12</td><td>7680</td><td>799</td><td>122</td><td>1.59</td><td>15.27</td><td>3.34</td></tr>
<tr><td>32</td><td>IDS*</td><td>672</td><td>40</td><td>0</td><td>0.00</td><td>0.00</td><td>0.00</td><td>187</td><td>12</td><td>0</td><td>0.00</td><td>0.00</td><td>0.00</td></tr>
<tr><td>33</td><td>job*</td><td>117,232</td><td>13,146</td><td>623</td><td>0.53</td><td>4.74</td><td>2.02</td><td>22,583</td><td>2537</td><td>675</td><td>2.99</td><td>26.60</td><td>18.48</td></tr>
<tr><td>34</td><td>JSA</td><td>118</td><td>8</td><td>0</td><td>0.00</td><td>0.00</td><td>0.00</td><td>184</td><td>14</td><td>5</td><td>2.72</td><td>35.71</td><td>0.14</td></tr>
<tr><td>35</td><td>*money*</td><td>129,601</td><td>7197</td><td>47</td><td>0.04</td><td>0.65</td><td>0.15</td><td>16,662</td><td>1468</td><td>110</td><td>0.66</td><td>7.49</td><td>3.01</td></tr>
<tr><td>36</td><td>*paid*</td><td>70,692</td><td>4993</td><td>53</td><td>0.07</td><td>1.06</td><td>0.17</td><td>9569</td><td>1070</td><td>89</td><td>0.93</td><td>8.32</td><td>2.44</td></tr>
<tr><td>37</td><td>pay*</td><td>170,672</td><td>21,514</td><td>102</td><td>0.06</td><td>0.47</td><td>0.33</td><td>24,752</td><td>1180</td><td>96</td><td>0.39</td><td>8.14</td><td>2.63</td></tr>
<tr><td>38</td><td>penn*</td><td>27,146</td><td>5344</td><td>28</td><td>0.10</td><td>0.52</td><td>0.09</td><td>1247</td><td>332</td><td>1</td><td>0.08</td><td>0.30</td><td>0.03</td></tr>
</table>

(continued)

Table 5.3 (continued)

		Daily Mail						*Guardian*					
		No. of hits	All PNCs ±10	PNCs post analysis	% of total hits	% of all PNCs	PNC pmw	No. of hits	All PNCs ±10	PNCs post analysis	% of total hits	% of all PNCs	PNC pmw
39	pension*	42,851	721	4	0.01	0.55	0.01	9081	665	44	0.48	6.62	1.20
40	personal independence payment	59	9	2	3.39	22.22	0.01	76	1	0	0.00	0.00	0.00
41	PIP	623	124	0	0.00	0.00	0.00	196	15	0	0.00	0.00	0.00
42	poor*	36,648	3991	264	0.72	6.61	0.86	9675	1283	307	3.17	23.93	8.40
43	*poverty*	8689	608	241	2.77	39.64	0.78	5288	745	245	4.63	32.89	6.71
44	price*	82,198	12,654	7	0.01	0.06	0.02	7428	1071	31	0.42	2.89	0.85
45	redundan*	3920	414	141	3.60	34.06	0.46	1484	97	42	2.83	43.30	1.15
46	rehous*	227	63	13	5.73	20.63	0.04	144	43	38	26.39	88.37	1.04
47	rent*	22,241	5076	56	0.25	1.10	0.18	4572	840	251	5.49	29.88	6.87
48	*salar*	15,107	1337	5	0.03	0.37	0.02	2140	194	34	1.59	17.53	0.93
49	*sanction*	9505	1136	2	0.02	0.18	0.01	1934	125	17	0.88	13.60	0.47
50	*scroung*	608	67	10	1.64	14.93	0.03	311	23	5	1.61	21.74	0.14
51	(single father* |single-fat*)	183	22	1	0.55	4.55	0.00	9	2	2	22.22	100.00	0.05
52	(single mother* |single-mot*)	2653	336	22	0.83	6.55	0.07	235	56	28	11.91	50.00	0.77

(continued)

Table 5.3 (continued)

		Daily Mail						*Guardian*					
		No. of hits	All PNCs ±10	PNCs post analysis	% of total hits	% of all PNCs	PNC pmw	No. of hits	All PNCs ±10	PNCs post analysis	% of total hits	% of all PNCs	PNC pmw
53	(single parent* |single-par*)	919	78	5	0.54	6.41	0.02	334	19	7	2.10	36.84	0.19
54	social* exclu*	66	11	4	6.06	36.36	0.01	153	31	6	3.92	19.35	0.16
55	*spend*	107,417	4882	11	0.01	0.23	0.04	18,357	2433	51	0.28	2.10	1.40
56	starv*	6248	377	8	0.13	2.12	0.03	408	37	3	0.74	8.11	0.08
57	struggl*	43,776	4336	88	0.20	2.03	0.29	5298	579	92	1.74	15.89	2.52
58	*subsidi*	4649	708	5	0.11	0.71	0.02	1221	202	4	0.33	1.98	0.11
59	*tax*	130,913	16,495	57	0.04	0.35	0.18	28,920	3711	99	0.34	2.67	2.71
60	vulnerable*	14,527	1453	6	0.04	0.41	0.02	4794	318	49	1.02	15.41	1.34
61	*wage*	17,340	1877	79	0.46	4.21	0.26	5352	691	260	4.86	37.63	7.12
62	*welfare*	17,666	1967	71	0.40	3.61	0.23	7726	779	132	1.71	16.94	3.61
63	work*	449,073	36,893	378	0.08	1.02	1.23	75,934	10,564	93	0.12	0.88	2.55
64	(work capability assessment*| WCA*|work-capability-assessment)	160	10	0	0.00	0.00	0.00	362	2	0	0.00	0.00	0.00
	Total	3,344,458	434,930	3659	0.11	0.84	11.88	535,419	68,809	6746	1.26	9.80	184.67

words of one of our search terms. Although labour intensive, we made this decision because we wanted our analysis to include all realisations of discourses of poverty co-occurring with PNCs for our chosen queries and we wanted to test GTA on a large scale in order to streamline the method for future projects

Whilst the half a million hits seems like a lot of data to manually analyse, the number of concordance lines was reduced somewhat when we automatically eliminated geoparser errors (i.e. PNCs which were not actually places) and PNCs which were not within the UK (e.g. Canada, Morocco, and France). The number of hits were further decreased by the removal of national-level UK place-names (UK, (Great) Britain, England, Wales, Scotland, and Northern Ireland); although these hits do not form part of the present analysis as they are not geographically specific enough for our purposes, we have kept this data for future work on discourses of poverty. It is worth investigating whether 'UK poverty' is discussed in similar or different terms to the localised poverty we are focused on here.

A third set of hits which could easily be eliminated related to erroneous query hits. As the queries were broad, there were occasions where queries returned hits which were not directly related to our initial set of search terms. For example, <*wage*> returned relevant hits such as *wage* and *wages*, but also returned *sewage*, whilst <*tax*> returned *taxpayer(s)*, but also *taxi*. One response to these erroneous hits would be to write more specific queries, but we wanted our analysis to be as comprehensive as possible and did not want to miss anything significant, but unpredicted, in our analysis of poverty and place. In any case, as the geoparser outputs are viewed as spreadsheets, unwanted query hits are easily filtered out and eliminated.

We determined whether PNCs occurred within discourses of poverty by looking at the wider co-text of the PNC and its related query term. In order to keep this process consistent, one author analysed all the concordance lines. Whilst reading the concordance lines in this way was somewhat subjective, there was no other (computational) method that we could use to ensure the PNCs that we would eventually plot (see the following chapters) were used within discourses of poverty.[8] In any case, most of the concordance lines in the geoparsed output were either related to discourses of poverty, as in (3–4), or clearly not about poverty, as in (5).

3. Until recently, Bo worked behind the bar of a West London pub and says she struggles to **pay** her bills 'just like everyone else' (DM news, Apr 2012).
4. He was already aware of a problem in South Shields, where around 610 young people have been claiming **Jobseeker's** allowance for six months or longer (G news: politics, July 2012).
5. In Bournemouth, where private **income** has increased ten-fold, the number of patients waiting too long for operations has risen (G news: society, Nov 2014).

However, we had to make some decisions about what actually constituted discourses of poverty. Whilst we wanted to keep the scope of our analysis broad, there were occasions where our search terms occurred but references to poverty were implied or secondary to the aim of a given text. As shown in (6–7), when reporting on criminal cases and court proceedings, the *Daily Mail* had a tendency to state whether a defendant was unemployed or in receipt of government benefits.

6. Prosecutor Gareth Hughes told Manchester magistrates that the out of **work** hotel chambermaid spat on each car, yanked off a wing mirror, damaged two others and bent back windscreen wipers (DM news, July 2011).
7. Taylor smashed windows with a hammer before pulling out the knife at Fleetwood **Job** Centre (pictured) in Lancashire. The **jobseeker**, who has 59 previous convictions, was jailed for 42 weeks (DM news, Mar 2015).

[8]It is possible to avoid this issue by only selecting texts related to the research topic at hand, rather than working with such broad corpora.

In (6), the fact that the defendant is 'out of work' is inconsequential to the charges against them, and similarly in (7) the jobseeker status of the accused—which implies receipt of Jobseeker's Allowance—bears no causality to their actions. The explicit mention of employment status or implicit references to benefits within a wider discourse of crime serves to make conceptual and ideological links between crime and benefits and portray benefits recipients as deviant. A relationship between crime and benefits receipt was also made explicitly in the *Daily Mail* corpus, through the (over)reporting of benefit fraud, as shown in (8–10). There was also a tendency to capitalise on big-money cases by reporting on the same case multiple times.

8. an asylum seeker from Sierra Leone fraudulently stolen (sic) more than 400,000 in **benefits** while holding down two **jobs** in <u>London</u> (DM news, Sept 2012).
9. Benefit cheat: Kelvin Kaloo, of <u>Dunstable</u>, Bedfordshire,[9] claimed nearly 100,000 in **handouts** from <u>Brent</u> Council and Central <u>Bedfordshire</u> Council (DM news, Jan 2013).
10. The Mail regularly highlights the most outrageous abuses of an insanely over-indulgent system, including the Afghan family of seven, living in a £1.2 million **house** in <u>Acton</u> and costing taxpayers £170,000 a year in **benefits** (DM news, Feb 2010).

However, benefit fraud is not automatically or necessarily directly related to poverty; reports of benefit fraud in the *Daily Mail* tend to focus on extreme examples where claimants had fraudulently obtained many thousands of pounds. Someone with such wealth at their disposal cannot really be considered poor or in poverty. Thus, the decision was made to remove hits relating to crime and benefits fraud from the analysis. We consider the significance of the topics and discourses which are related to discourses of poverty, such as crime and immigration (see 10) in more detail in the conclusion.

---

[9]Where two place-names co-occurred in this way, we only included the most local place-name in our analysis to avoid duplicating PNCs.

Table 5.4 Queries with low/zero PNCs

<table>
<tr><th>No. PNCs</th><th>Daily Mail</th><th>Guardian</th></tr>
<tr><td>0</td><td>IDS*
PIP
JSA
(Work capability assess-ment*|WCA*|Work-capability-assessment)</td><td>IDS*
personal indepdenence payment
PIP
(Work capability assess-ment*|WCA*|Work-capability-assessment)</td></tr>
<tr><td>1</td><td>(single father*|single-fat*)
(single parent*|single-par*)</td><td>DLA
penn*</td></tr>
<tr><td>2</td><td>DLA
(fitness to work|fitness-to-work)
personal independence payment
sanction</td><td>ESA*
fit for work
(single father*|single-fat*)</td></tr>
<tr><td>3</td><td>–</td><td>starv*</td></tr>
<tr><td>4</td><td>pension*
social* exclu*</td><td>*subsidi*</td></tr>
</table>

Some search terms were clearly more related to discourses of poverty and place than others. As shown in Table 5.4, four queries returned no relevant PNCs in the *Daily Mail* and four returned no relevant hits in the *Guardian*. Similarly, there were several queries that, when geoparsed and manually analysed, returned fewer than 5 PNCs used within discourses of poverty.

All of the search terms producing small numbers of PNCs were those that we added to the list of search terms originally generated using collocation data. This result suggests that the method of using collocate analysis to select query terms is robust at identifying the key terms in discourse which index particular ideologies. However, one issue that complicates this finding somewhat is that most PNCs returned for <(single father*|single-fat*)> were related to poverty as were 100% of the PNCs for <fit for work> both of which were addded to the list of search terms but did not appear in the collocate lists for either newspaper.[10]

[10]The query relating to single fatherhood also had a 100% return in the *Guardian*, compared to a 4.55% return in the *Daily Mail*.

11. Almost a third of people in Burnley and Aberdeen were **fit for work** and 38% had the potential to work with the correct support (DM news, Apr 2011).
12. Today Chris, an accountant from Dronfield, Derbyshire, is a **single father**. He went bankrupt and lost his home paying out half a million pounds in his fight for answers into his wife's death (DM news, Jan 2014).
13. Lashbrook is a **single father** living in south Kilburn with his baby daughter, who is now almost two. Out of work following a construction work injury in 2010, this is the fourth time he has been forced to turn to Sufra for help (G news: socety, Apr 2014).

Thus, we can posit that when these newspapers mention place in relation to *fit for work* (a type of assessment for government benefits) they overwhelmingly do so to talk about poverty. On the other hand, however, many of the queries in Table 5.4 are the names of particular UK government benefits—Personal Independence Payment (PIP) and Employment Support Allowance (ESA)—but these queries did not return high percentages of PNCs. This, it seems from the raw data that there is no strong relationship between particular benefits and place, although as the analysis in the following chapters shows, there were exceptions to this finding.

Taking proportion into account, what we can say about search terms that returned low numbers of PNCs is that, fundamentally, these search terms are not associated with particular locations in our corpora. We can take this one step further by comparing the overall percentages for all queries combined; only 0.11% of the *Daily Mail* and 1.27% of the *Guardian* query hits related poverty to place. The implications of this finding for critical discourse analysis are significant: they suggest that poverty, which is treated as a measurable phenomenon (see Sect. 5.1), is not locatable. Discourses of poverty may be drawn upon to talk about a UK or global picture, and may include terms such as *single-parent, social exclusion*, and *sanction*, but discussion on such a wide geographical scale means that poverty is made somewhat abstract, somewhat elsewhere, and somewhat other. Focusing on the local aspects of poverty make it less of a social phenomenon and more of an observable, concrete reality. Because poverty is not consistently associated with place, the use of place-names in reports about poverty become salient, insofar as they are anchoring a text to a particular location. Thus, by extracting PNCs, we can interrogate the significance of place-name mentions for discourses of poverty.

On the other hand, there were queries that returned relative high numbers of PNCs. <job*> returned the highest number in both corpora (623 in the *Daily Mail* and 677 in the *Guardian*). As well as relevant hits for *job* and *jobs* (which tended to refer to job losses) as shown in (14–15), this query also returned hits for *jobseeker* and *Jobseeker's Allowance* (16–17) which quantified the number of people claiming benefits, discussed the ratio between job applicants and vacancies, and ranked the areas with the highest proportion of JSA claimants (19).

14. dozens of workers could lose their **jobs**, particularly in Chirk near Wrexham and Marlbrook in Herefordshire (DM news, July 2010).
15. A section of the Lambeth website suggests **claimants** may need to find a **job** to replace benefits (DM news, Feb 2013).
16. Figures published this week showed that 4045 18-to-24 year olds in East Lancashire were claiming **Jobseeker's Allowance** last month (DM news, Apr 2010).
17. In Haringey, Lewisham, Waltham Forest and Hackney, people claiming **jobseeker's allowance** outnumber **job** vacancies by more than 20 to 1 (G news: society, Aug 2011).
18. Many claimants in Birkenhead who have trouble with their **benefits** end up at Mersey Advice, a welfare rights charity five minutes walk (sic) from the **jobcentre** dubbed by staff "the fourth emergency service in Birkenhead" (G news: society, June 2012).
19. four of the worst **jobless claimant** blackspots are in Birmingham constituencies (G news: society, Jan 2012).

The top 10 queries by raw frequency are given in Table 5.5. Terms including <*poverty*> and <poor*> are expected, given that they label either the phenomenon of poverty or those experiencing poverty. The occurrence of <job*>, <work*>, <redundan*>, <pay*>, and <*wage*> indicates that terms relating to employment, and the money gained from employment, are particularly prominent within discourses of poverty and place. There is also a related set of terms concerning benefits

Table 5.5 Queries with highest raw values of PNCs

Top PNCs	*Daily Mail*	No.	% of all hits	*Guardian*	No.	% of all hits
1	job*	623	0.53	job*	675	2.99
2	work*	378	0.08	*home*	595	1.49
3	*depriv*	324	7.40	*depriv*	383	19.66
4	poor*	264	0.72	*benefit*	382	21.40
5	*poverty*	241	2.77	*afford*	355	23.78
6	redundan*	141	3.60	poor*	307	3.17
7	pay*	102	0.06	hous*	291	0.87
8	*claim*	99	0.03	*wage*	260	37.63
9	(food bank*|food-bank*|food-bank*)	99	6.95	rent*	251	5.49
10	*home*	96	0.02	*poverty*	245	4.63

receipt (<*claim*>, <*benefit*>) which suggest that poverty and place is discussed in terms of welfare payments. Terms including those relating to *food banks* and <*afford*>, and the evaluative label <depriv*> indicate that discourses of poverty and place also concern a lack of money and a need for basic necessities, such as food.

Finally in Table 5.5, there are four terms associated with housing, <*home*>, which occurs in the top ten for both corpora, <hous*>, and <rent*>. The fact that three housing-related terms occur in the *Guardian* but there is only one in the *Daily Mail* could indicate that discourses of poverty and place in the *Guardian* focus more on the topic of homes/housing. Indeed, the two newspapers did treat these terms differently. PNCs co-occurring with *house* and *home* in the *Daily Mail* were just as likely to refer to the sale of a multi-million pound properties (20) as they were to refer to poverty. Such aspirational mentions of housing and place did not tend to occur in the *Guardian.* In any case, examples like (20) were eliminated during manual analysis as they do not relate to poverty.

20. Or for £1.85 million they could have Perryston House, an eight-bedroom **home** on Ayrshire's 'golf coast' (DM news, Dec 2014).
21. It was completely **unaffordable** to working-class families like us." Tower Hamlets is one of the most **deprived** boroughs in London, but the housing crisis has hit here too (G news, Feb 2012).
22. British housebuyers, particularly first-time buyers, could find themselves **priced** out of London, where **house prices** have risen to a three-year high (DM news, Aug 2013).
23. A single mother with three children was placed by her local council in a £1.5m mews **house**, left, in Kensington, west London (DM news, Aug 2012).

Where the two newspapers converge is in their discussion of UK house prices, particularly the unaffordability of houses in London. However, whilst the *Guardian* takes the position that rising house prices are excluding poorer groups of society from some areas (21), the *Daily Mail*, whilst acknowledging the difficulties of getting on the property ladder (22), uses the high prices of particular areas of London to suggest that people claiming Housing Benefit should not be able to live there (23). Thus, whilst UK property prices are not necessarily related to poverty—not being able to afford a house in central London does not automatically make one poor—references to benefits recipients having access to properties that would be unaffordable for many imply that perhaps those who claim benefits are receiving too much money. Of course, what is not considered in examples such as (23) is that many people in receipt of Housing Benefit, especially in London, are in paid employment and, furthermore, if they were to lose Housing Benefit (or have it capped) they may have to relocate, which might also lead to unemployment.

5.3 Summary

This initial analysis of multiple geoparsed search terms has shown that, despite differences between the two corpora, there are repeated key elements which appear to sit at the core of discourses of poverty and place: employment, money, housing, and benefits. The process of expanding GTA to consider how multiple search terms work together within wider discourses is fundamentally still in its infancy. However, the method detailed above for determining suitable search terms based on collocates of a primary node seems robust. Indeed, where additional queries were generated in response to wider reading, they tended to be less fruitful than those terms which collocated with <*poverty*>. One potential way to eliminate less fruitful terms in future GTA-based discourse analysis would be to only include search terms which were bidirectional collocates (e.g. words which are collocates of *poverty*, but which also had *poverty* as a collocate). However, for analysis on large, non-specialised corpora this may decrease the number of potential search terms too much. To decrease interference from erroneous query hits, it would be advisable to work with lemmas (although this depends on the availability of lemmatised corpora) or run a process of trial and error where different query syntax is tested before geoparsing. As this analysis is the first of its kind, we chose not to do this in order to demonstrate some of the issues that arise when geoparsing multiple search terms. Fundamentally though, the occurrence of erroneous hits only affected the proportional measures, as reported in Table 5.3.

The most difficult part of the process is deciding which concordance lines to accept as realisations of discourses of poverty and which to eliminate. This required some subjective judgement. It is possible that other scholars would choose to draw different boundaries than the ones we have used. For example, they might include reports of benefit fraud, or they might exclude generic references to job losses. Indeed, not all job losses lead directly to poverty, and cases where an individual lost an extremely-well-paid job were not included in our analysis. However, generic references to job cuts, job losses, and redundancies tended to be quantified ('800 job losses', '10,000 prison and probation jobs cut'), which suggested that a large number of people would end up unemployed and not earning a wage. As such, we opted to keep them in our analysis.

In order to structure our analysis of the different elements of discourses of poverty and place, we grouped our search terms into the subsets shown in Table 5.6. Unavoidably there were some queries that were difficult to categorise. Terms such as <*salar*> and <*wage*> clearly relate to employment, but they have been allocated to the Money subset because *salary* and *wage* relate directly to the money received for employment, as does the term <*pay*>. However, <*pay*> can also relate to the payment of benefits, as well as the payment of wages. Therefore, we decided to keep all of these related terms together in one subset.

Having established these subsets, we can see that, proportionally at least, the *Daily Mail*'s coverage of poverty and place tends to focus on employment and evaluation more than people and food, whereas the *Guardian* hits are spread more evenly across subsets. In both corpora, food, people, and social unity appear to be more marginal elements and, as such, we do not look at these subsets in great detail here. The following chapters take a closer look at what is actually written about poverty and place, and where these different elements—employment, benefits, money, and housing—are geographically located by each newspaper.

Table 5.6 Subsets of search terms

		Daily Mail		*Guardian*	
		No.	%	No.	%
Employment	*employ*, job*, redundan*, work*	1180	34.56	1036	15.92
Money	*afford*, *austerity*, *cost*, earn*, *expens*, income*, *money*, *paid*, pay*, penn*, price*, *salar*, *spend*, *wage*	514	15.06	1542	23.70
Benefits	*allowance*, *benefit*, *claim*, credit*, cut*, *disab*, DLA, dole*, Duncan Smith*, ESA*, fit for work, (fitness to work|fitness-to-work), handout*, IDS*, JSA, personal independence payment, PIP, *sanction*, *subsidi*, *tax*, *welfare*, (Work capability assessment*|WCA*|Work-capability-assessment)	446	13.06	1397	21.47
Food	(food bank*|foodbank*|food-bank*), (hunge*|hungr*), starv*	121	3.54	139	2.14
Housing	*home*, hous*, rehous*, rent*	253	7.41	1175	18.06
Social unity	*charit*, *communit*, *equali*	109	3.19	263	4.04
Evaluation	{beg}, *depriv*, *entitl*, hardship*, poor*, *scroung*, social* exclu*, struggl*,vulnerable*	763	22.35	875	13.45
People	pension*, (single father*|single-fat*), (single mother*|single-mot*), (single parent*|single-par*)	28	0.82	80	1.23
	Total	3414		6507	

References

Paterson, L. L., D. Peplow, & K. Grainger. 2017. Does Money Talk Equal Class Talk? Audience Responses to Poverty Porn in Relation to Money and Debt. In A. Mooney & E. Sifaki (eds.). *The Language of Money and Debt: An Interdisciplinary Approach.* Basingstoke: Palgrave, pp. 205–232.

Stubbs, M. 2001. Texts, Corpora, and Problems of Interpretation: A Response to Widdowson. *Applied Linguistics* 22 (2): 149–172.

6

Locating (Un)Employment in the National Press

Having established the key terms associated with poverty in our corpora, this chapter focuses on two of the subsets of search terms identified in Chapter 5. We take employment—a topic closely related to poverty—as a case study and how show how discourse analysis and GTA can be combined. The chapter begins by contextualising discussions of (un) employment within their wider social context and also considers the linguistic co-text of hits returned by the query <*employ*> (Sect. 6.1). Section 6.2 discusses the similarities in the geographical distribution of PNCs for the query <*employ*> and the Employment subset more broadly. This is followed by an analysis of the language used in the Employment subset (Sect. 6.3) and the Money subset (Sect. 6.4).

6.1 Social and Linguistic Context of Unemployment

We begin with an overview of the wider social context within which the texts in our two corpora were produced. After the global financial crisis in 2008, the UK unemployment rate was 6.4% and rose to a peak of 8.4% in the final quarter of 2011. Since that point, unemployment levels have

L. L Paterson and I. N Gregory, *Representations of Poverty and Place*,
https://doi.org/10.1007/978-3-319-93503-4_6

fallen, moving below 7% in the first quarter of 2014, and statistics from the third quarter of 2016 place it at 4.8% (ONS 2016a). However, despite the statistics suggesting positive overall trends, 4.8% equates to 1.6 million people. During the time period covered by our corpora Lansley and Mack (2015: 90–91) note cases where over 1700 people applied for eight jobs in a coffee chain-store in Nottingham in 2013, 1300 applied for twenty fixed-term Christmas positions in retail in the Midlands in 2010, and thirty cinema jobs in West Bromwich in 2013 received 2000 applications.

Unemployment can be measured in a number of different ways. The International Labour Force definition includes everyone aged over 16 who is not in employment and is either available to start work within the next two weeks, waiting to start a new job within the next two weeks, or has been actively looking for work in the last four weeks (ONS, n.d. (a)). This is the measurement used by the 2011 census (ONS 2014). An alternative measure of unemployment is to look at workless households, defined as households that contain at least one person aged between 16 and 64 where no-one aged 16 or over is in employment (ONS, n.d. (b)). Figure 6.1 shows these two different measures of unemployment, at slightly different dates. The maps show strongly similar patterns, although there is more worklessness in rural areas, compared to unemployment which tends to be a more urban phenomenon. Table 6.1 measures these similarities formally using correlation analysis. It shows that the two measures are strongly correlated, and both also correlate closely with Carstairs scores. Therefore, a relationship clearly exists between geography and unemployment and, by extension, poverty, which is persistent between different definitions.

Unemployment tends to be lower in the South-East and higher in urban areas including London, South Wales, the West Midlands, the North-West and North-East of England, and central Scotland. These differences are marked. For example, in 2015, Lansley and Mack (2015: 116) noted that in 'areas such as Hartlepool in the North-East of England, and north and east Ayrshire in Scotland, the ratio of unemployed to job vacancies has remained three times higher than the national average'. In addition to formally-defined unemployment, the ONS indicates that there were a further 8.89 million people who were 'economically inactive' and unable to work in the third quarter of 2016 (ONS 2016b: 3). This group includes students, people looking after family members (especially

Fig. 6.1 Different definitions of unemployment using **a** the 2011 census definition and **b** workless households 2015. Legends use quintiles

Table 6.1 Correlation coefficients between measures of poverty, unemployment, and worklessness at local authority district level. Excludes Northern Ireland

	Census unemployment 2011	Workless households, 2015
Carstairs Score, 2011	.949**	.609**
Census unemployment 2011	–	.602**

**Significant at $p < 0.01$

children), and people who have taken early retirement, as well as those who have long-term illnesses. Most of those categorised as long-term sick, or caring for family members will be in receipt of some form of government benefit, such as Child Benefit, Personal Independence Payments, Carer's Allowance, and/or Employment and Support Allowance (ESA). Due to the coalition government's cuts to the welfare budget, those in receipt of such benefits may have seen their payments of decrease or cease entirely. Thus, poverty does not merely relate to unemployment, it also shares a relationship with so-called economic inactivity.

To analyse (un)employment, as depicted in the news sections of our two corpora, we can start at the macro level and compare the collocates of <*employ*> for each newspaper. By beginning with the corpora—not just focusing on the immediate co-text of PNCs—we can provide evidence for each newspaper's general stance on this issue, which we can use in close analysis of their representation of (un)employment at particular locations. We can also, of course, compare the PNCs for <*poverty*> and <*employ*> directly. There are 87,550 hits for <*employ*> in the news section of *Daily Mail* (a normalised frequency of 283.73 pmw). In comparison, there are 17,042 hits in the *Guardian* news Section (466.52 hits pmw). From this we can deduce that, overall, the *Guardian* uses the lemma EMPLOY[1] relatively more frequently than the *Daily Mail*.

However, such a broad-stroke analysis sheds light on why we cannot reduce poverty discourses to individual search terms; the use of EMPLOY

[1]Small capitals denote lemmas: all forms of a word, such as *employ, employee, unemployed, employment*, etc.

does not cover all potential references to employment. Reference could be made to particular job titles or alternative terms like *job* or *work* may be used. Hits for the query <*work*> show that the *Guardian* uses this term 2078.65 times pmw, whereas the *Daily Mail* uses it 1455.4 times pmw. Similarly for JOB the figures are 618.2 and 379.93 respectively. Despite the limitations of such statistics (we can 'employ common sense' and 'work out at the gym', neither of which relate to employment, but are included in the normalised frequencies[2]) the fact that the *Guardian* has higher normalised frequencies for all these employment-related terms is evidence that the *Guardian* appears more concerned with (un)employment than the *Daily Mail*.

Taking a closer look more specifically at unemployment, we can start to see nuances in how the term is used by each newspaper. The query <(unemployment|unemployed)> returns 13,453 hits in the *Daily Mail* (43.60 pmw) and 4357 hits in the *Guardian* (119.27 pmw), suggesting that the latter refers to unemployment relatively more frequently. To highlight the semantic fields associated with unemployment, we manually categorised the top 100 collocates in each newspaper (Table 6.2). There were 50 shared collocates, 35 were unique to the *Daily Mail* and 37 were unique to the *Guardian* (7 grammatical terms and numbers were removed).

Overwhelmingly, the groups of collocates suggest that, similarly to poverty (see Chapter 5), unemployment is discussed by both newspapers in terms of its measurability: 24 of the 50 shared collocates occur in this category. However, despite both the *Daily Mail* and the *Guardian* appearing to focus on unemployment *rates, statistics* and *levels*, the collocates unique to the *Daily Mail* appear to focus on *falling* unemployment (1) whilst the *Guardian* tends towards collocates like *mass* and *risen*, which emphasise increases in unemployment (2).

1. The quarterly fall in overall **unemployment** was mainly among 16 to 24-year-olds, with **unemployment** in this age group down by 42,000 to 917,000 (DM news, July 2011).

[2]Complex queries could reduce some of this noise, but the normalised frequencies are merely a litmus test for each newspapers' coverage of employment.

Table 6.2 Top 100 lexical collocates of *unemployment*

	Shared collocates	Unique to DM 100	Unique to G 100
Measurement	falling, figures, growth, high, higher, highest, increase, inflation, level, levels, long-term, low, lower, lowest, million, number, quarter, rate, rates, rise, rising, rose, soaring, statistics	fall, fallen, falls, fell, median, more, overall, per cent, per-cent, record	average, increasing, mass, risen
Work	employment, job, jobs, unemployed, unemployment, work, workers	Hiring	placements, programme, scheme, schemes, vacancies, working
Benefits	allowance, benefit, benefits, claiming, dole, jobless, jobseeker		claimants, jobcentre, joblessness, jobseekers, welfare, workfare
Money	poverty, wages	debt, income, prices	incomes, insurance, low-paid, paid, pensions, unpaid
Policy	cuts, economic, economy, recession	austerity, government, recovery	
People/ Demographics	people, young, youth	Americans, graduate, graduates, Labor, Obama, population	disabled, over-50s, under-25s
Locations		country, Eurozone, Spain, UK	areas
Time	Months	currently, seasonally, since	year
Homes	Housing	Household	homelessness
Action	Tackle	Hits	find, help, helping, hit, living
Evaluation		crisis, struggling, stubbornly	deprivation, poor, scarring, sickness

2. We are the undiscovered generation. With the number of **unemployed** under-25s rising to almost 1 million this year (G news: society, Mar 2010).
3. Mr. Kirby said the recent fall in **unemployment** was a 'hiatus rather than a turning point', forecasting that nearly 450,000 workers will lose their jobs over the next two years (DM news, Feb 2010)

This does not mean that the *Daily Mail* ignores increases in unemployment rates or long-term trends, as is evidenced by the newspapers' shared collocates and (3). However, analysing the collocates in this way emphasises that, whilst the newspapers are working with similar lexical resources, the discourses surrounding *unemployment* in both corpora are somewhat different. For example, unemployment collocates with more terms relating to benefits (*claimants, jobcentre*, etc.) in the *Guardian*, whilst the *Daily Mail* links unemployment to government policies (*austerity, government, recovery*). A subset of unique collocates in the *Daily Mail* includes *Americans, Obama, Eurozone*, and *Spain*, which suggest consideration of unemployment in different nation states (similar to the findings in Chapter 5). In order to focus more closely on the geographical aspect of poverty discourses in both corpora, we turn to the PNCs for employment-related search terms in the *Daily Mail* and the *Guardian*.

6.2 Poverty and Place in the Employment Sub-set

Beginning with <*employ*>, there are only 223 and 38 PNCs in the *Guardian* and *Daily Mail*, respectively, which relate to poverty. Thus, the overwhelming conclusion is that neither newspaper systematically associates the term employment and poverty with particular locations in the UK. Figure 6.2 shows the distribution of <*employ*> PNCs for both newspapers. It is clear that both newspapers are heavily concentrated on London and the south-east: 32% of the *Daily Mail*'s PNCs are in London rising to 61% in the south-east. Despite having far more PNCs, the *Guardian* is even more London-centric with 72% of its <*employ*> PNCs in London and 75% in the south-east as a whole. The *Guardian* does, however, have around 5% of its PNCs in both Scotland (mainly Edinburgh) and Northern Ireland (all in Belfast, which did not occur for <*poverty*>) whereas the *Daily Mail* has no coverage of <*employ*> in either of these areas. Neither newspaper pays much attention to Wales; there are two *Daily Mail* PNCs in Merthyr Tydfil and one *Guardian* PNC in Cardiff. Within England, both newspapers have minor subsets in the north-east; the *Daily Mail* has six PNCs (16%) in and around Newcastle, while the *Guardian* has a cluster of fourteen PNCs centred on Hull.

Comparing the PNCs to the measures of unemployment reported in Fig. 6.1, it is clear that there is little relationship between the newspapers' geographical coverage of (un)employment, and quantitative measures of its distribution. None of the ten districts with the highest rates of worklessness (see Fig. 6.1) are in London. The *Guardian* has only three PNCs these ten districts, two in Glasgow and one in Liverpool, while the *Daily Mail* has two, both in Merthyr Tydfil. Using the statistics for unemployment the emphasis on London is perhaps slightly more justifiable as three of the ten districts (outside Northern Ireland) with the highest unemployment rates are in London. Nevertheless, there is little to justify the newspapers' concentration on London and their apparent lack of interest in other areas.

However, focusing on <*employ*> alone cannot tell us the whole story. To address wider discourses of (un)employment, we turn to the Employment subset, which consists of the results for four related queries (<*employ*>, <job*>, <redundan*>, and <work*>). As discussed in Chapter 5, all PNCs returned by these queries, but not used within discourses of poverty were eliminated. For example, <job*> occurred in unrelated hits such as 'paint job' or 'did a good job'. By manually removing these hits, we thinned our dataset so that we only plotted PNCs where there was a three-way relationship between the search terms, poverty, and place. As a result, we removed noise from our data and provide a nuanced picture of the geographical aspect of discourses of poverty and employment in the UK media. The PNCs for the Employment subset are shown in Fig. 6.3.

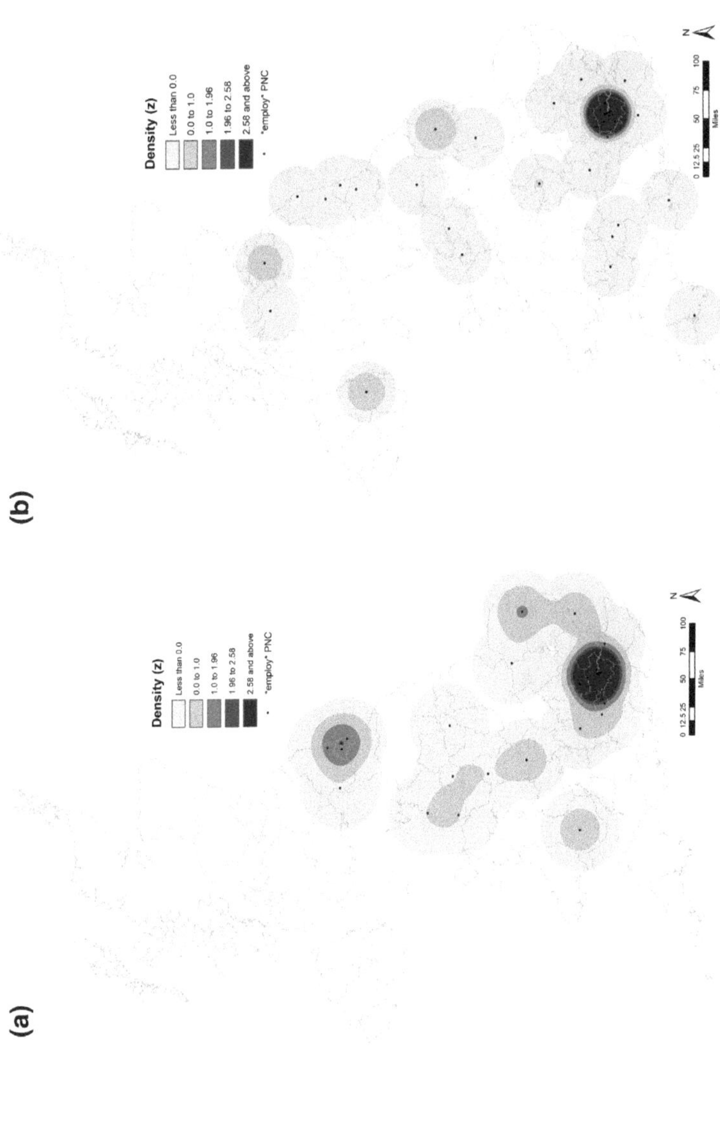

Fig. 6.2 Density smoothed maps of <*employ*> PNCs in **a** the *Daily Mail* and **b** the *Guardian*

The *Daily Mail* has a total of 1185 PNCs comprising 360 unique place-names, whilst the *Guardian* has 1038 PNCs comprising 272 unique place-names. The fact that there are repeated PNCs (39 for Birmingham in the *Guardian*, for example) suggests that particular places are more associated with discussions of (un)employment than others. Figure 6.3 shows that the pattern for the *Guardian* is quite similar to that for <*employ*> in Fig. 6.2, being dominated by London (41% of PNCs), although other urban centres such as Birmingham, Liverpool and Manchester also emerge. The pattern for the *Daily Mail* is, however, significantly more complex. Although still London-centric, only 21% of the *Daily Mail*'s PNCs are in London and there are also major clusters around Birmingham, across the north of England, and in Glasgow. This pattern of more geographical complexity in the *Daily Mail* is also found when a Kulldorf's spatial scan statistic is used to identify places with more (hotspots) or fewer (cold spots) PNCs than would be expected from the background geography found in the two corpora (Fig. 6.4). As described in Chapter 4, this background geography was determined using a 5% sample of PNCs for <the> in each corpus.

The *Guardian* has hotspots around Liverpool, Humberside (centred on Hull), and in the north-east of England, particularly in Middlesbrough and Sunderland. Interestingly, London is not a hotspot, suggesting that the PNCs in the Employ subset actually represent the background geography of the *Guardian* corpus rather than any particular association between London and unemployment. Much of the south of England and of Scotland are cold spots suggesting that the *Guardian* does not associate these places with unemployment. The *Daily Mail* does have a hotspot in London but it is in north-east London, whilst much of the rest of London is a cold spot. Elsewhere, there are clusters stretching from Birmingham to Nottingham, one in Liverpool stretching north through much of Lancashire, another in areas east of Barnsley and Wakefield to Hull and Scunthorpe, and in Middlesbrough and Newcastle, and Glasgow. There are also smaller clusters associated with a single place-name: Swindon is associated with redundancies at the Honda car plant there, and Aberdeen is associated with a pilot scheme for Incapacity Benefit reassessment.

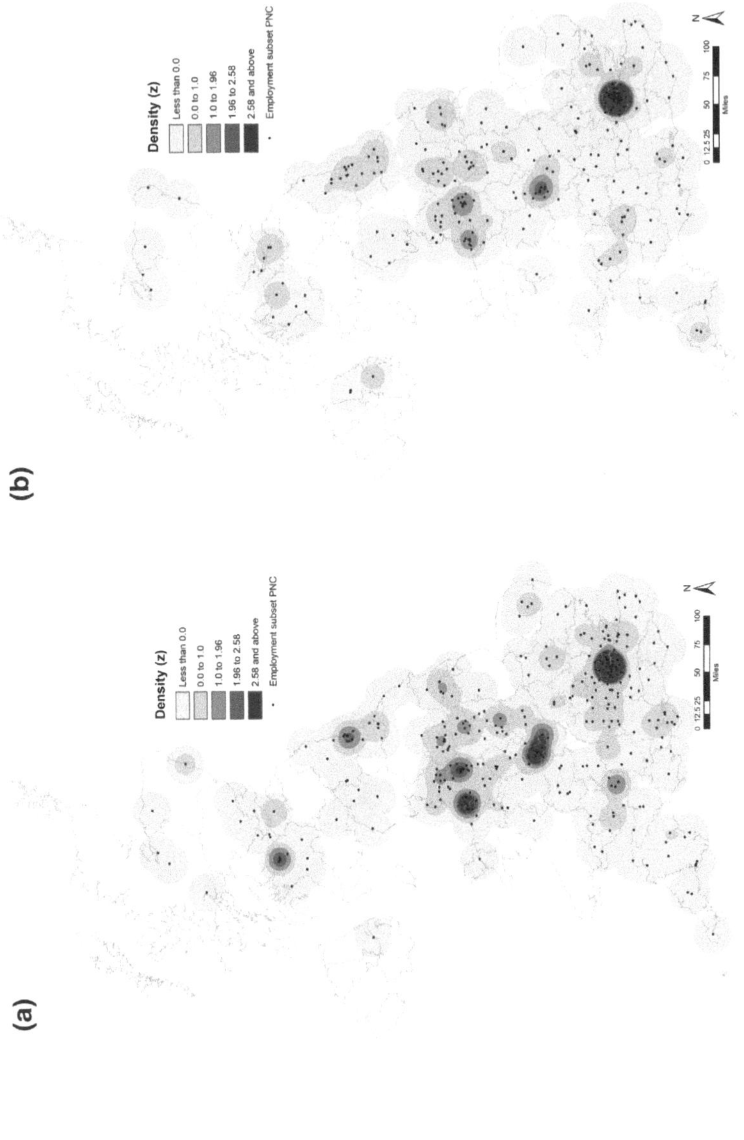

Fig. 6.3 Density smoothed maps of PNCs in the Employment subset in **a** the *Daily Mail* and **b** the *Guardian*

Fig. 6.4 Kulldorf clusters of PNCs in the Employment sub-set in **a** the *Daily Mail* and **b** the *Guardian*

6.3 Locating the Language of Unemployment

In order to understand how the locations referred to were used within discourses of poverty (and employment) we began with PNC keyword analysis—a form of contrastive concordance analysis—as described in Chapter 4. PNC keywords are a robust way to ascertain how the newspapers are internally different in relation to their coverage of London and the rest of the UK. Comparing the PNC keywords for each newspaper can also act as a test of how similar they are in their coverage of (un)employment. However, as noted in Sect. 6.1, although the newspapers may draw on the same lexical resources, they do not necessarily represent a given topic in the same way. To compare the newspapers in detail and facilitate triangulation, we analysed samples of concordance lines, following the method proposed by Baker (2006). This involved taking a random sample of 50 concordance lines[3] from the Employ subset for each newspaper and undertaking manual analysis to identify key themes, trends, categories, etc. Following the initial analysis a further randomly-selected batch of 50 concordance lines were tested against the patterns found in the original 50. The analysis proceeded in batches of 50 concordances until no further patterns were found. This procedure was repeated for all subsets (Employ, Money, Benefits, Housing, and Evaluation) which are discussed across the following chapters. In most cases 250 concordance lines was sufficient to identify the major trends in each subset and also highlighted some more minor trends in the data.

Table 6.3 shows the PNC keywords for the Employ subset in the *Daily Mail*. To maintain consistency in the analysis, the PNC keywords have been split into those relating to London and those relating to the rest of the UK. However, as the Kulldorf analysis has shown, there was not always such a dichotomy in the data. In order to avoid homogenising data for the rest of the UK, particular places of interest are explored in the following close analysis.

[3] A random number generator was used to generate samples. No concordances were analysed more than once.

Table 6.3 PNC keywords in the Employment subset in the *Daily Mail* ($n \geq 5$)

Place	Sig.	PNC keywords
London	<0.01	months, without, who, end, or, can
London	<0.05	I, west, live, outside, back, hundreds, east, go, week, into, families, Tesco, headquarters, more, that, than
Rest of UK	<0.01	plant, at, per, police, lost, fit, near, had, capable, cent, third, midlands, bae, said, losing
Rest of UK	<0.05	factory, biggest, department, town, planning, claimants, ten, sites, systems, even, redundant, Tata, vacancy, places, refinery, former, Honda, hall, blow, hours, led, tests, products, work

In London, PNCs that included *Tesco* referred to unpaid internships and related to campaigns against companies who advertise vacancies but only offer expenses and/or Jobseeker's Allowance (4). References to such vacancies are not restricted to London, and they also occur in the *Guardian*, which reports on legal proceedings relating to unpaid placements. The *Daily Mail* reports job losses across many different sectors in London: terms like *retail, firefighter, bankers, Deutsche bank, Homebase, Argos, BBC, fitters, Ford, UBS, parcel, showrooms* and *HQ* were PNC keywords which met the threshold for statistical significance, but did not occur 5 or more times (cf. criteria for Table 6.3). Many of the job cuts/redundancies reported are actual. However, there are also reports of threats to jobs and proposed redundancies (as is also found in the *Guardian*, see below).

4. Right to **work** campaigners disrupted *Tesco*'s Westminster branch after the company advertised for workers in exchange for expenses and Jobseeker's Allowance (DM news, Feb 2012).
5. Meanwhile, in Tower Hamlets, the poorest borough in London and arguably the most deprived in Britain, 58 **employees** have **job** titles which contain the words 'climate change' or 'global warming' […] You couldn't make it up (DM news, Mar 2010).
6 Beggars belief: Despite hundreds of **jobs** being axed, Westminster Council is recruiting an extra 50 traffic wardens. One of Britain's largest councils is to spend nearly £2million to increase its squad of traffic wardens—while axeing (sic) more than 500 jobs (DM news, Nov 2010).

Despite the *Daily Mail* reporting on job losses, which it generally evaluates negatively, the converse positive evaluation for job creation does not hold true; the *Daily Mail* negatively evaluates particular types of job, especially those relating to climate change (5) and the recruitment of new traffic wardens (6). The use of 'you couldn't make it up' in (5) indicates a negative stance towards jobs relating to climate change. By mentioning poverty in relation to these particular jobs, the *Daily Mail* positions this type of job creation as opposed to or irrelevant to addressing poverty in Tower Hamlets. By implication, poverty is somehow a 'real' issue, whilst climate change is seen as less important. However, there is no evidence that the climate change jobs mentioned in (5) were in any way related to anti-poverty initiatives; the *Daily Mail* has made this faux-connection. Similarly, the use of 'axed' in (6), as opposed to more a neutral verb such as 'cut', positions the *Daily Mail* as opposed to job cuts, but jobs for new traffic wardens are somehow unsatisfactory (see the use of 'despite') and the phrase 'spend nearly 2million' implies such jobs will cost too much or that money is better spent elsewhere.

PNC keywords for the rest of the UK are dominated by references to job cuts; terms like *plant, lost, products, near, losing, planning, systems, sites, Tat, BAE, Honda, refinery, places,* and *police* all refer to real or planned redundancies. Locating these in space, Nissan is associated with creating jobs in Sunderland, whilst Vauxhall (Luton, Elsmere Port), BMW (Longbridge), Honda (Swindon), BAE Systems (Brough), Tata (Scunthorpe), Kraft/Cadbury (Somerdale, Bristol, York), Twinings (North Shields) and Imperial Tobacco (Nottingham) are reported to be cutting jobs across England. The *Daily Mail* states that, before losing their jobs, Twinings workers in North Shields were expected to 'train up their Polish replacements', noting that the workers 'have accused bosses of "rubbing salt into the wound"'. The *Daily Mail* thus takes an implied negative stance on the relocation of jobs to Poland; the use of the quotation from unnamed workers allows the *Daily Mail* to express dissatisfaction that jobs in Britain are being moved elsewhere, but they never need to state this explicitly.

The PNC keywords *per, cent, ten, even,* and *vacancy* refer to the number of people receiving government benefits, particularly Jobseeker's Allowance, or the number of vacancies in a given area. The *Daily Mail* focuses on job availability by reporting that Aberdeen is the place where there are 'the greatest number of jobs available in construction'. In this instance, reporting on locations where jobs are available (and focusing on just one industry) works within the wider ideology that jobs are available if people want them. However, no consideration is given to the difficulties of relocating for work or the fact that not all jobseekers are trained in construction. The focus on available jobs in Aberdeen is contrasted with a set of PNC keywords associated with the reassessment of recipients of Incapacity Benefit.[4] *Fit, capable, third, biggest, claimants, test,* and *work* are used to discuss the numbers of people being declared fit for work after reassessment (7), particularly in Aberdeen and Burnley where pilot studies were conducted (8).

7. Of 14,640 claimants, 5180 were fit. THE TOP 20 '**WORKSHY**' AREAS Birmingham 5180 Glasgow City 3950 Liverpool 3280 Manchester 3030 County Durham 2970 Leeds 2570 Bradford 2430 Sheffield 2180 Stoke-on-Trent 1900 Wakefield 1880 Kirklees 183 (DM news, May 2013).
8. A pilot trial reassessing claimants who took up incapacity benefit before 2008 found that nearly 30 per cent were fit for **work**. New tests of claimants in Aberdeen and Burnley found that 29.6 *per cent* should not be on sickness benefits at all (DM news, Feb 2011).

The use of 'workshy' to refer to all who have been assessed and deemed fit for work homogenises people having benefits removed, independent of the reasons for which they were reassessed as fit to work. The naming and shaming of areas, all of which are notably in Scotland or the north of England, does not take into account the overarching employment and health profiles of these regions, and further implies that (large numbers of) people in receipt of Incapacity Benefit are somehow devious.

[4]Incapacity Benefit was replaced by Employment Support Allowance (ESA) and existing claimants were reassessed from 2010 onwards to determine if they met the criteria for ESA. The reassessment process included a paper-based and/or face-to-face Work Capability Assessment (WCA) with a third-party contractor.

The *Daily Mail*'s focuses on the number of people without a job (9) or claiming benefits is supported by concordance analysis, and it has a tendency to rank locations (10). Areas in the north of England are labelled as 'jobless ghettos' and there is even a list of 'BENEFIT BLACKSPOT AREA WORK-AGE ADULTS ON BENEFITS' which is capitalised to draw readers' attention. The *Daily Mail* includes a list of the 'worst ten places to find work' but this is part of the same article about construction jobs in Aberdeen (see above). Thus, the overarching effect is that the *Daily Mail* states that there are jobs available for those who want them in places like Aberdeen (which it describes as 'one of the three happiest places in the UK'). It endorses the behaviour of those who use unusual techniques to attain jobs (see (12) below), whilst ranking and negatively evaluating those who receive government benefits.

9. Glasgow had the highest proportion of **workless** families—with 28.6 per cent of households without a **job**. Nearby Ayrshire is in second—with 28.5 per cent of families in the area out of **work**. Without students Nottingham sits in third place—with a **jobless** rate of 27.5 per cent (DM news, Nov 2014).
10. Birmingham is listed among the five British cities suffering the most from the blight of **worklessness**. It is placed fourth in the new ONS **worklessness** table (DM news, Sept 2013).
11. Jeff Randall reported from **unemployment** blackspot Merthyr Tydfil, where he discovered people who were so accustomed to living in a dependency culture that they couldn't even be bothered to catch a bus a few miles to Cardiff, where **jobs** were available (DM news, Mar 2015).

Example (11) shows these elements working together in relation to location. The premodification of Merthyr Tydfil as an 'unemployment blackspot' is combined with the homogenisation of benefits recipients as people who are 'accustomed to living in a dependency culture'. These people are negatively evaluated because they 'couldn't even be bothered' to travel for work. To support this position, and reinforce the implied notion of laziness, the commute to Cardiff is presented as 'a few miles', though the actual distance is 24 miles and the journey takes over an hour by public transport. Thus the framing of this issue by the *Daily Mail* does not take into account whether individuals could actually make the journey to Cardiff (people may be restricted by caring duties, for example), nor do they address the underlying issue that there are apparently not enough jobs in Merthyr Tydfil. Furthermore, (11) is an example of reference to generic benefits recipients; Sky reporter Jeff Randall met 'people' who are never named, and the use of 'discovered' is sensationalist, as it implies that Randall has found something or someone which has been hidden.

The *Guardian* also reports on Merthyr Tydfil and employment in Cardiff, but presents the same story reported by the *Daily Mail* in a different way. The *Guardian* positions the story as Iain Duncan Smith's denial of having a 'get on yer bike moment', which intertextually refers to the famous quotation from Conservative MP Norman Tebbit in the 1980s, that his father had 'got on his bike and looked for work, and kept looking 'til he found it'. This statement was controversial as unemployment rates reached 12% in the 1980s and Tebbit's view was taken to endorse the neoliberal notion that those who were unemployed were held back not by socioeconomic constraints, but their own lack of initiative. By referencing Tebbit, the *Guardian* makes links between the Conservative policies of the 1980s and coalition policies on employment and welfare from 2010 onwards.

Concordance analysis also brought to light instances where the *Daily Mail* focused on the employment status of individuals, with multiple reports of people committing suicide because they lost their jobs. In these cases, job loss is presented as causing suicide with no contextual factors noted; the *Daily Mail* quotes the partner of one suicide victim as saying 'I've no doubt in my mind the reason Michael took his own life was because he lost his job'. Reports of individuals posting job requests on sandwich boards (12), billboards, hand-held signs, and Facebook are evaluated positively. In the article (12) is taken from, the jobseeker is described as 'dedicated', 'determined', someone who 'has gone the extra mile' and who wants to 'make an honest crust'. He is also directly quoted as saying 'I don't want to claim benefits'. These examples make a direct link between one's employment status and identity (especially in the case of the reported suicides) and sit well within capitalist ideologies.

12. Desperate: **Jobless** Martin Bailey from Nottingham who has resorted to wearing with a sandwich board (sic) to try and attract potential employer (DM news, Jan 2013).
13. But at Burnley Crown Court **jobless** Lumb was spared jail again after claiming he was stealing six steaks to feed his new pet dog as his state benefits had been cut (DM news, Sept 2014).
14. These are the 11 children of an unemployed mother who has provoked outrage after it was revealed a taxpayer-funded £400,000 council home is being specially built for her family. The picture was released as it was also claimed that **jobless** Heather Frost, 37, of Churchdown, Gloucestershire, has paid for her partner to have flying lessons (DM news, Feb 2013).

Despite its occurrence in (12) the use of 'jobless' to premodify a name or occupation is rarely used positively in the *Daily Mail*, and there are repeated links between this naming technique and crime (13). For example, a mother receiving an antisocial behaviour order is described as 'Jobless and single', even though her employment and relationship statuses are irrelevant to the legal proceedings reported. There are also examples of a 'jobless decorator', an 'out of work hairdresser', and a 'jobless factory worker', the latter of whom is the victim of assault. Jobless is used in this position to refer to criminals, dads, 'a squatter', a 'homeless drifter', and there are multiple references to the wedding of a 'jobless couple'. The use of this naming technique in (14) also taps into wider discourses about benefits recipients; there is an implicature here that someone who is unemployed, parent to a large number of children, and living in council-owned accommodation should not be in a position to buy flying lessons. Her status as a 'jobless' woman and 'unemployed mother' positions her as a 'flawed consumer' (Bauman 2004) and the purchase of flying lessons by someone in a 'taxpayer-funded' home taps into discourses of the undeserving poor (Katz 2013). The term jobless is not used in this way in the *Guardian*, where it occurs only seven times in premodifying position and tends to refer to generic 'jobless households' in Liverpool, Nottingham, and Glasgow.

Thus, interrogation of the language used by the *Daily Mail* to discuss unemployment, redundancies, and the links that it makes (implicitly or not) between job availability and benefits receipt suggests that the newspaper's treatment of such issues is underpinned by ideologies of neoliberalism—insofar as benefits recipients and the unemployed are responsible for their own lot, independent of wider social factors such as job availability. Furthermore, and in direct contradiction to the individualisation required by its apparent neoliberal stance, the *Daily Mail*'s homogenisation of those who are out of work and/or in receipt of government benefits through the construction of so-called 'workshy areas' facilitates the negative evaluation of entire groups of people without consideration of individual circumstance. When individuals are mentioned, they tend to be extreme (newsworthy) examples, such as parents to large families or people claiming large amounts of benefit (see Sect. 7.2) which are used to justify the newspaper's stance on such issues. Such individuals are not treated as exceptions to the norm (which statistically they are—most people do not have 11 children), but are given as indexical examples of 'the unemployed' or 'benefits claimants'. This allows the *Daily Mail* to both ignore heterogeneity and to present welfare receipt as a single problem, which is associated more with deviance than with wide-spread redundancies and low vacancy rates.

In considering how the *Guardian* treats (un)employment, poverty, and place (Table 6.4), there is more of a focus on the Living Wage Campaign, which is discussed in detail in Sect. 6.4. However, repeated references to minimum wage thresholds 'in London' and 'outside London' increase the number of PNCs relating to this issue. Such labels (inside/outside London) show how the geoparser cannot differentiate between direct references to a place and references to elsewhere which use a place-name as a starting point. The use of 'outside London' reinforces the need for close analysis to supplement geoparsing and foregrounds the apparent dichotomy between London and elsewhere.

Close reading of concordance lines indicated that there were also references to job losses in the NHS and the London fire brigade and a focus on the number of jobseekers for each available vacancy in particular areas, with the *Guardian* concentrating on those area where the ratio is high (15), which contrasts with *Daily Mail*'s focused on the availability of jobs in Aberdeen.

Table 6.4 PNC keywords in the Employment subset in the *Guardian* ($n \geq 5$)

Place	Sig.	PNC keywords
London	<0.01	living, if, outside, north, you, who
London	<0.05	his, against, people, south, from
Rest of UK	<0.01	centres, losses, face, loss, council, households, union, plant, constituency, county, sector, trade, biggest, told, programme, applied, public, greater, unison, beneath, our, variation, large, labour, cut, economy, how, today, redundancies, photograph, lab, midlands
Rest of UK	<0.05	authorities, unemployed, plans, even, chasing, Sodexo, expects, seeking, transferred, notices, applying, risk, year, every, include, cuts, over, residents, managers, department, john, policy, PWC, following, without, maintenance, moment, himself, chief, shed, Pfizer, valleys, announced, been, call, regional, yes, AR, vacancy, next, government, top

15. In Hackney, there were fewer than 500 vacancies for more than 11,000 claimants, while in Lewisham just over 10,000 people were after 487 available **jobs** (G news: society, Aug 2011).

Outside of London, job cuts and redundancies are associated with the most PNC keywords (*losses, council, face, sector, economy, Pfizer, plant, biggest, redundancies, midlands, announced, include, notices, Sodexo, call, expects, chief, shed, seeking, risk, PWC, next, top, transferred*) but focus more on police work, the MoD, and council-based positions than the industrial occupations noted in the *Daily Mail* (see above). In particular, cuts and changes to the NHS 111 service (a non-emergency telephone line) are localised to Bristol, Sheffield, Wakefield, Nottingham, Hull, Stafford, Chelmsford, and Newcastle, which also accounts for *centres, loss, union, large, Unison,* and *trade.* A further cluster of PNCs concern unemployment rates and workless *households* (including *variation, regional* and *today*) and involve repeated comparisons between Liverpool, Nottingham, and Glasgow (where the number of workless households is reported to be 1/3) and average rates of 1/9 elsewhere. The *Guardian* focuses particularly on the number of people *chasing every vacancy* and *applying* unsuccessfully for large numbers of jobs. Thus they are embodying the neoliberal attitude that the *Daily Mail* seems to expect, but the *Guardian* notes that they are unsuccessful because of the lack of jobs, not their lack of effort. A similar theme is drawn upon when claimants of Jobseeker's Allowance are broken down by *constituency*: Birmingham, Belfast, Middlesbrough, and Liverpool are associated with particularly high rates of people claiming this benefit.

Whilst the *Guardian* acknowledges job cuts in the private sector, it is more likely than the *Daily Mail* to report on cuts and redundancies in the public sector—in particular council-based employment and the NHS—and it is also more likely to mention unions. However, as shown in the *Guardian*'s general treatment of employment (Sect. 6.1), whilst the *Guardian* does report on actual job losses (16), many references to job cuts are only proposed (17) or 'could' occur. Jobs are quantified and described as 'at risk', or 'under threat', whilst cuts are 'expected' or 'planned', and 'redundancy estimates' are made. The *Guardian* has a tendency to report redundancies at the point of announcement, not at the point where redundancies are made and they are not as likely as the *Daily Mail* to state explicitly that jobs will be 'axed', but rather draw on epistemic modality and/or conditionals (see 'unless a buyer can be found' in 18) to avoid explicitly stating that cuts will occur.

16. Job losses so far include Sunderland housing provider Gentoo, axing 275 of its 1800 staff; 1400 **jobs** after the collapse of Leeds-based housing maintenance firm Connaught last year (G news: society, Mar 2011).
17. Beneath "Are **job** cuts proposed?" it is a yes in Sunderland, yes in Darlington, yes in Durham, yes in Gateshead, yes in Hartlepool and yes, yes, yes, yes in Newcastle, Northumberland, Redcar and Cleveland (G news: politics, May 2010).
18. The company that boasts the world's best-selling brand of haggis will close its meat processing plant near Edinburgh with the loss of 1700 **jobs** unless a buyer can be found (G news: news, Oct 2012).

The *Guardian* also reports on potential job creation, both generically (19) and using specific examples, such as (20), which relates to the construction of the HS2 train line. Most examples of job creation refer to London (or particular areas of London), whilst reports of job creation in the rest of the UK tend to revolve around HS2 and/or the manufacture of new trains. Again epistemic modality is used, insofar as the 'economy could generate' jobs, and reports of job creations are 'claimed' by third parties such as 'council leaders'.

19. Over the next four years, London's economy could generate 385,000 new **jobs** (G news: news, Jan 2011).
20. Council leaders have claimed a 20-minute cut in journey times between Leeds and Manchester would be worth £6.7bn and create nearly 30,000 **jobs** across the north of England (G news: society, Nov 2014).

The *Guardian* reports on the number of people claiming government benefits, particularly JSA (21) and Housing Benefit. As well as noting which areas have high rates of benefits claimants, the *Guardian* contextualises such reports by stating the number of available vacancies in areas of high unemployment. Furthermore, example (22) debates the accuracy of such figures by reference to the newspaper's own research—'even these figures mask the true competition for work'—and reports that high jobseeker-to-vacancy rates are a UK-wide phenomenon, not restricted to London or urban centres. The *Guardian*'s position on unemployment rates and the number of benefit claimants is thus in direct contradiction to the *Daily Mail*'s position that there are jobs if people want them, and that relocating/commuting (to Aberdeen or Cardiff, for example) would decrease unemployment rates.

21. In Haringey, Lewisham, Waltham Forest and Hackney, people claiming jobseeker's allowance outnumber **job** vacancies by more than 20 to 1 (G news: society, Aug 2011).
22. The worst-affected areas are spread all across the country: Clackmannanshire in Scotland has 35 **jobseekers** for every vacancy; the Isle of Wight has 21; Haringay (sic), London, 19; and Inverclyde 18. Research by the Guardian suggests even these figures mask the true competition for work (G news: society, Apr 2012).

The *Guardian*'s treatment of unemployment sits within their wider position on benefits (see Chapter 7); there are no reports in the Employ subset of people abusing or fraudulently claiming benefits, nor are there links to flawed consumerism.[5] Rather the *Guardian* reports on government policy and alleged targets for the number of benefit recipients expected to be sanctioned. It uses direct quotation (23) or summarised testimony (24) to justify reporting on the alleged targets. The use of 'ordered', 'threatened', and 'disciplinary action' position staff who oppose sanctions as both vulnerable to management and implicitly sympathetic to benefits claimants, whilst the description of (a subset of) benefits claimants as 'weak and vulnerable' places them in direct contrast to the negatively evaluated 'unscrupulous staff'. Thus, overall the *Guardian*'s position on (un)employment, poverty, and place, acknowledges neoliberalism but rejects it in favour of foregrounding structural inequalities and other social constraints; this is to be expected given the left-leaning nature of the publication.

23. Further new evidence of targets is revealed, which includes: An email from a **Jobcentre** manager in <u>Derbyshire</u> to say sanction referrals are top priority. "By end Sept we should have been at 5.5% (G news: society, Mar 2013).
24. A former personal adviser at a <u>Leicester</u> **Jobcentre**, says he was ordered by managers to send more claimants for sanction, and was threatened with disciplinary action when he questioned the policy. Unscrupulous staff would target weak and vulnerable claimants for sanctions, he states (G news: society, Jan 2015).

The PNC keyword and concordance analysis highlights the topics each newspaper focuses on in relation to poverty, place, and employment. However, it can also show what the newspapers do not do. With the exception of the *Guardian*'s focus on the Living Wage Campaign, there are no explicit links between the Employment subset and money. Very few of the query terms that comprise the Money subset occurred in the PNCs for the Employment subset, suggesting little overlap in terms of

[5]Whilst potential PNCs concerned only with benefit fraud were eliminated (as discussed in Chapter 5) there were some remnants of references to benefit fraud where it was mentioned alongside other issues relating to poverty, such as homelessness, loss of employment, and people being unable to pay their household bills.

how these issues are drawn upon within discourses of poverty and place. Given that the terms in the Employ subset and the Money subset were all collocates of <*poverty*>, and that employment is a primary way of obtaining money, this absence of overlap is somewhat unexpected. Nevertheless, it demonstrates that the different subsets may be used to contribute to newspaper discussions of poverty in different ways. The final section of this chapter focuses specifically on the Money subset.

6.4 Analysing Money Talk

The Money subset contains 14 queries[6] but resulted in fewer PNCs than the Employment subset. The *Guardian* has 885 PNCs and the *Daily Mail* has 378, the geography of which is quite similar to the Employ subset. The density smoothed and Kulldorf maps for the Money subset are shown in Figs. 6.5 and 6.6. The *Guardian* is particularly London-centric with 60% of its PNCs in or near London while the *Daily Mail* is somewhat dispersed, also having clusters around Birmingham and Manchester.

In both cases, inner London is a hotspot when compared to the newspapers' background geography. With the *Guardian*, this is the only major hotspot, but the *Daily Mail* also has a significant hotspot in the north-west of England that includes Manchester, Liverpool, and Burnley. In both cases much of Scotland and Northern Ireland are cold spots suggesting that money terms relating to poverty are not associated with these places. In the *Guardian*, much of England is also a cold spot which emphasises just how London-centric its coverage of this theme is.

To understand how the distributions in Figs. 6.5 and 6.6 relate to discourses of poverty, we turn again to the PNC keywords. To keep the analysis consistent we conducted a comparison between London and the rest of the UK. However, as shown in Fig. 6.6, the Money subset

[6] <*afford*>, <*austerity*>, <*cost*>, <earn*>, <*expens*>, <income*>, <*money*>, <*paid*>, <pay*>, <penn*>, <price*>, <*salar*>, <*spend*>, <*wage*>.

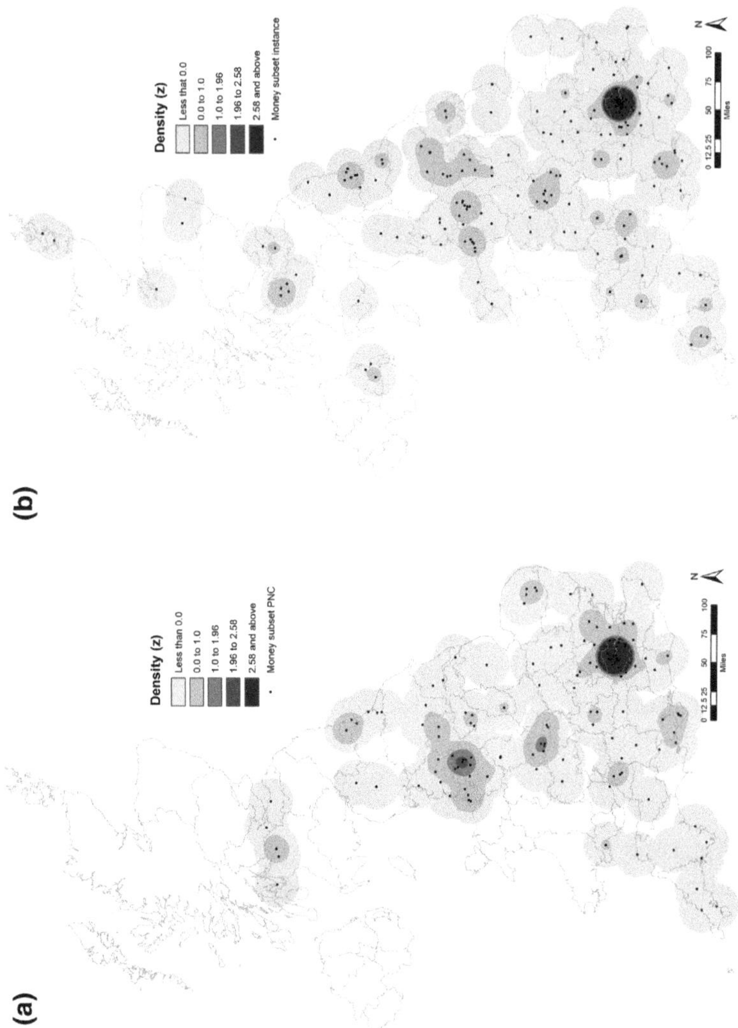

Fig. 6.5 Density smoothed maps of PNCs in the Money subset in **a** the *Daily Mail* and **b** the *Guardian*

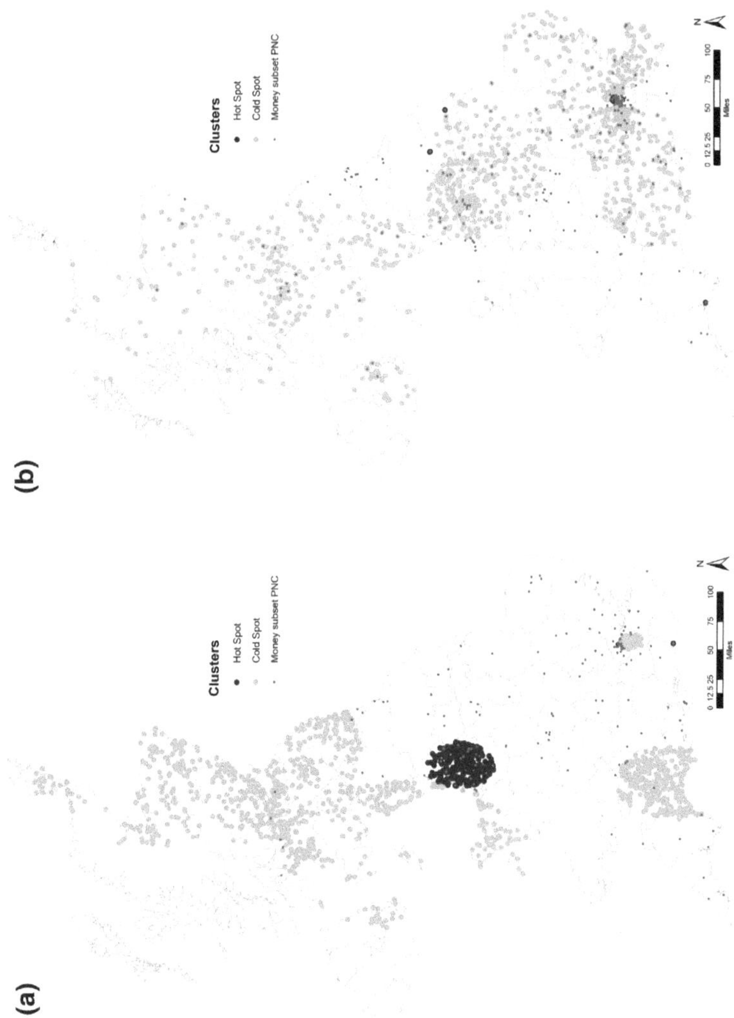

Fig. 6.6 Kulldorf clusters of PNCs in the Money subset in **a** the *Daily Mail* and **b** the *Guardian*

Table 6.5 PNC keywords in the Money subset in the *Daily Mail* ($n \geq 5$)

Place	Sig.	PNC keywords
London	<0.01	living, hour, be, wage, per, an
London	<0.05	–
Rest of UK	<0.01	left, after, from, her, biggest, told, save, beggar, nurse, loan
Rest of UK	<0.05	home, feminist, fines, awkwardly, university, went, failed, claimed, t-shirt, having, such, she, just

Table 6.6 PNC keywords in the Money subset in the *Guardian* ($n \geq 5$)

Place	Sig.	PNC keywords
London	<0.01	living, hour, wage, the, that, an, pay, than, workers, can, minimum
London	<0.05	is, do, we
Rest of UK	<0.01	different, council, west, charities, from, city, town, claimed, strong, labour, recording, never, claimants, springing, trustees, commuter, little, 'minimum, calculating, response, millions, county, midlands, unemployed, took, five, extra, jobseekers, up
Rest of UK	<0.05	years, like, measures, advice, rather, growth, pounds, average, week, about, spend, coach, and, give, some, also, another, combined, respectively, face, MP, hundreds, campaigns, increases, already, place, conference

is not always realised as such a geographical dichotomy. Furthermore, there were more similarities than differences between the newspapers. Thus the analysis is structured by theme, rather than by source. The PNC keywords for the *Daily Mail* are given in Table 6.5 and for the *Guardian* in Table 6.6.

The primary theme in the PNC keywords is a focus on the Living Wage Campaign, which encourages employers to pay their workers a minimum hourly wage to support an acceptable standard of living. Figures for the living wage currently stand at £8.45 across the UK and £9.75 in London. In the *Daily Mail* it is referred to using *living*, *hour*, *per*, and *wage*, and is associated particularly with Labour, then Labour leader Ed Miliband, and Conservative MP Boris Johnson, who was Mayor of London at the time. The living wage is reported on extensively by both the *Daily Mail* and the *Guardian*, and although there is a focus on London (amplified somewhat by the repetition of 'in London' and 'outside London'), there are references to other UK locations. In the *Guardian, hour, living, minimum, pay, wage, campaigns, different, minimum, never, response, springing,* and *up* all relate to the Living Wage Campaign, which is described as moving beyond London with action: '*springing up* in other cities—Glasgow, Leeds, Oxford, Preston, Norwich'.

The *Daily Mail* PNCs also refer to firefighters 'who are *paid* 28,000 a year plus the 5021 London weighting, [and] claim they must supplement their **income**', and supermarkets who pay low wages which are topped up by benefits.[7] Thus, an increase in wages 'would reduce the need for in-work benefits' and reduce taxpayer costs (25). Although the *Daily Mail* notes that 'half of people living in some areas earn less than living wage', references to such locations is generic ('areas'). When specific places are mentioned, focus is on those areas where the highest percentage of people earn the living wage (26). This is similar to the focus on available jobs in Aberdeen and Cardiff noted in Sect. 6.3. It is also in direct contrast to the *Guardian*'s reporting on the number of people not being paid the living wage (27).

25. Citizens UK is calling for London *living wage* to be spread to *rest* of Britain. It claims rolling out £9.15 an *hour wage* would reduce benefits by £6billion (DM news, Apr 2015).
26. Just 5.6 *per cent* of people working in Poplar and Limehouse (East London) earn less than the *living* **wage** followed by 5.8 *per cent* in Runnymede and Weybridge (Surrey), 7.3 *per cent* in South Cambridgeshire and also 7.3 *per cent* in Islington South (DM news, Apr 2014).
27. Fiona Twycross, Labour's economy spokeswoman in the London Assembly, said: "Poverty **pay** is a growing problem in London. In 2007 there were 420,000 people paid below the London *Living* ***Wage*** (G news: news, Mar 2014).

The strong focus on the living wage in both newspapers suggests a direct relationship between poverty and minimum hourly pay. The premodification of *wage* by *living* taps into the measures of poverty that Lansley

[7]In the *Guardian, pay* includes references to retail workers, particularly those employed by Sainsbury's. Thus, there are parallels between the *Guardian* and the *Daily Mail*'s coverage of retail wages.

and Mack (2015) attempted to capture in their *Breadline Britain* surveys (see Chapter 1) and are underpinned by a presumption that there is a relative, society-defined acceptable standard of living. The implications of the term 'living wage' are that those who do not receive a particular hourly rate of pay are somehow unable to live within UK society's accepted norms.

Both newspapers are pointing in the same direction in relation to the Living Wage Campaign. But they differ in who they present as the overall beneficiaries; the *Daily Mail* frames it as positive for taxpayers and a way to reduce the total welfare bill, whilst the *Guardian* labels it 'A campaign to help the low-paid' and focuses on the workers who will benefit from higher wages, which they equate to a higher standard of living. Although the *Guardian* does note that 'Employers in Brent could save as much as 5,000 if they ***pay*** all *workers* at least 9.15'. The ideology underpinning the Living Wage Campaign is that all workers, independent of the type of job they do, should have access to a minimum standard of living and that such access can be achieved through setting minimum hourly rates of pay. Furthermore, the existing minimum wage is considered too low (the *Guardian* claims that the national minimum wage is 'a poverty wage in London') and has not kept up with the cost of living. This means that wages below the living wage threshold(s) are conceptualised as directly contributing to poverty.

Concordance analysis highlights that a concept closely related to the living wage is the cost of living (in London). In the *Guardian*, terms like *rent* and *report* relate to increasing London rents, benefits recipients paying a percentage of market rents, and people being evicted because of the benefits cap. *High rent* is also directly to blame for poverty: 'There are families in London with a *high* level of *rent*, who just *do* not have enough **money** left'. The *Daily Mail* relates *rent* to the benefits cap (see Sect. 7.3), evictions, and people paying market rents, and reports extreme cases such as (28). The construction of (28) as 'worrying' is evaluative, but the agent who performs the action of worrying is obscured. Furthermore, by using 'worrying' as a premodifier not as a subject complement, the argument that the case is worrying is difficult to dispute.

28. Last Sunday, this newspaper reported the worrying case of a family living in a £2million Kensington townhouse, the £8000-a-month rent being **paid** directly though housing benefit (DM news, July 2010).
29. Families in well-heeled suburbs have been warned to brace themselves for an influx of thousands of benefits claimants (DM news, Oct 2010).

Words like *claimants* and *will* also refer to the benefits cap as well as the living wage, and the *Daily Mail* reports that 'Experts' claim 'cuts "*will* force 200,000 benefits *claimants* out of London and into the suburbs"'. However, the *Daily Mail*'s stance on this issue does not relate to the difficulties that families may face if they need to relocate, but rather frames the issue as in (29). Here we see that the problem is not that families may have to move because they cannot afford to live in London, and/or are experiencing financial hardship, but rather the families themselves *are* the problem for encroaching on 'well-heeled suburbs' where it is implied they do not belong. The framing of the *Daily Mail*'s report as a warning for people of relatively higher socioeconomic status to 'brace themselves' presents benefits claimants as undesirable, and the use of 'influx' draws on the negative semantics of water metaphors identified in discourses of immigration by Baker et al. (2008).

Migrants are mentioned explicitly in relation to low-pay and a higher welfare bill (the family in (28) are labelled as 'former asylum seekers'). Repeated references to a report that 'the 20 per cent lowest paid [in London] had seen wages fall by 15 per cent on average' are immediately followed by one of the sentences in (30), published across two different years.

30a. It added that schools in some areas of the country had seen a 'marked increase in the number of migrant pupils' (DM news, July 2014).

30b. Earlier this month, official figures showed that the number of Romanians and Bulgarians working in the UK had increased by a third in a single year to 173,000 (DM news, May 2015).

30c. Driving down the *wage* of natives pushes up the overall welfare bill since they are likely to be paid more in tax credits and other handouts to compensate (DM news, Nov 2014).

In each of these examples, a causal link is made between low wages and immigration (more specifically migrants, particularly from Bulgaria and Romania). In (a) and (b) this link is implied through reference to migrant children (or presumably their parents) and migrant workers, whereas in (c) the link is implied through the use of 'natives'. The 'natives' are not positioned as 'driving down' their own wages, but rather an unnamed force—contextually understood to be migrant workers—is performing this action. No other potential causes for declining wages are considered. Migrants are blamed not only for low wages, but their presence 'pushes up the overall welfare bill' because 'natives' must 'compensate' using 'tax credits and other handouts'. Thus, clear links are made here between poverty and its causes and the immigration of foreign nationals into the UK. This link represents endorsement of the *Daily Mail*'s generally-anti-immigration stance.

Outside London, the *Daily Mail* PNC keywords are more difficult to cluster. *Beggar, awkwardly, feminist*, and *t-shirt* are associated with a campaign where politicians were asked to wear a t-shirt with the logo 'This is what a feminist looks like' and an occasion where Ed Miliband gave money to a beggar while at the Labour Party conference. *Failed* refers to repossession after defaulting on mortgage payments. *She* and *her* link to stories about individual women and the benefits they claim: White Dee (who appeared in Channel 4's *Benefits Street*) is mentioned, as is someone in Wythenshawe where '*Shameless*, the Channel 4 comedy about feckless families living on benefits' was filmed. There are also mentions of individual women committing benefit fraud, shoplifting, choosing a future *university*, and a woman 'suing the Government' because she was given a voluntary work placement. This focus on stories about particular women again supports the notion that the *Daily Mail* is more likely to associate poverty with individual circumstances than the *Guardian*, with further implications that women behaving badly (shoplifting, etc.) are bringing poverty upon themselves.

There are also a cluster of PNC keywords below the threshold of 5 occurrences which refer to payday loans (*biggest, hotspot, search, showed, Wonga.com*), with a particular focus on Altringham in Greater Manchester (31). Although *loan* itself was more likely to refer to crime, particularly as a catalyst for armed robbery. The *Guardian* too focuses on payday loans (32). Both newspapers take the stance that such loans are negative and neither single out any individual as responsible when discussing this topic.

31. Google's data showed Altrincham was the biggest hotspot for the search terms '**payday** loans' and 'Wonga.com' (DM news, July 2014).
32. In Plymouth alone, the *council* estimates 5000 people are *using* **payday** lenders (G news: news, July 2013).

In the *Guardian*, *city* refers specifically to Birmingham and its history of moving from 'a high-wage, low-unemployment city to a low-wage, high-unemployment city' between the 1970s and 1980s. James Turner Street (*Benefits Street*) is also mentioned, as are reported cuts at Birmingham *city council*, and reports of compensation for underpaid female staff. In the case of the female staff, however, the story was not presented as individual narratives, but rather reported on wider action by the council to deal with complaints about low pay from a large group of women. *Council* (and *county*) locate discourses of poverty in space, with references to Birmingham city council, pay cuts by Southampton city council, the prosecution of Torbay council for not paying the minimum wage, and Shropshire county council's employment practices (33).

33. A Conservative-led *council* has sent letters of dismissal to its entire workforce, telling them they will be re-hired the next day only if they agree to a **pay** cut. Shropshire *county council* gave its 6500 staff notice of their dismissal on 30 September, but offered them immediate re-employment if they accepted a 5.4% pay cut as well as changes to their sick-pay arrangements (G news: society, July 2007).

Councils are thus portrayed by the *Guardian* as the agents behind the causes of poverty (low wages, the gender pay gap, and job cuts), although in (33) an overarching social actor is implied through references to the council being 'Conservative-led'. The *Guardian*'s focus on public sector cuts is again evidence of their opposition to Conservative and coalition-led policies to cut council budgets under the guise of austerity. Thus, the shrinking of the state is the implied cause of poverty and, as such, the ability to decrease poverty is not in the hands of the individuals who are experiencing it.

The locations mentioned above are contrasted with more positively-slanted stories such as the creation of jobs involving Corby council and Essex county council, and the City of York council's pledge to pay the living wage. *Recording, strong, growth, increases*, and *respectively* are PNC keywords because they occur in repeated *Guardian* reports about increases in disposable income in Hull, Sheffield, Bradford, Shropshire, Staffordshire, Herefordshire, Worcestershire, and Warwickshire, which are compared to decreases in Manchester and York. Similarly *average* refers to the lowest average wage (34) and is linked to four locations in the north of England.[8] References to the north-west are also linked to transport and the concept of a 'rust belt' of traditionally industrial locations (35) which is somewhat cut off from the rest of the UK.

34. The four constituencies with the lowest *average* **wage** are in *north-west* England; those working in Blackley and Broughton, Preston and Middlesbrough earn an average **salary** of between £323 and £330 per *week* (G news: society, June 2012).
35. Meanwhile, public investment in job-creating transport is needed by the *workless* of the *north-western* "*rust belt*" to *access* **better-paid** jobs in Preston, Manchester, Liverpool and Leeds (G news: politics, July 2010).

The focus on the lowest paid, presented as weekly wages (34) as opposed to annual salary, complements the *Guardian*'s focus on the

[8] The reference to Middlesbrough in (34) is misleading as it is in the north-east, not the north-west as stated.

highest jobseeker to vacancy ratios (Sect. 6.3). It is another example of contrast between the *Guardian* and the *Daily Mail* and evidence that the *Guardian* presents a bleaker view of poverty in the UK by focusing on the lowest paid areas, whilst the *Daily Mail* foregrounds more positive statistics and, by extension, downplays links between poverty and place.

6.5 Summary

Whilst the analysis of the single query <*poverty*> in Chapter 4 demonstrated the core concepts of geoparsing and GTA and illustrated the nuanced differences in how the *Guardian* and *Daily Mail* use a particular lemma, this chapter has begun to show that analyses of individual terms is only the starting point for discourse-level GTA. Whilst a focus on unemployment facilitated a three-way comparison between the *Guardian*, *Daily Mail*, and official statistics, it is clear that poverty discourses are made up of more than individual terms or concepts which are directly measurable.

By taking a closer look at how subsets of our queries are used by each newspaper we have demonstrated that although the *Guardian* and the *Daily Mail* (perhaps unsurprisingly) report on similar topics, their use of the query terms and PNC keywords differs. The *Daily Mail* reports on job losses, focusing particularly on locations associated with manufacturing (particularly the automotive industry). But it also foregrounds references to locations where jobs are available. The *Guardian* reports on those places where the jobseeker to vacancy ratio is particularly high, and despite the PNCs clustering in London, unemployment is not presented as a particular problem restricted to the capital. Job losses are reported across England (but less so in Scotland, Wales and Northern Ireland), with a particular focus on public sector redundancies. By analysing the language choices of each newspaper, and the stances that such choices indicate, we can begin to detail the *Daily Mail* and the *Guardian*'s orientation to wider discourses of poverty and place.

In the Money subset, the dominance of coverage of the Living Wage Campaign suggested that it is a key issue within discourses of poverty.

But each newspaper used this campaign in slightly different ways. In the *Guardian* it was seen as a way to tackle poverty and low pay and increase workers' access to a minimum standard of living, whereas in the *Daily Mail* it was seen as a way to decrease the amount of money paid in in-work benefits and reduce the burden on taxpayers (although there were no explicit links to tax cuts). In both approaches, there are links to welfare payments and the identities of benefits recipients. We consider the Benefits subset, and the related Housing subset, in the following chapter.

References

Baker, P. 2006. *Using Corpora in Discourse Analysis*. London: Continuum.

Baker, P., C. Gabrielatos, M. KhosraviNik, M. Kryzanowski, T. McEnery, & R. Wodak. 2008. A Useful Methodological Synergy? Combining Critical Discourse Analysis and Corpus Linguistics to Examine Discourses of Refugees and Asylum Seekers in the UK Press. *Discourse and Society* 19 (3): 273–306.

Bauman, Z. 2004. *Work, Consumerism and the New Poor*. Buckingham: Open University Press.

Katz, M. B. 2013. *The Undeserving Poor* (second edition). Oxford: Oxford University Press.

Lansley, S., & J. Mack. 2015. *Breadline Britain: The Rise of Mass Poverty*. London: Oneworld.

ONS. 2014. 2011 Census Glossary of Terms. https://www.ons.gov.uk/ons/guide-method/census/2011/census-data/2011-census-data/2011-first-release/2011-census-definitions/2011-census-glossary.pdf. Accessed 24/2/2017.

ONS. 2016a. Unemployment Rate: Sourced from the Labour Market Statistics Time Series Dataset. https://www.ons.gov.uk/employmentandlabourmarket/peoplenotinwork/unemployment/timeseries/mgsx/lms. Accessed 2/12/2016.

ONS. 2016b. Statistical Bulletin: UK Labour Market: Nov 2016. https://www.ons.gov.uk/employmentandlabourmarket/peopleinwork/employmentandemployeetypes/bulletins/uklabourmarket/november2016. Accessed 2/12/2016.

7
Characterising Poverty in Place: Benefits Receipt in Britain

The previous chapter explored two of our four major poverty-related subsets: terms related to Employment and Money. This chapter focuses on the other two major subsets: Benefits and Housing. Section 7.1 provides an overview of the wider context of benefits receipt in the UK. This is followed by analysis of PNCs relating to the Benefits subset in the *Daily Mail* (Sect. 7.2) and the *Guardian* (Sect. 7.3). As shown in Chapter 5, references to benefits and the cost of housing are core components of discourses of poverty and place. Whilst the former may have been expected, given the apparent relationship between poverty and the welfare state, the centrality of housing and rent was not necessarily predicted. It was somewhat expected that links would be made between poverty and homelessness, but, as shown in Sect. 7.4, the relationship between poverty and housing more often concerns the general cost of living and high household costs. Section 7.5 summarises how the different subsets analysed in Chapter 6 and this chapter relate statistically to each other and to quantitative measures of poverty including the Carstairs, worklessness, and unemployment data introduced in earlier chapters.

L. L Paterson and I. N Gregory, *Representations of Poverty and Place*,
https://doi.org/10.1007/978-3-319-93503-4_7

7.1 The Social, Political, and Linguistic Context of Benefits Receipt

In line with the analysis of employment in Chapter 6, it is important to note the wider context of our corpora. In 2010—the start of the period covered by our corpora—the total number of people claiming out of work benefits was estimated to be 1,496,400, but by 2015 this figure had dropped to 797,800 (ONS 2017). Conversely, there were 4,651,106 Housing Benefits claimants in January 2010, which rose to 4,894,992 in January 2015 (DWP 2018). Official statistics from the Family Resources Survey 2013/14 show that 55% of 'UK working age adults who are in receipt of state support' are in some form of employment (DWP 2016). Discussing trends in poverty from the 1980s to the present day, Lansley and Mack (2015: 81) note that 'the most striking shift has been the rise in poverty among those *in work*' and claim that those experiencing child poverty are likely to 'have at least one person in the household in full-time work' (2015: 87).

Research on the portrayal of benefits receipt by the media shows the topic is controversial. Multiple arms of the mass media make associations between benefits receipt and fraud, poor work ethic, scrounging, and a money for nothing attitude. For example, Lundström (2013) found evidence of anti-benefits sentiment in the UK press, whilst Paterson et al. (2016) showed how members of the UK public used the television programme *Benefits Street* to make negative generalisations about people who receive government benefits. Similar sentiments were also found by Baker and McEnery (2015) and van der Bom et al. (2018) in their analyses of the discourses drawn upon by people tweeting about *Benefits Street*. Importantly, the representations of benefits receipt presented in the mass media (as seen in programmes such as *Benefits Street, On Benefits and Proud,* and *Benefits Britain*) are used to justify government actions that potentially impact all benefits recipients. The example below is taken from the Hansard record and includes an exchange in the House of Commons between Conservative MP Phillip Davies and Secretary of State Iain Duncan Smith:

> **Philip Davies (Shipley) (Con)**: Has the Secretary of State managed to watch programmes such as "Benefits Street" and "On Benefits & Proud"? If so, has he, like me, been struck by the number of people on them who manage to combine complaining about welfare reform with being able to afford to buy copious amounts of cigarettes, have lots of tattoos, and watch Sky TV on the obligatory widescreen television? Does he understand the concerns and irritation of many people who go to work every day and pay their taxes but cannot afford those kinds of luxuries?
> **Mr. Duncan Smith**: My hon. Friend is right: many people are shocked by what they see. That is why the public back our welfare reform package, which will get more people back to work and end these abuses. All these abuses date back to the last Government, who had massive spending and trapped people in benefit dependency. (Hansard 2014)

The position set out in this exchange is that benefits recipients illegitimately spend their money on tattoos and televisions, which causes 'irritation' for working people who do not have the money to buy such items. Direct contrast is made between benefits recipients and hard-working, taxpayers who are 'shocked' by *Benefits Street*, despite the fact that many benefits recipients are in work. The language used is highly evaluative; their (presumably expensive) televisions are described as 'obligatory' and their consumption of cigarettes is 'copious'. It is ultimately implied that those receiving benefits should not be able to afford such 'luxuries'. The apparently flawed consumerism of benefits recipients, along with their 'complaining', are described as 'abuses' of a system which will be fixed by Conservative-led Welfare Reform. This is, thus, a clear example of how media depictions of benefits receipt (and poverty more widely) can be used as supporting evidence for government policy.

Having established the socio-political background within which the texts in our corpora were produced, we can also take an overview of how the *Guardian* and the *Daily Mail* discuss government benefits more generally. As a litmus test <*benefit*> returns 27,159 hits in the *Guardian* (481.51 pmw) and 61,165 hits in the *Daily Mail* (188.38 pmw), showing that the former is 2.5 times more likely to use the term. Of course, not all references to benefits will correspond to government welfare payments; the different forms of BENEFIT can be used much more generally, as in 'reap the benefits', 'feel the benefit' and to 'benefit from'. Nevertheless, the collocates of <*benefit*> suggest that it is predominantly used in reference to welfare payments. Table 7.1 lists the top 25 lemmatised collocates of <*benefit*> in both corpora (including the debate sub-corpora) calculated using log-likelihood, a span of ±5, minimum frequency of 5 and a minimum collocation frequency of 5.

The *Daily Mail* collocates include references to particular types of benefits (*child, tax, incapacity, disability, housing, credit, unemployment, pension, allowance, out-of-work*) but also include *cheat* and *fraud* (see example 1). The *Guardian*, whilst also collocating <*benefit*> with particular types of payment (*housing, incapacity, tax, child, credit, disability, universal, out-of-work, in-work, allowance, sickness, working-age*), does not collocate <*benefit*> as highly with fraud. *Fraud* and *cheat* occur in the *Guardian* collocates, but are ranked in 28th and 30th place. In contrast to the *Daily Mail*, the top *Guardian* collocates also include references to *sanction* (2), which occurs in 496th place in the *Daily Mail*'s collocate list. The *Guardian* also makes more distinctions between the employment status of benefits recipients (*out-of-work, unemployment, in-work, working-age*) than the *Daily Mail*, which includes only *unemployment* and *out-of-work* in its top collocates.

1. During the recession, benefit fraud boomed—with the amount paid to cheats up £300 million (DM news, Feb 2010).
2. A whistleblower said staff at his jobcentre were given targets of three people a week to refer for sanctions, where benefits are removed for up to six months (G news: politics, Apr 2011).

The different lenses of the two newspapers are also evidenced by their number one collocates, with the *Daily Mail* most closely associating <*benefit*> with *claim*. Analysing a random sample of 50 concordance lines, the collocation of *claim* and <*benefit*> tends to refer to changes in the rules for claiming benefits, fraudulent claims and/or prosecution, the amount of benefits individuals have claimed, the number of people claiming benefits, and the television programme *Benefits Street*.[1]

[1]For analysis of public attitudes to *Benefits Street*, see Paterson et al. (2016, 2017), and van der Bom et al. (2018).

Table 7.1 Top 25 collocates of <*benefit*>

Daily Mail	Collocate freq.	No. of texts	LL value	*Guardian*	Collocate freq.	No. of texts	LL value
1. Claim	5833	2971	17091.46	1. Cut	2022	1405	5997.733
2. Tax	3118	1847	12337.39	2. Cap	1010	547	5930.261
3. Child	5259	2284	11276.97	3. House	1719	983	5671.677
4. Cheat	1694	1002	10755.33	4. Housing	1137	694	5021.859
5. Incapacity	836	418	9829.756	5. Incapacity	483	287	4968.502
6. Cut	2364	1514	7592.809	6. Claimant	670	518	4109.355
7. Cap	1263	669	7497.109	7. Tax	1511	1027	4021.37
8. From	8131	6449	7354.443	8. Child	1835	927	3765.821
9. Disability	1070	625	7029.107	9. From	3249	2726	3219.434
10. Claimant	826	616	6425.181	10. Credit	688	519	2659.03
11. Housing	1159	723	6325.772	11. Disability	524	363	2395.079
12. System	1716	1210	5477.948	12. Claim	1065	789	2317.219
13. Fraud	1126	614	5395.454	13. System	879	681	1888.258
14. Receive	1783	1298	4628.842	14. Payment	455	372	1773.977
15. Credit	1083	684	4471.915	15. Welfare	560	483	1686.019
16. Unemployment	773	501	4451.995	16. Universal	373	271	1674.223
17. Benefit	1294	521	4021.045	17. Out-of-work	168	140	1613.822
18. Payment	839	710	3489.682	18. Unemployment	391	278	1571.237
19. Welfare	797	652	3346.398	19. Receive	577	458	1466.983
20. House	2205	1279	3314.952	20. Sanction	315	207	1339.746
21. Pension	896	692	3313.436	21. In-work	157	113	1301.04
22. Allowance	611	470	3308.073	22. Allowance	334	297	1284.783
23. Pay	1919	1452	3253.795	23. Sickness	161	116	1122.974
24. Will	4102	2916	3144.391	24. People	1675	1274	1118.954
25. Out-of-work	287	211	3064.144	25. Working-age	141	105	1043.226

In contrast, the *Guardian*'s top collocate is *cut* and an analysis of a random sample of 50 concordance lines indicates a focus on Housing Benefits, the coalition government's actions to decrease the amount of benefits paid to individuals (and thus the total welfare bill), and the contrast between tax cuts for high earners and benefits cuts for the poor. The opposite analysis (*cut* in the *Daily Mail* and *claim* in the *Guardian*) shows that the former focuses on Housing Benefit, cuts to child benefit for people earning over £60,000 (which it notes has strong public support), cuts in Greece and America, and the reported speech of MPs such as Phillip Hammond (then Defence Secretary) and Nick Clegg (then Deputy Prime Minister), see (3). The *Guardian*'s use of *claim* refutes arguments that EU nationals arrive in the UK *en masse* only to claim benefits (4), and that claiming benefits is a lifestyle choice (5). It focuses on Housing Benefit and notes benefit fraud, but to a lesser extent than the *Daily Mail*.

3. Deputy Prime Minister Nick Clegg said the decision to cut child benefit was 'excruciatingly difficult' Nick Clegg, the Deputy Prime Minister, suggested yesterday that many of those losing child benefit do not see themselves as well off (DM news, Oct 2012).
4. The European commission (sic) is also growing increasingly frustrated with the UK government for claiming that "benefit tourism" is a massive problem while not supplying any verifiable data to support the claim (G news: news, Oct 2013).
5. Osborne will be called to the Commons to answer an urgent question from Bob Russell, a Liberal Democrat who objected to Osborne's assertion that he would reduce the number of people who claim welfare benefits as a "lifestyle choice" (G news: news, Sept 2010).

However, focusing just on <*benefits*> may be somewhat misleading, as the *Daily Mail* also systematically refers to welfare payments as 'handouts'. There are 326 hits of <*handout*> in the *Guardian* (5.78 pmw) and 3132 (9.65 pmw) in the *Daily Mail*. Its top collocates are *food, photograph, state, cash* and *relying* in the *Guardian* and *state, welfare, photo, undated,* and *claiming* in the *Daily Mail*, suggesting that both newspapers use the term to refer to benefits, but that the *Daily Mail* does this proportionally more often. Thus, as discussed in Chapter 5, a single search term cannot tell us the whole story. To this end, we turn to the Benefits subset (cf. Table 5.7).

7.2 Benefits and Geography in the *Daily Mail*

The Benefits subset contains 22 queries and includes terminology relating to benefits receipt and the names of different of government benefits (excluding pensions): <*allowance*>, <*benefit*>, <*claim*>, <credit*>, <cut*>, <*disab*>, <DLA>, <dole*>, <Duncan Smith*>, <ESA*>, <fit for work>, <(fitness to work|fitness-to-work)>, <handout*>, <IDS*>, <JSA>, <personal independence payment>, <PIP>, <*sanction*>, <*subsidi*>, <*tax*>, <*welfare*>, and <(Work capability assessment*|WCA*| Work-capability-assessment)>. Despite containing the most queries, the Benefits subset returned only the fourth-highest number of PNCs for any subset in the *Daily Mail* (446), and the second-highest in the *Guardian* (1397) (cf. Table 5.7). Given that the *Guardian* corpus was much smaller than the *Daily Mail* corpus, we can deduce that the *Guardian* discusses benefits in relation to place much more often than the *Daily Mail.* There are 322 different locations in the *Guardian* data and 164 in the *Daily Mail.*

Figure 7.1 shows the density smoothed pattern and the Kulldorf map for the *Daily Mail*, whilst Fig. 7.2 (Sect. 7.3) shows the corresponding maps for the *Guardian.* The spatial pattern for the *Daily Mail* is quite similar to that for the Money subset (Sect. 6.4), in that it has clusters in London, Birmingham, north-west England and Glasgow. The Kulldorf map emphasises these clusters for the Benefits subset more than for the Money subset.

To interrogate the different geographical distributions of the Benefits subset, we again began with the PNC keywords and conducted contrastive concordance analysis combined with close reading of a random sample of concordance lines. The PNC keywords have been split into London and the Rest of the UK to maintain consistency, but this distinction is rather artificial for the *Guardian* in particular (Sect. 7.3). Table 7.2 shows the PNC keywords for the Benefits subset in the *Daily Mail.*

Cuts refers to the government attempting to 'balance the books' and co-occurs with *payments* and *credits* (in particular working tax *credits*). There are also references to the *Welfare* Reform Bill (2012), and *support* relates to the amount of (financial) services that workless families can claim. The *Daily Mail* contrasts speeches made by Conservative George Osbourne (who was Chancellor of the Exchequer) and Labour's Ed Miliband (then party leader), reporting on Osbourne's aim to restrict the amount that people can claim and Milliband's 'pledge' to increase tax credits.

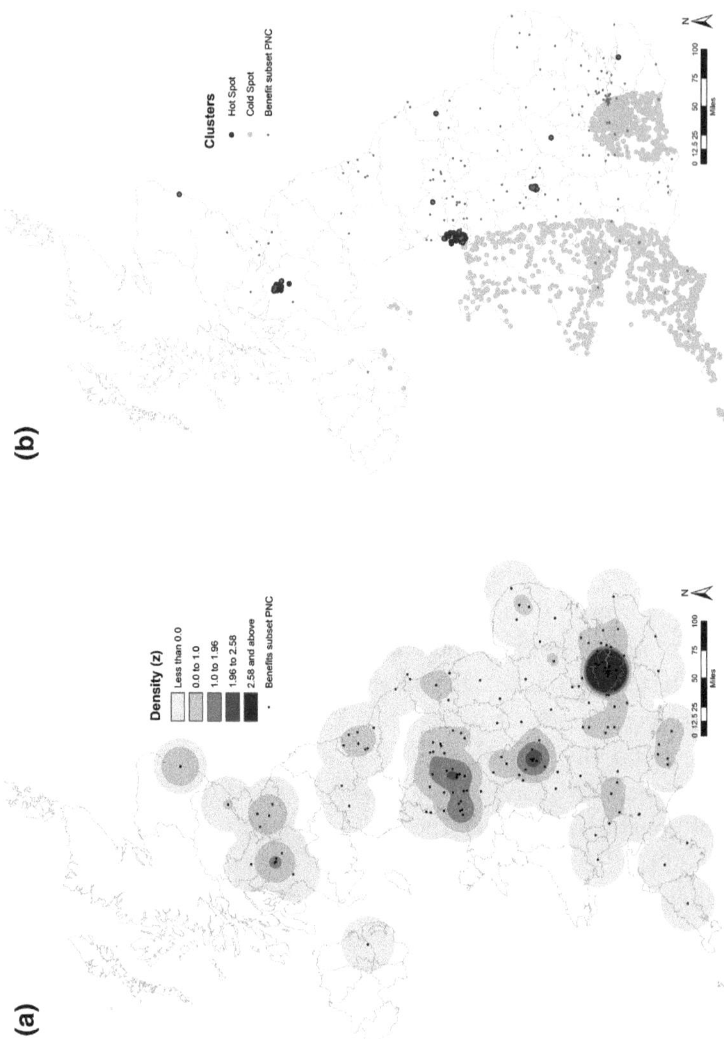

Fig. 7.1 Density smoothed and Kulldorf maps of PNCs in the Benefits subset in the *Daily Mail*

Table 7.2 PNC Keywords in the Benefits subset in the *Daily Mail* ($n \geq 5$)

Place	Sig.	PNC keywords
London	<0.01	cuts, credits, housing, to, a, payments
London	<0.05	welfare, support, an
Rest of UK	<0.01	cent, per, residents, of, claiming, town, abolish, receive, his, one, drug, country
Rest of UK	<0.05	incapacity, existing, number, suggest, show, new, also, left, tests, near, office, numbers, on, job, life, stopped, figures, biggest, 'on, 'we, alcohol, around, showed, lived, future, only, highest, him, market, car, single, pilot, problems, third, capital, trial, addictions, came, should

However, there is little variation in the topics associated with the London PNCs; they are dominated by references to Housing Benefit and the affordability of London. *Housing* refers almost exclusively to Housing Benefit and the amount of this benefit that people living in London are claiming. Whilst the *Daily Mail* notes that the capital is unaffordable for many (especially in terms of rent), it focuses on extreme examples of people claiming large amounts of Housing Benefit, and/or being able to live in expensive properties due to Housing Benefit.

6. Nasra Warsame and seven of her children were living in a 1.8 million house in <u>Westminster</u> at *a* cost to **taxpayers** of £1600 a week. Her husband Bashir Aden and her eighth child were living in *an* 'overspill' property, also on *housing* **benefit** (DM news, Jan 2010).

Although example (6) was published in an article in 2010, making it eligible for inclusion in our corpus, it is heavily based on an article published in November 2009, which was headlined 'Taxpayers pay £1600-a-week for family of ex-asylum seekers to live in luxury five-storey home' (Ballinger 2009). This is just one example of the *Daily Mail* recycling its content and repeating sensational stories about benefits claimants. Whilst the *Daily Mail* never takes an explicit stance on the family discussed within the article or their receipt of benefits, close analysis indicates a particular preferred reading of the text. The agents in the headline are the taxpayers (perhaps short hand for the *Daily Mail*'s target readership and thus, by extension, an example of synthetic personalisation) who are positioned as providing for a family in need of Housing Benefit. However, there is a sense that taxpayers actually have no say in how taxes are spent, that £1600 is too much to pay in benefits (it is sensational enough to warrant a headline), and that the family's 'ex-asylum seeker' status is somehow significant to their receipt of Housing Benefits. Their case is presented as newsworthy through the foregrounding of amounts of money that would be unaffordable for many (£1600 a week in rent, 1.8 million house, annual rent of £83,200).

The number of children the couple have is made central to the story, as the family were moved from a previous property, which the council deemed too small. It is also noted that the family is split between two houses, both paid for by Housing Benefit. They are repeatedly referred to as 'ex-asylum seekers', 'A Somali family', and 'the former asylum seeker', who 'fled unrest in Somalia in 1991 and claimed asylum in Britain', although they have received citizenship and 'all of their children were born here'. As the family are UK citizens, there is no direct relationship between their route to citizenship and their claiming Housing Benefits, yet their Somali heritage is repeatedly referred to in order to link their benefits claim to a wider context. A context which is further illuminated towards the end of the article, when a seemingly unrelated story is also reported (7).

7. Last year it was revealed Afghan single mother Toorpakai Saiedi and her seven children were given a £1.2 million property complete with 100 ft. garden by Ealing council in West London. Mrs Saiedi, 35, received £170,000 a year in benefits. Some £150,000 of that is paid to a private landlord for the seven-bedroom house (Ballinger 2009).

Here an unrelated example, discussing a different family, from a different country, living in a different area of London, is included in the story about the family in central London. No contextual information is provided as to how these two examples may be linked; it is left for the reader to fill in the blanks. A correlation between asylum seekers and large claims for Housing Benefit is therefore implied, and furthermore, the article draws upon the wider discourse that asylum seekers are 'benefits tourists' taking advantage of the UK system (a position opposed by the *Guardian*). We see many of the same techniques used to describe the woman in (7) as were used to discuss the Somali family: she is labelled an 'Afghan', her number of children is foregrounded, as are large sums of money. Furthermore, she was reportedly 'given' an expensive house. This is factually inaccurate as she does not own the house, rather she has been provided with Housing Benefit to pay rent. Nevertheless, there is an underlying implication that she is somehow not deserving of the home she has.

To situate the original article within wider discourses of poverty, descriptions of the Somali family's house paint it as extremely desirable: it is 'luxury', 'fully-furnished', 'within walking distance of the West End'; it has 'two leather sofas, a flat screen television and a glass coffee table' and 'a large glass sculpture situated in the middle of a courtyard'. Similarly the property referred to in (7) was 'complete with [a] 100ft garden'. These descriptions draw on discourses of the deserving and undeserving poor, with the implication that, if someone is poor enough to need Housing Benefit, they should not be able to afford to live in such a property and, significantly for discourses of poverty and place, in such a prime location. But what neither of these examples consider is that the families mentioned do not represent average benefits claimants, rather they are at the extreme end of the spectrum for benefits receipt. Yet these are the examples that the *Daily Mail* presents to its readers to justify its wider stance on welfare reform and the endorsement of Conservative-led policies.

Whilst only one article, the naming of particular (individual) benefits recipients who are unrepresentative of wider benefits claimants is a tactic which has been noted by Lundström (2013) as typical of reports on benefits recipients in the tabloid press (and in the *Daily Mail* in particular). Other extreme examples include (8), which is underpinned by the notion that people receiving benefits should not reside in 'exclusive' areas alongside celebrities. The notion of an 'exclusive' area is of great relevance to discourses of poverty and place as it presupposes that one's economic standing can grant access to particular locations which are (or should be) off limits to those who have less (8).

8. Behnaz and Emmanuel Scotts received £2670 *a* month in *housing* benefit, which helped *to* pay for their four-bed apartment in the exclusive Chelsea Harbour. The couple received jobseekers' **allowance** of £64.30 *a* week each—which Hammersmith and Fulham Council said meant it was forced *to* pay them *housing* benefit. They were able to live in the same blocks as singer Robbie Williams and sir (sic) Michael Caine (DM news, Mar 2012).
9. London councils have acquired rental properties in Luton, Northampton, Broxbourne, Gravesend, Dartford, Slough, Windsor, Margate, Hastings, Epping Forest, Thurrock and Basildon in preparation for **welfare** *cuts*, the Guardian has found (DM news, Nov 2012).

Ideologies concerning who should (not) live in a particular place are linked to multiple locations: links are made between government welfare policies and councils preparing to move their tenants to areas with cheaper rent (9). Thus, the relationship between welfare cuts and geography extends beyond London. However, whilst the London PNC keywords tended to cluster around welfare reform and Housing Benefit, elsewhere the picture was more mixed.

Abolish refers to campaigns against the so-called Bedroom Tax (a term used for the coalition government's Removal of Spare Room Subsidy policy which decreased the amount of Housing Benefits available to people seen to be under occupying their properties—see Sect. 1.2). In particular the bedroom tax appears to be associated with Scotland, but this is due to the multiple PNCs generated by repeated reports, including (10), which comes from a speech made by Ed Miliband to Scottish voters before the Scottish Independence Referendum in 2014.

10. He will claim: 'We will *abolish* the bedroom **tax**. *Abolish* it in Dundee, in Glasgow, but also in Carlisle, Newcastle and Nottingham' (DM news, Sept 2014).

This example demonstrates the importance of considering PNCs in their wider context. The *Daily Mail* is not making explicit links here between the bedroom tax and these particular locations, rather they are reporting the words of a third party who does make these connections.

Where the *Daily Mail* does take an explicit stance is in the reporting the number of people receiving benefits. *Per cent, existing, incapacity, number, tests, third, trial,* and *residents* refer to the jobless rates in different areas, the number of people receiving benefits, and the outcomes of fitness-to-work (re)assessments. The *Daily Mail* shows a tendency to list the 'best' and the 'worst' areas for benefits receipt or worklessness (11–14). Notably, the places with the highest rates are in the north of England, whilst the areas with fewer claimants are all relatively affluent areas in the south of England (see 11). Additionally, the *Daily Mail* claims that towns 'claiming the most sickness benefit are in Wales and County Durham' in contrast with places like Uttoxeter (14) where employment rates are high.

11. The news was particularly grim for young people in the north, with 10 *per cent* of 16–24-year-olds in Hull, Grimbsy and Middlesbrough *on* the Jobseekers **Allowance.** This compared with less than two *per cent* in Cambridge and Oxford and less than four *per cent* in Reading, Southampton and Bournemouth (DM news, Jan 2010).
12. Manchester has 71,000 who have never been in work and Liverpool has 52,000. Bradford is next with 50,000, then Sheffield on 46,000, Tower Hamlets has 42,000 and Cardiff 41,000. **Taxpayers'** Alliance boss Matthew Sinclair told The Sun: 'These are truly shocking *figures* which underline the importance *of* reforming the welfare system in order to make work pay once and for all (DM news, Feb 2013).
13. The UK's welfare capital is the Isle of Wight but, when payments to the elderly are excluded, Liverpool is the *biggest* **claimer** of **benefits** (DM news, Sept 2013).
14. A record surge in employment means in *one* town almost no-one is on the dole. In the Staffordshire *market* town of Uttoxeter just 34 people are **claiming** Jobseekers (DM news, July 2014).

To take another extreme example, the *Daily Mail* claims that 99.1% of working age people on the Cottsmeadow Estate in Birmingham (15) 'live off state handouts', with only one person in a full-time job, whilst the rest are described as in (16).

15. The Cottsmeadow Estate is *one of* five communities where more than 90 *per cent of* adults are on some form of **benefits.** The Egerton Street area of Oldham, where 110 out *of* 113 (or 97.3 *per cent*) *of residents* claim state benefits, was second *on* the list (DM news, Jan 2011).
16. *Figures* from the Department for Work and Pensions reveal that among *residents*, 50 are listed as *on* the dole, 30 are signed off sick and get incapacity benefits, 20 pocket lone-parent payments and five claim other handouts (DM news, Jan 2011).

The choice of verbs in (16) is particularly illuminating in terms of the *Daily Mail*'s evaluation of benefits recipients; the negatively-loaded 'pocket', which could have implications of criminality, and the non-standard form 'on the dole' alongside the use of 'handouts' (discussed above) are used within the scope of something that the *Daily Mail* (via the DWP) 'reveal'. Furthermore, the article is framed under the headline 'Britain's most workshy estate' despite the fact that, as stated in the article, many of those receiving benefits were lone parents caring for children (and thus doing unpaid work), and people who were too sick to work. The percentage number of claimants is 'staggering' and the statistics are presented as evidence which will 'heap further pressure on ministers to stamp out the something-for-nothing culture that spiralled under Labour'. Here there is a presupposition that a 'something-for-nothing culture' exists in (particular locations in) Britain, and a further implication that such a culture is realised by benefits receipt. The blame for this culture is placed on previous Labour governments; thus a high number of benefits claimants is seen as a sign of an overgenerous state.

The so-called workshy and the Labour party are not the only groups the *Daily Mail* holds accountable for the number of people receiving benefits. The article that (11) is taken from includes a hyperlink to a second article headlined 'Migrants ARE driving down wages of the poor, as Equalities watchdog blames East European influx' (Slack 2010). Thus, whilst there is no blame (other than individual laziness) in the original article for why there are more people claiming Jobseekers' Allowance in some areas over others, blame is implied through links to other articles which are hyperlinked from the first. This is another aspect that needs to be considered when using corpora of online texts. The *Daily Mail* makes (implied) causal links between immigration and poverty using hyperlinks. A corpus analysis would not normally focus on such practices; it is only through the wider interrogation of context that the significance of hyperlinking can be teased out and examined.

Across the other PNCs, the *Daily Mail* makes repeated references to the television programme *Benefits Street* (the first series of which was filmed in Birmingham, accounting somewhat for it being a hotspot on the Kulldorf map, Fig. 7.1). It reports on proposals for geographically means-tested benefits that are calculated based on the cost of living where you live (a policy which did not become part of the Welfare Reform Act, but can be seen in a limited sense in the different levels of benefits cap inside and outside London). It also highlights which areas of the UK have high levels of drug and alcohol dependency: *drug, alcohol, addictions, highest, lived*, and *problems* all relate to this topic and are given as reasons for people claiming benefits in particular geographical locations (17).

17. Bournemouth has the *biggest* proportion of **claimants** of **ESA** for people with *alcohol* and *drug addictions*, with around *one* in 14 people in the Dorset town who are handed the **benefit** abusing *alcohol*, while *one* in 20 have *drug addiction* problems. Other areas with a high percentage of **claimants** with *drug* and *alcohol addictions* include Edinburgh, Glasgow, Aberdeen and Bristol. Meanwhile, the *biggest* proportion of **claimants** due to stress is South Hams in Devon, closely followed by Tamworth in Staffordshire and Richmond in North Yorkshire (DM news, Mar 2015).

In devoting a report to the reasons for Employment Support Allowance claims, the *Daily Mail* groups together those claiming benefits for addictions, as shown above, and other conditions such as stress, and obesity. Those claiming ESA for these reasons are described as 'being handed £100 a week' and their claims (and health conditions) are somewhat delegitimised. ESA is described as being 'awarded to those who have an illness or disability that affects their ability to work' but this is contrasted with the claim that 'Now, according to new figures… 56,000 people with alcohol problems receive ESA, while 36,650 drug addicts are also claimants'. The use of 'now' as a qualifier suggests that alcoholism, drug addiction, obesity, and stress, do not meet the (*Daily Mail*'s) definition of 'illness or disability'. Thus, whilst there is nothing illegal about claiming ESA for these conditions—and, as such (17) is not reporting on benefit fraud—the claims are seen as somehow illegitimate and the *Daily Mail* is positioned as making moral judgements about claimants with these issues and conditions.

As part of the article (17) is taken from (Newton 2015), the *Daily Mail* provides a map of the 'booze' and 'drug hotspots' and a table ranking the top ten worst offenders. This 'name and shame' approach homogenises people in two ways. It groups together all benefits claimants with particular health issues and treats them as interchangeable, and does the same for all people living in a particular area. Associating an area with alcoholism or drug taking contributes to an overall negative characterisation of that location; not everyone in Bournemouth is accused of being an alcoholic, but Bournemouth is categorised as a place where alcoholics live. The *Daily Mail* does not attempt to offer potential solutions to problems associated with alcoholism (although stopping benefits is implied) nor does it consider the wider social factors, health profiles, employment opportunities, etc. which may go some way to explaining why certain places may be more (or less) affected by alcoholism, etc.

7.3 Benefits and Geography in the *Guardian*

The density smoothed and Kulldorf maps for the Benefits subset in the *Guardian* (Fig. 7.2) show a very different pattern to the same maps for the *Daily Mail* (Fig. 7.1). While its Employment and Money subsets are highly London-centric (see Chapter 6), the pattern for the Benefits subset is much more dispersed, with clusters around London, Birmingham, north-west and north-east England, and Glasgow. These clusters, as well as Aberdeen, are also apparent as hotspots on the Kulldorf map.

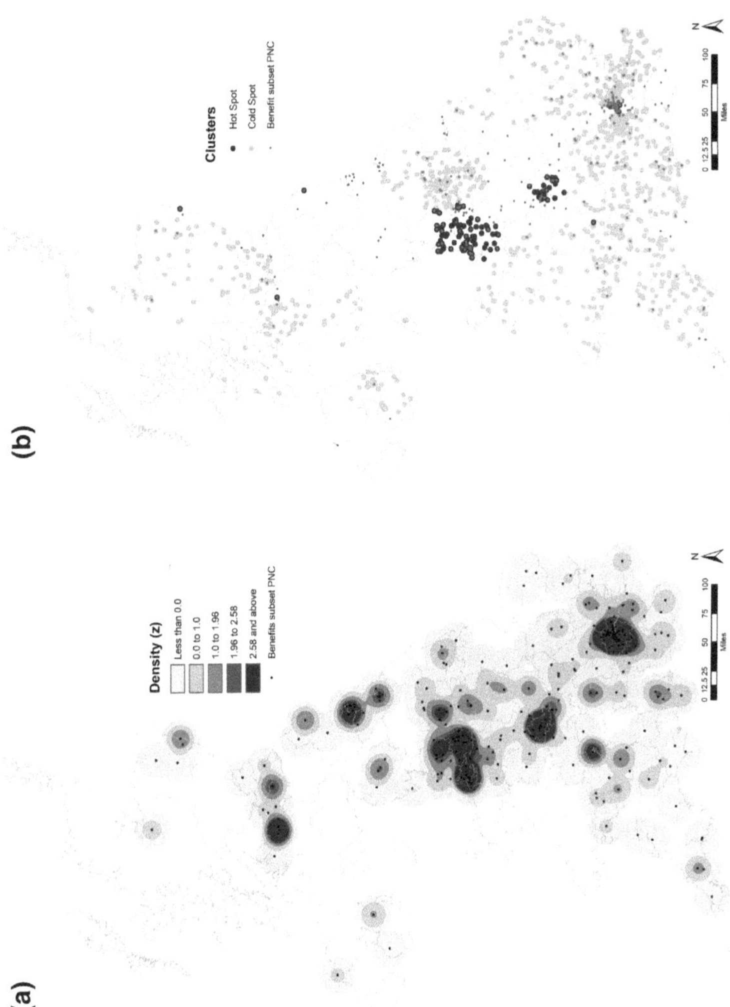

Fig. 7.2 Density smoothed and Kulldorf maps of PNCs in the Benefits subset in the *Guardian*

Table 7.3 PNC Keywords in the Benefits subset in the *Guardian* ($n \geq 5$)

Place	Sig.	PNC keywords
London	<0.01	cap, housing, will, week, benefit, through, families, not, total, cuts, many
London	<0.05	their, these, borough, coalition, to, that, across, against, reforms, homes, make, than, impact, so, changes
Rest of UK	<0.01	street, city, incapacity, lowest, party, constituency, began, council, lab, county, service, centre, estate, jobs, near, lain, end, visit, testing, addresses, highest, and, former, all, worst, since, claims, support, jobseeker, welfare, unrest, go, July, channel, Liz, minimum, starts, existing, IB, igniting, forces, DWP, increased, photograph, years, he, huge, staff
Rest of UK	<0.05	seats, no-go, bounds, involved, leaders, looking, trial, chasing, town, economically, mid, son, tests, office, needed, project, northern, warning, jobcentre, Scotland, national, allowance, system, at, time, tomorrow, my, losses, away, lost, jobcentres, plans, UK, its, according, care, health, one, universal, man, posts, employment, off, authority, must

The PNC keyword *benefit* (Table 7.3) refers to benefit *cuts* (particularly to Housing Benefit) and the benefits *cap*.[2] Even though *across* occurs as a PNC keyword in the London PNCs, it most often occurs in the cluster 'across the country' (as well as in 'across London') and is used to demonstrate the wide ranging impact of the benefits cap, particularly in relation to Housing Benefit, the bedroom tax, and high rent prices. The benefits cap is described as affecting people across England and Wales but the *Guardian* also presents it as a local issue which will disproportionately affect London (18). The *cap* is 'forcing people out of London', with the implication that homelessness is the only alternative, because people cannot 'keep a roof over their heads'. There are also reports of private landlords pre-emptively evicting tenants receiving Housing Benefit to protect against arrears resulting from the cap.

[2]The benefits cap refers to the limit of state benefits payable to most working age adults. Although there are exceptions—recipients of particular benefits may be exempt—current figures stand at £20,000 per year, per couple or single parents, and £13,400 per single childless person. The figures for people living in Greater London are slightly higher, standing at £23,000 and £15,410 respectively (gov.uk, n.d.).

18. The acute *housing* shortage in the capital means market rents outstrip **benefit** *cap* levels in cheaper outer London boroughs including Haringey, Waltham Forest, and Barking and Dagenham (G news: society, Nov 2012).
19. Ministers were accused last night of deliberately driving **poor** people out of wealthy inner cities as London councils revealed they were preparing a mass exodus of low-income *families* from the capital because of coalition *benefit cuts* (G news: politics, Oct 2010).
20. Bromley, Croydon, Enfield and Haringey—*will* have overall **benefits** capped at £26,000 a year, with the scheme becoming nationwide in December. Opponents have warned *that* it could cause a mass movement of poorer *families* out of parts of London or other expensive areas, disrupting children's education (G news: society, Mar 2013).

Changes also refers to Housing Benefit and a 'mass exodus' of *families* from inner to outer London, for which the *coalition* government are held responsible (19). The *Guardian* focuses on the potential impacts of the benefits cap on *families*, as opposed to *claimants* or *recipients*. This naming technique, which is reinforced by references to the number of school children who may have to move (20), presents benefits recipients as part of wider family and social networks.

Against is used to report on protests opposing cuts to disability payments in particular (and austerity more widely). The *Guardian* reported on these protests during their organisation—'Thousands of people will demonstrate in Westminster on Wednesday *against* **cuts**'—and after the event. The choice to report on the planned peaceful protest (labelled as 'civil disobedience') serves a dual purpose; it is a report of a planned political event, but it also acts to publicise the planned protest to its readership, who presumably share the *Guardian*'s anti-cuts (and anti-austerity) stance. Furthermore, by foregrounding protests opposing disability cuts, the *Guardian* highlights government cuts to services for those who are presented as most vulnerable (21). Thus, the amount of sympathy for benefits recipients can be maximised. Such reports contrast with the *Daily Mail*'s reports of people receiving sickness benefits for conditions such as alcoholism, obesity, and stress (see 17).

21. Far from protecting the vulnerable, these cuts are bearing down disproportionately on those with disability." Wheelchair user Tony Vanterpool, 53, from Brampton in Cambridgeshire, said he had come to protest at the **cutting** of his *mobility* allowance of £17 a month (G news: society, May 2011).

Outside London, *allowance* refers to JSA and housing allowance. However, the number of PNCs is greatly increased by (22), which includes multiple place-names, and also accounts for the occurrence of *Lab* as a PNC keyword. In contrast to the absence of Belfast in the <*poverty*> PNCs (Chapter 4), *highest* refers to repeated reports that Derry and West Belfast have the highest number of out of work benefits recipients (with 23 including an uncharacteristic use of the term *dole*).

22. 11 Birmingham, Hall Green (Lab) 12.5%; 12 Belfast North (DUP) 12.4%; 13 Kingston upon Hull North (Lab) 12.4%; 14 Nottingham North (Lab) 12.3%; 15 Wolverhampton South East (Lab) 12.3%. The *lowest jobseeker*'s **allowance** (G news: society, Jan 2012).
23. Derry is *one* of the UK's most impoverished (*and* youngest) cities. Nearly 10% of its working population are on the **dole** *and*, apart from west Belfast, the *city* has the *highest* numbers on *welfare* benefits (G news: news, May 2013).

The Benefits subset includes some mentions of benefit fraud (within the wider context of poverty) but these are treated as anomalous individual cases—there are no references, for example, to the total welfare bill or fraud rates. The *Guardian* also reports on *Benefits Street*, which it terms 'controversial' and 'the current crucible of Britain's social conscience'. However, the programme is not sensationalised or held up as representative of wider trends in benefits receipt. *Estate, he, Iain, Centre, photograph*, and *visit* are responsible for the PNCs in the Easterhouse area of Glasgow; they refer to Iain Duncan Smith visiting the area in 2002. *Began, existing, health, IB, incapacity* and *testing* refer to benefits reassessment in Burnley and Aberdeen (see Sect. 6.3). *Testing* also refers to the roll out of *Universal* Credit, a key component of the Welfare Reform Act; as shown in (24), the *Guardian* reports on initial trials of Universal

Credit, but there is little direct evaluation of the policy in the PNCs. By contrast, other elements of welfare reform, particularly the bedroom tax, are evaluated negatively.

24. *Universal* credit went live on 29 April with just *one jobcentre*—Ashton under Lyne—accepting clams for *universal* **credit** and three other *jobcentres*, Wigan, Warrington and Oldham, *testing* the system (G news: society, Jul 2013).
25. The *council* estimates that the money spent by the taxpayer in mitigating the effects of the bedroom **tax** in Newcastle far outstrip the £3 m a year the *DWP* saves in housing benefit (G news: society, Mar 2015).
26. Pauline Jones, 54, was also hit with the double blow of *council* tax and bedroom tax after she had downsized from a three-bedroom house to a two-bedroom in South Ockendon, Essex. Struggling before the £22 monthly *council* **tax** bill and the £14 weekly bedroom tax reduction, she's resorted to using food banks to keep herself afloat (G news: society, Jan 2014).

Example (25) reports that the bedroom tax is economically inefficient, and (26) shows how the bedroom tax affects individuals. In this case, a direct link is made between welfare reform and the use of foodbanks. Furthermore, the woman in (26) has 'won an appeal' against the bedroom tax because one of her rooms was 'too small to be classed as a bedroom'. The implication here is that the bedroom tax is based on unsuitable criteria and is thus not sound policy. The *Guardian* further criticises policy in (27) suggesting that welfare reform penalises the poorest areas. Similarly, (28) argues that housing allowance policy is inadequate because rates are set centrally by the government. Criticism of the government is also evidenced by *council, county* and *services* which invariably refer to councils taking money away from people, and cutting jobs (Sect. 6.3) and, ultimately, services.

27. An analysis by Birmingham *city council* that shows the more deprived an area, the deeper the **cut**. *According* to the Birmingham analysis, Liverpool is the region *worst* affected by the government's cuts (G news: society, May 2012).

28. On the Mersey, 21,000 people collecting local housing *allowance* will only be able to afford 12,000 homes in Liverpool. Because *welfare* is set at Westminster, the **cuts** will also be felt in *Scotland* (G news: society, Jan 2012).
29. The Homeless Link survey suggests that 41% *councils* in England are making "disproportionate cuts" to homelessness services. This includes Tory-controlled Cornwall *county council*, which has imposed **cuts** of 40% on local homeless charities (G news: society, Mar 2011).

To support its anti-cuts stance, the *Guardian* uses individual examples of hardship (26) and makes links between benefits cuts and food poverty, but it also draws upon research from independent bodies. Whilst the research in (29) may support the *Guardian*'s general position it is used specifically to reference 'Tory-controlled' councils. There is clearly no ambiguity about where the *Guardian* lays the blame for (benefits-related) poverty and hardship.

7.4 Housing Costs and Relative Poverty

The Housing subset shows one of the biggest differences between the two newspapers. The *Daily Mail* has relatively little geographical interest in housing and poverty with only 253 PNCs, but this is of course mitigated by the preceding discussion of Housing Benefits. The *Guardian*, by contrast, has 1175 PNCs. The *Daily Mail*'s geographical spread (Fig. 7.3) broadly follows the newspaper's background geography as shown on the Kulldorf map. The only clusters occurring are relatively small and are found around Birmingham (19 PNCs), Hull (14), Bournemouth (12), Brighton (8), and Orpington and Sidcup (6) to the south-east of London. The cluster in south-west Wales can be ignored as it has only one PNC.

Of these, the Birmingham cluster is driven, at least in part, by discussion about *Benefits Street* (*James Turner Street* are all PNC keywords). The Bournemouth cluster concentrates on examples of families claiming to want better housing to accommodate their large families

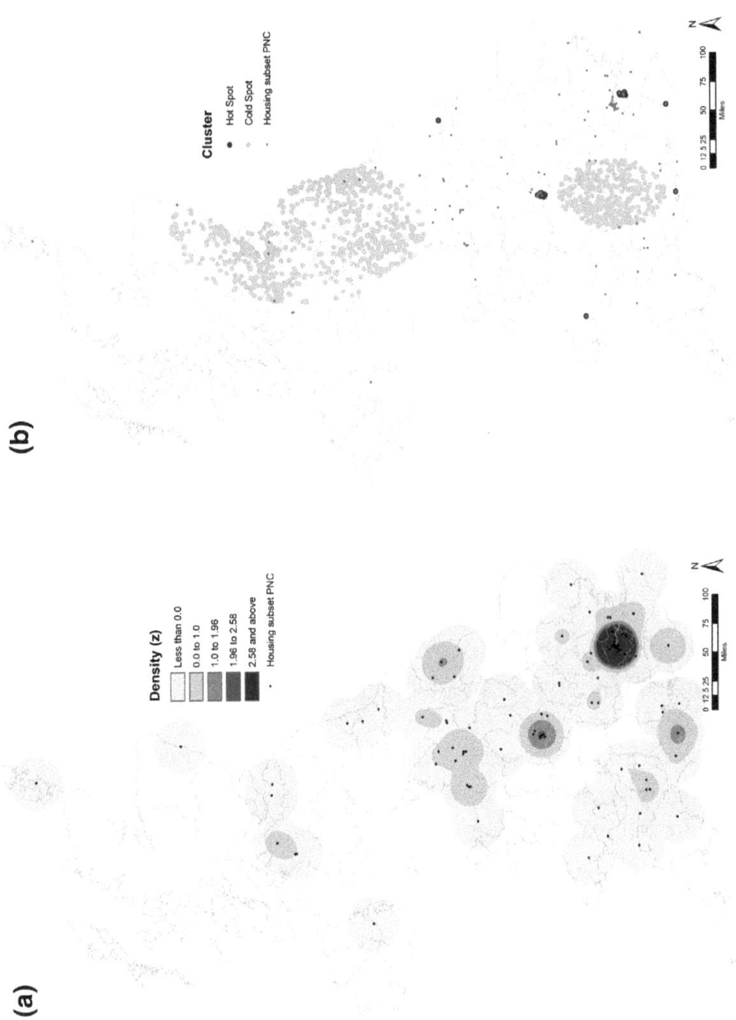

Fig. 7.3 Density smoothed and Kulldorf maps of PNCs in the Housing subset in the *Daily Mail*

Table 7.4 PNC Keywords in the Housing subset in the *Daily Mail* ($n \geq 5$)

Place	Sig.	Keywords
London	<.01	–
London	<.05	council
Rest of UK	<.01	she, other, street, three-bedroom, association
Rest of UK	<.05	month, works, million, damp, James, into, moved, mother, across, no-one, turner, seen, inside, and, from

(cf. Sect. 7.2). In Brighton and Hull, articles concentrate on problems with homelessness, with the Hull cluster in particular being caused by reports of families being displaced out of London by the benefit cap. The Sidcup/Orpington cluster focusses on a particular story, this time sympathetic, of a homeless family who fail to meet the criteria for local authority housing despite having lost their income as a result of redundancy (30).

30. Homeless: Carole Karawaiez and her husband Norman stand next to the car they are sleeping in with their son and daughter. The couple had their **home** in Sidcup, Kent, repossessed 10 years ago (DM news, Aug 2013).

The limited scope of the stories covered in relation to these clusters is also reflected in the low number of PNCs in the *Daily Mail* Housing subset (Table 7.4).[3]

As the pattern of PNCs seems to largely follow the *Daily Mail*'s background geography, this results in a strong bias towards London: 41.1% PNCs in the Housing subset are in London. The London PNC keywords cannot tell us much, but the concordance analysis showed that London was associated with the affordability of housing, the difficulties of paying rent or housing costs (31), and/or no longer being able to afford such costs (32). There are also references to the role of councils and the responsibility to house families. Thus, there is a much overlap between the Benefits subset and the Housing subset. These stories are

[3]For the Housing subset in the *Daily Mail* it was only necessary to closely read 150 concordances due to the relatively small number of hits in this subset (cf. Sect. 6.3).

typically sympathetic to the plight of people struggling to pay for housing in London, especially when the working status of the individuals concerned is mentioned (see 'young professionals' in example 31).

31. One of thousands of young professionals forced to still live with his parents because he can not afford to **rent** in London (DM news, Apr 2015).
32. Many of the tenants have been living in the building for over 10 years and claim they will have to find somewhere to live outside London as they can no longer afford to pay Brixton **rent** prices (DM news, Apr 2015).

Outside London the PNC keywords are somewhat more varied. *She* is associated with stories about women in poverty. The occurrence of feminine pronouns and female-gendered nouns occurs elsewhere (cf. Chapter 4) and suggests that the *Daily Mail* has more of a tendency to write stories about individual women than the *Guardian*. In this subset, reports are sometimes sympathetic, especially when their subjects are seen as hard-working women (33), but the *Daily Mail* is far less sympathetic when poor women have large numbers of children (34).

33. I owe money to everyone including £800 to the housing *association* for the **rent** which is one of the highest in Exeter. I am a single working mum *and* I am not entitled to any financial help (DM news, May 2011).
34. A single mother with eight children who receives £2000 a *month* in state handouts has complained *she* is struggling to make ends meet. Marie Buchan, 31, whose children range in age *from* 12 to two months, lives in a *three-bedroom* **housing** *association* house in Selly Oak, Birmingham, but says it's not big enough and has applied for a bigger one (DM news, Dec 2013).

The mother in example (33) is described as a 'Hostage in her own home' because she wants to move out of a property that is too big for her, but cannot, despite 'pleading' with the council. Much of the article consists of direct quotation, where she notes that 'red tape and a lack of common sense' means she cannot move but is unable to afford her rent. Whilst the mother in (34) is also directly quoted, a larger proportion of the article is given to the *Daily Mail*'s description of her circumstances: they mention that she has been in court for rent arrears and is unable to pay fines for using a bus lane on ten different occasions, and note the amount of benefits that she receives. The same woman is also mentioned in another *Daily Mail* article which reports that a 37-year-old mother of eleven 'who never worked and claimed around £60,000 a year in benefits, appeared in a documentary series on Channel 5 called On Benefits and Proud'. Thus, two independent stories are used together to facilitate the *Daily Mail*'s contrast between deserving, working mothers, and undeserving, entitled mothers who have too many children. This tendency to append unrelated stories, as also shown with the Somali and Afghan families in Sect. 7.2, does not occur in the *Guardian* PNCs.

As well as associating housing with poverty far more than the *Daily Mail*, the *Guardian* also has a much stronger geographical patterns, as shown in Fig. 7.4. There is a major cluster of PNCs in London, which is statistically significant against the corpus' background geography, and contains 57.0% of the PNCs in the Housing subset. The West Midlands is the second-densest area in terms of density smoothing but this contains only 4.3% of PNCs. The Kulldorf maps shows a number of small, localised hotspots outside London including Newcastle-upon-Tyne (22 PNCs), Luton (12), Caerphilly (11), Slough/Windsor (60), and Solihull (6). The dominance of cold spots, however, suggests just how polarised the pattern is, with most of the country receiving very little attention in terms of housing (with the exceptions of the clusters noted above, the M62 corridor, and Kent and East Sussex).

The PNC keywords for London (Table 7.5) reveal that the *Guardian*'s coverage of poverty and housing in the capital is very much associated with unaffordability, high, rising, or 'soaring' rents, and the related roles of the benefit cap, private landlords, and the authorities. There are also multiple PNCs concerning people being forced to move out of London to cheaper areas (as was the case in the *Daily Mail*), homelessness (35), and (the attempted abolition of) soup runs (36).

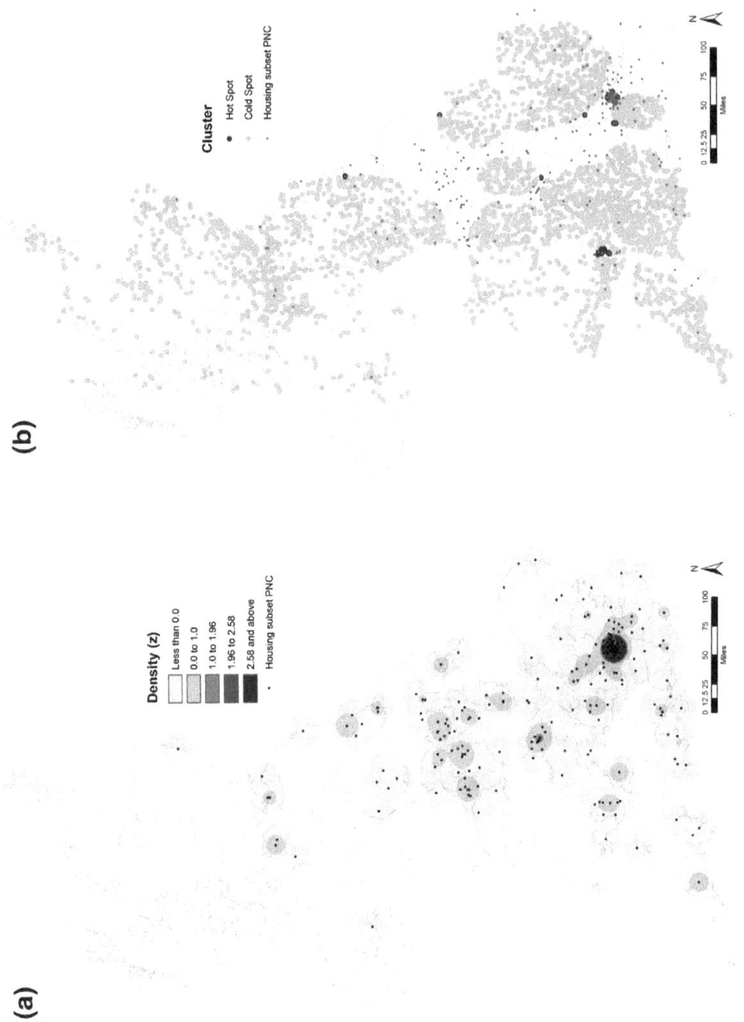

Fig. 7.4 Density smoothed and Kulldorf maps of PNCs in the Housing subset in the *Guardian*

7.5 Comparisons with Quantitative Indicators

This chapter and the previous one have explored the geographies of themes related to poverty as represented in the two newspapers using four subsets of terms, those related to: Employment (see Sects. 6.2 and 6.3), Money (Sect. 6.4), Benefits (Sects. 7.2 and 7.3), and Housing (Sect. 7.4). These have been shown to have different geographies from each other, across the two newspapers. Section 4.4 explored comparing PNCs from the search term <*poverty*> with a quantitative geography of poverty as measured using Carstairs scores at local authority district level. In this section we return to this approach to explore how closely the two newspapers' representation of the four sets of poverty-related themes relates to quantitative measures. There are several issues that this analysis explores: firstly, the extent to which newspapers seem to concentrate their coverage of poverty on areas that have high rates of poverty. Second, whether the newspapers concentrate their coverage on areas with high rates of unemployment, which would seem to suggest that they associate poverty with people being out of work, or on areas with high rates of poverty, which suggests more of an acceptance that in-work poverty also exists. To explore this theme, as well as comparing poverty to Carstairs scores, a relatively broad measure of poverty (see Sect. 4.4), we also use two measures of lack of work, namely the census definition of unemployment as recorded in the 2011 census, and worklessness, households that contain people of working age and where nobody is in employment, as measured in 2015. These two measures are shown in Fig. 6.1. Table 6.1 showed that all three measures are closely correlated but the maps reveal that there are some differences in the patterns. Our third topic is the extent to which the two newspapers differ in both respects.

Comparisons between the *Guardian's* four subsets and the three measures of poverty are shown in Table 7.6. Note that in all cases PNCs referring to high-level units have not been included (see Chapter 4). In each case three comparisons are made: with all PNCs and all local authority districts, only PNCs in districts with above average poverty as measured by a Carstairs scores of greater than 0.0, and only districts that contain at least one PNC. The table shows that all four PNC

Table 7.6 Spearman's rank correlation coefficients comparing numbers of *Guardian* PNCs with three measures of poverty at local authority district level

	Carstairs 2011	Worklessness 2015	Unemployment 2011
All Employment PNCs	.231**	.092	.145**
Carstairs > 0.0	.090	−.022	−.031
Employment PNC > 0	.255	.181	.187
All Money PNCs	.299**	.184**	.220**
Carstairs > 0.0	.239**	.089	.122
Money PNC > 0	.246**	.134	.148
All Benefit PNCs	.388**	.273**	.342**
Carstairs > 0.0	.458**	.239**	.350**
Benefit PNC > 0	.407**	.295**	.349**
All Housing PNCs	.379**	.229**	.323**
Carstairs > 0.0	.410**	.117	.255**
Housing PNC > 0	.498**	.180*	.427**

**Significant at $p < .01$

subsets consistently correlate more strongly with the Carstairs measure of poverty rather than either of the two measures of unemployment. Areas with high deprivation scores are most closely correlated with the Benefits and Housing subsets, with Money next and Employment being the weakest. The Benefits subset has a stronger correlation than Money except when districts with no housing PNCs are excluded, where the relationship between housing and Carstairs, at 0.498, gives the highest of any of the coefficients. This suggests that when the *Guardian* talks about districts in relation to housing, it pays more attention to (some, but not all) districts with higher rates of poverty.

Table 7.7 repeats this analysis using PNCs from the *Daily Mail*. As with the *Guardian*, correlations are strongest with Carstairs scores than the other two measures. However, the two measures are statically significant more commonly than in the *Guardian*. In direct contrast to the *Guardian*, the *Daily Mail*'s Employment subset has the strongest correlation with Carstairs, in the *Guardian* this was the weakest. Housing and Benefits have similar correlations of around 0.29, while the Money subset has the lowest correlation.

The two tables suggest a very different emphasis from the two newspapers on their attitudes to districts with high rates of poverty. The higher a district's rate of poverty the more emphasis the *Guardian* gives

Table 7.7 Spearman's rank correlation coefficients comparing numbers of *Daily Mail* PNCs with three measures of poverty at local authority district level

	Carstairs 2011	Worklessness 2015	Unemployment 2011
All Employment PNCs	.419**	.335**	.357**
Carstairs > 0.0	.264**	.251**	.167*
Employment PNC > 0	.345**	.317**	.295**
All Money PNCs	.234**	.211**	.183**
Carstairs > 0.0	.214**	.201**	.077
Money PNC > 0	.309**	.318**	.234**
All Benefit PNCs	.288**	.248**	.264**
Carstairs > 0.0	.191**	.222**	.165*
Benefit PNC > 0	.185	.294**	.127
All Housing PNCs	.296**	.225**	.217**
Carstairs > 0.0	.223**	.175*	.092
Housing PNC > 0	.347**	.098	.294*

**Significant at $p < .01$

it in relation to housing and benefits. The *Daily Mail* associates these districts with terms related to employment. Both newspapers' PNCs correlate with Carstairs scores more strongly than measures of unemployment suggesting that they do understand that poverty is more complex than simply being out of work. This is, however, less pronounced in the *Daily Mail* suggesting that it pays less attention to in-work poverty.

7.6 Summary

Unlike the Employment and Money subsets discussed in the previous chapter, the Benefits and Housing subset show much more overlap in terms of theme. Although different in their geographies, the dominance of Housing Benefit in the Benefits subset draws on very similar topics to the Housing subset. There is a strong focus on affordability of housing and housing costs, particularly in London, although the two newspapers position themselves differently in terms of this broad issue. The *Daily Mail* foregrounds extreme Housing Benefit claims in order to question whether or not people should be able to live in an area supported by Housing Benefits which would be unaffordable to most people. It constructs a dichotomy between Housing Benefit recipients and 'hardworking people', without acknowledging that this benefit is not restricted to those who are out of work. By referring to those not receiving Housing Benefit as 'hardworking' and those receiving benefits as 'workshy' the *Daily Mail* is endorsing a neoliberal ideology which positions people as able to achieve the social status and financial security they desire if only they work hard enough. It implies that those who are receiving Housing Benefit, and benefits more widely, are merely inadequate workers. Relatedly, there is little sympathy for addicts, or people receiving sickness benefits because they are out of work due to stress. By contrast, the *Guardian*'s coverage of the affordability of housing and dependence on Housing Benefits does not encourage a neoliberal agenda. It focuses on how government policy is exacerbating hardship due to cuts to the benefits system. The *Guardian* focuses on the social responsibility of the government to provide for those in food poverty and those who are homeless, whilst also noting that certain areas (in London) are unaffordable for most.

Our final chapter looks at the overall patterns in our data and so we combine all the PNCs for each of our subsets. Instead of focusing on different themes, the following chapter centralises geography and looks at the different aspects of poverty that each newspaper associates with particular locations. These range from large urban centres—especially London—to smaller cities and larger towns; there is no real pattern of rural poverty evident in our data. The maps we produce represent snapshots of the geographies of poverty in the UK in the twenty-first century as reported in the largest newspapers in the UK. Thus, they are indicative of how people talk about poverty, who is classed as being in poverty, and thus indicate the dominant ideologies of poverty associated with a particular geographical location.

References

Baker, P., & T. McEnery. 2015. Who Benefits When Discourse Gets Democratised? Analysing a Twitter Corpus Around the British *Benefits Street* Debate. In P. Baker & T. McEnery (eds.). *Corpora and Discourse Studies: Integrating Discourse and Corpora*. Basingstoke: Palgrave, pp. 244–265.

Ballinger, L. 2009. Taxpayers Pay £1,600-a-Week for Family of Ex-asylum Seekers to Live in Luxury Five-Storey Home. *Mail Online* 20/11/09. http://

www.dailymail.co.uk/news/article-1231795/Taxpayers-pay-1-600-week-family-ex-asylum-seekers-live-luxury-storey-home.html. Accessed 22/1/2018.

DWP. 2016. Freedom of Information Requests 2016-398/2026-397. https://www.gov.uk/government/uploads/system/uploads/attachment_data/file/502566/389-397-2016.pdf. Accessed 13/11/2016.

DWP. 2018. Housing Benefit caseload statistics. https://www.gov.uk/government/uploads/system/uploads/attachment_data/file/659362/housing-benefit-caseload-data-to-august-2017.ods. Accessed 23/03/2018.

GOV.UK. nd. Benefit Cap. https://www.gov.uk/benefit-cap. Accessed 23/11/2017.

Hansard. 2014. Topical Questions, 13 January 2014, Vol. 573. https://hansard.parliament.uk/Commons/2014-01-13/debates/14011313000007/WorkAndPensions. Accessed 4/1/2018.

Lansley, S., & J. Mack. 2015. *Breadline Britain: The Rise of Mass Poverty*. London: Oneworld.

Lundström, R. 2013. Framing Fraud: Discourse on Benefit Cheating in Sweden and the UK. *European Journal of Communication* 28 (6): 630–645.

Newton, J. 2015. More than 100,000 Benefit Claimants Across the UK Are Being Handed £100 a Week After Being Assessed as Unable to Work Because of Addiction, Obesity and Stress. *Mail Online* 22/05/15. http://www.dailymail.co.uk/news/article-3006248/More-100-000-benefits-claimants-UK-handed-100-week-assessed-unable-work-addiction-obesity-stress.html. Accessed 14/3/2018.

ONS. 2017. Statistical bulletin: UK labour market Jan 2017. https://www.ons.gov.uk/employmentandlabourmarket/peopleinwork/employmentandemployeetypes/bulletins/uklabourmarket/jan2017. Accessed 23/03/2018.

Paterson, L. L., L. Coffey-Glover, & D. Peplow. 2016. Negotiating Stance Within Discourses of Class: Reactions to *Benefits Street*. *Discourse & Society* 27 (2): 195–214.

Paterson, L. L., D. Peplow, & K. Grainger. 2017. Does Money Talk Equal Class Talk? Audience Responses to Poverty Porn in Relation to Money and Debt. In A. Mooney & E. Sifaki (eds.). *The Language of Money and Debt: An Interdisciplinary Approach*. Basingstoke: Palgrave, pp. 205–232.

Slack, J. 2010. Migrants ARE Driving Down Wages of the Poor, as Equalities Watchdog Blames East European Influx. *Mail Online* 18/01/10. http://www.dailymail.co.uk/news/article-1244060/Migrants-ARE-driving-wages-poor-equalities-watchdog-blames-East-European-influx.html. Accessed 15/1/2018.

van der Bom, I., L. L. Paterson, K. Grainger, & D. Peplow. 2018. 'It's Not the Fact They Claim Benefits but Their Useless, Lazy, Drug Taking Lifestyles We Despise': Analysing Audience Responses to Benefits Street Using Live Tweets. *Discourse, Context & Media* 21: 36–45.

8

Geography-Based Discourses of Poverty

In this final chapter, we bring together all of the PNCs for each of our queries to establish overarching patterns of how each newspaper deals with poverty and place. References to poverty in this chapter, therefore, should be taken to refer to our entire dataset (including all of our queries and all PNCs directly related to poverty, as shown in Table 5.7). The analysis of the linguistic similarities and differences between the *Guardian* and the *Daily Mail* begins with PNC keyword analysis. As the preceding chapters have focused on particular subsets of queries, we do not intend to repeat data here. For this final chapter we draw on all PNCs to investigate how each newspaper discursively constructs poverty and place, and how particularly-salient places are related to poverty by each publication. Before focusing on which places the two newspapers concentrate on in their discussion of poverty, we first explore the extent to which the two newspapers discuss poverty and place overall (Sect. 8.1). Having established the overarching geographies of poverty and place in our corpora, we explore the topics that the two newspapers associate with different places. Our analysis begins with London (Sect. 8.2) before focusing on major urban areas (Sect. 8.3) and other locations (Sect. 8.4).

L. L Paterson and I. N Gregory, *Representations of Poverty and Place*,
https://doi.org/10.1007/978-3-319-93503-4_8

8.1 Poverty and Place in the Two Newspapers

Table 8.1 shows how frequently instances of poverty and place occur in the two corpora (normalised per million words to facilitate direct comparison). PNCs for *the*, calculated using a 5% sample of each corpus (as discussed in Chapter 4), have been used to give an indication of how frequently the two papers use place-names generally.

References to poverty are found more frequently in the *Guardian* than in the *Daily Mail*; the *Guardian* has 35% more hits for our queries. The second column in Table 8.1 shows that the *Guardian* also uses place-names about 14% more than the *Daily Mail*. When the number of poverty PNCs is compared (column three, Table 8.1), the disparity between the two newspapers becomes much greater: the *Guardian* associates poverty with place, as measured by the number of PNCs, more than fifteen times more often than the *Daily Mail*. As described below, the *Guardian* strongly associates poverty with London and places within it. However, even when London-based PNCs are removed, the *Guardian* still associates poverty with place eleven times more than the *Daily Mail* (column four, Table 8.1).

Figure 8.1 shows the distribution of all poverty instances for the *Guardian*. The density smoothed map reveals a highly London-centric pattern; London is the only cluster that scores above the $z > 2.58$ threshold (see Sect. 4.2) and 49.8% of the poverty PNCs are found in this cluster. Birmingham is the only other place to cross the $z > 1.96$ threshold. However this cluster only has 267 PNCs compared to 3407 in London. The Kulldorf map—generated when poverty PNCs

Table 8.1 Frequency of poverty and place mentions in the *Daily Mail* and the *Guardian*

	All poverty instances (normalised pmw)	PNCs for *the* from 5% sample (pmw)	All poverty PNCs (pmw)	Non-London poverty PNCs (pmw)
Daily Mail	10,855.0	143.6	12.0	8.3
Guardian	14,656.8	163.2	187.1	93.9
Ratio (G: DM)	1.35: 1	1.14: 1	15.64: 1	11.32: 1

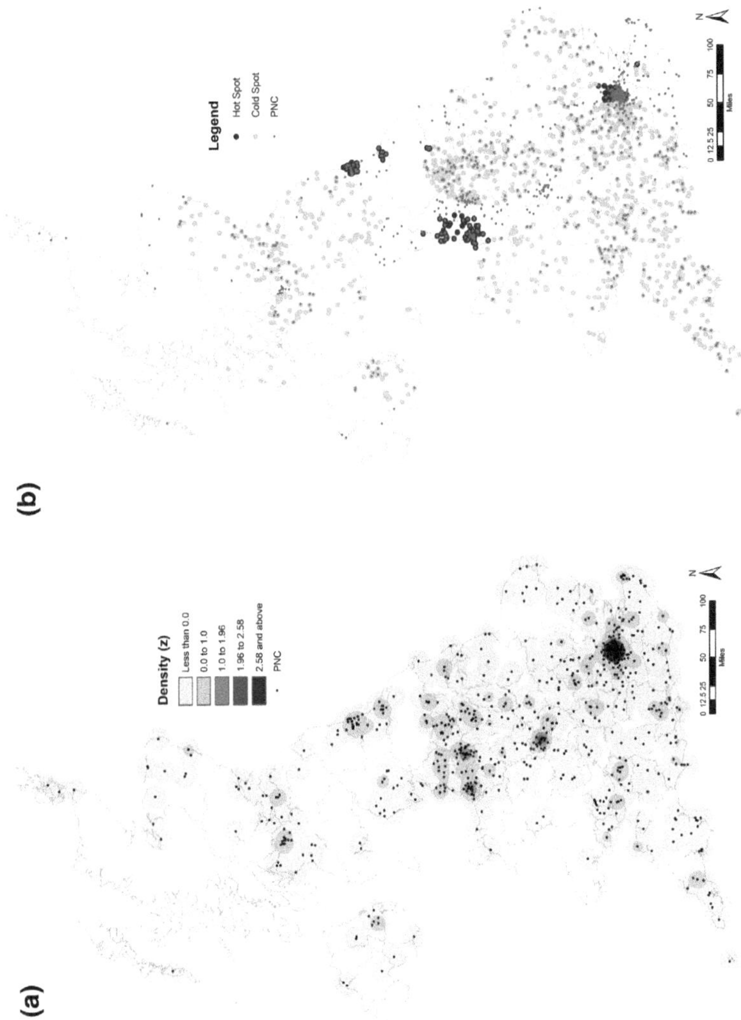

Fig. 8.1 Density smoothed and Kulldorf maps for all poverty PNCs in the *Guardian*

are compared to the background geography of their newspapers (calculated using a sample of PNCs for *the*, see Chapter 4)—complicates the idea of London as a hotspot somewhat. Areas of north, east, and south London are revealed as hotspots but London itself, represented by a point in the centre of London, is actually a cold spot. This suggests that the *Guardian* concentrates on poverty in specific parts of London (such as Hackney, Islington, Haringey, Tower Hamlets, Brixton, Lambeth, and Southwark) more than on London as a generic whole. Elsewhere there are hotspots around Merseyside, stretching east as far as Wigan and Warrington, and others around Newcastle, and slightly further south around Middlesbrough. There are smaller hotspots around York (46 PNCs), north of Merseyside in West Lancashire (46 PNCs), Kent and Maidstone (40 PNCs), and a much smaller one in Morecambe Bay (6 PNCs). The *Guardian* has no hotspots in Wales, Scotland, or Northern Ireland. The overwhelming finding in Fig. 8.1 is the extent of the cold spots. With a small number of exceptions, particularly in the south-east, almost all of the UK is a cold spot. This suggest that the *Guardian* strongly associates poverty with a small number of mainly urban places in England and largely ignores it elsewhere.

Figure 8.2 shows all of the poverty PNCs for the *Daily Mail*. There is also a London-centric pattern but noticeably less so than for the *Guardian*. Almost exactly a third of the *Daily Mail*'s 3687 PNCs are in London but there are other clusters in Birmingham, Liverpool, and Manchester that lie above the $z > 2.58$ threshold. The Kulldorf map shows major hotspots in London, particularly north and east London, the West Midlands, Merseyside, Greater Manchester (stretching north to include Rochdale, Blackburn, and Burnley), Middlesbrough, Newcastle, and Glasgow. All of these have over 50 PNCs. Smaller hotspots are found around Nottingham (40 PNCs), Hull (38), Aberdeen (31), Kent and Maidstone (28), Clacton (23), Stoke-on-Trent (17), Keynsham (16), Okehampton (14), Ebbw Vale in South Wales (12), and West Berkshire (10). As with the *Guardian*, cold spots dominate much of the map suggesting that the geography of areas associated with poverty is highly polarised.

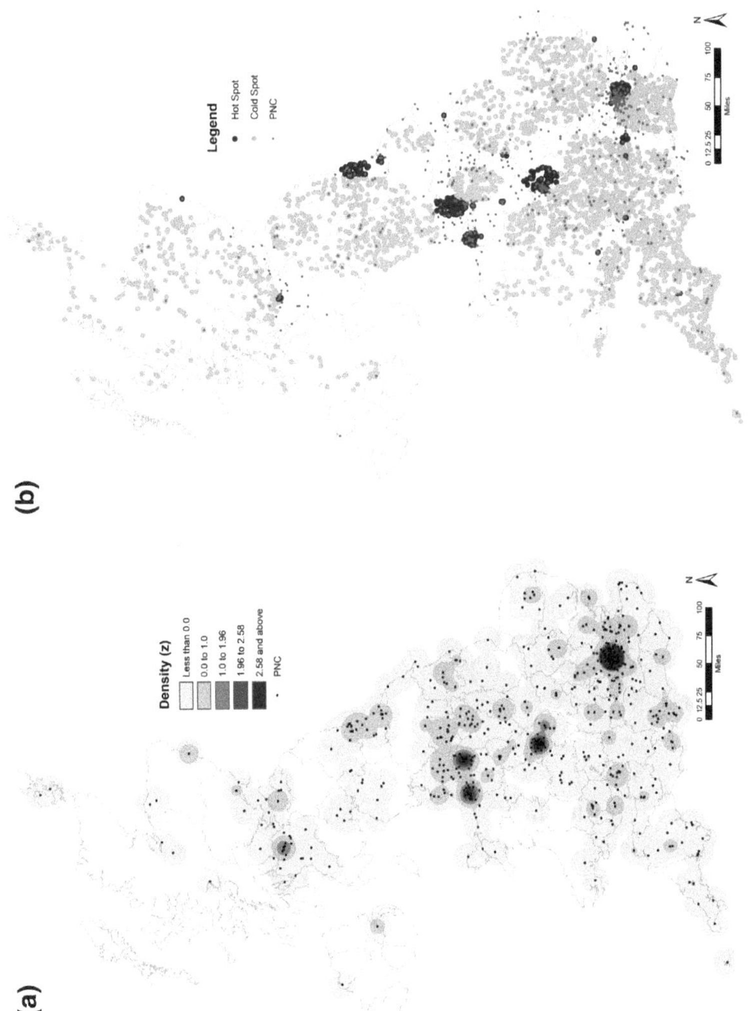

Fig. 8.2 Density smoothed and Kulldorf maps for all poverty PNCs in the *Daily Mail*

Figure 8.3 uses the spatial segregation analysis point comparison technique described in Sect. 4.2 to compare the distribution of all poverty PNCs from the *Guardian* and the *Daily Mail.* Figure 8.3a shows that, as expected, the area around London has significantly more *Guardian* PNCs than *Daily Mail* ones. Much of the rest of the map has more *Daily Mail* instances than *Guardian* ones. In particular, the *Daily Mail* concentrates more on an area stretching from Birmingham and Nottingham (in the midlands) to Liverpool and Manchester (in the north). This pattern is potentially problematic, however, because the *Guardian*'s overwhelming concentration on London means, almost by definition, that its PNCs are under-represented elsewhere. For this reason, Fig. 8.3b repeats the analysis but with PNCs within Greater London excluded. This shows a noticeably more even pattern between the two newspapers outside London, but the differences are still statistically significant.

Taking the analyses from Fig. 8.3 together suggests that, beyond London, the major cities do not receive significantly more attention from either newspaper, with the exception of Manchester which has statistically significantly more *Daily Mail* PNCs at the $p < 0.05$ level. The *Guardian* associates the south Midlands (including Oxfordshire, Aylesbury, Milton Keynes, and Chipping Norton), York, Sheffield, and Cornwall with poverty significantly more than the *Daily Mail.* Other areas with significantly high *Guardian* PNCs include Belfast, Consett (just north of Newcastle), east Glasgow, south Cumbria, and Weymouth, but these are represented by only small numbers of PNCs—35 in Belfast, fewer than twenty in all other cases. Thus, they can tell us less about the newspapers' representation of poverty than might initially seem possible. The *Daily Mail* has a complex pattern that includes clusters around Coventry (79 PNCs), northern East Anglia (74), Swindon and West Berkshire (36), Scunthorpe to the south of Hull (11), Okehampton in Devon (17), and south-west Scotland (5). Considering Figs. 8.1–8.3 together reveals the following:

- Both newspapers strongly associate London with poverty, but the *Guardian* does this to a far greater extent than the *Daily Mail.*
- Both newspapers also associate Merseyside, Birmingham, Newcastle, and Glasgow with poverty. Arguably, the *Daily Mail* associates these with poverty more than the *Guardian* but this is driven, at least in

(a) (b)

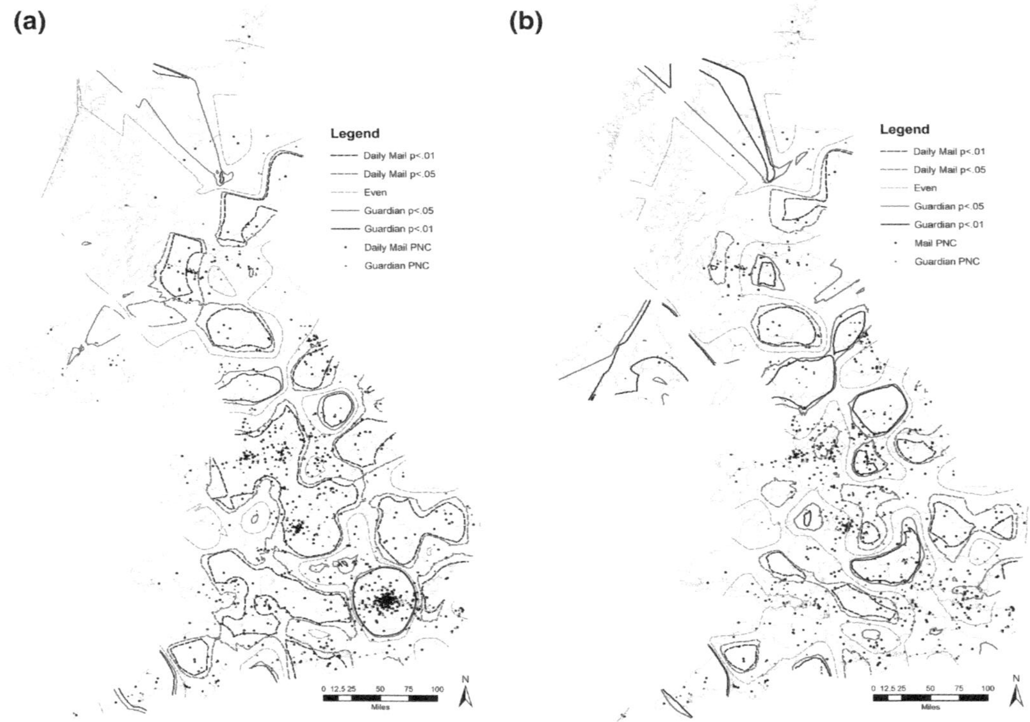

Fig. 8.3 Spatial segregation analysis comparing all poverty PNCs for the *Guardian* and the *Daily Mail*: **a** All PNCs **b** PNCs outside London

part, by the *Guardian*'s over-emphasis on London. Of these city areas, Merseyside is most associated with poverty based on the number of PNCs in its Kulldorf hotspots in both newspapers.

- Manchester reveals a contrast between the two newspapers, being a density smoothed cluster and Kulldorf hotspot in the *Daily Mail* but a cold spot in the *Guardian*. It has weakly significantly more instances in the *Daily Mail* than the *Guardian* even after London has been removed from the comparison. This is a somewhat surprising finding, given the *Guardian*'s history as a Manchester-based newspaper.
- Away from the major cities, Middlesbrough, Hull, and Kent and Maidstone attract attention from both newspapers.
- Cornwall and, to a lesser extent, Sheffield, the south Midlands, and Belfast are associated with poverty by the *Guardian* more than the *Daily Mail* but, according to the Kulldorf analysis, they are not significant, suggesting that the *Guardian* does not strongly associate them with poverty.
- Similarly, the *Daily Mail* gives more attention to northern East Anglia and Coventry than the *Guardian* does, but these are not hotspots so, again, they do not receive a significant amount of interest from the *Daily Mail*.
- York is an area that the *Guardian* associates with poverty but the *Daily Mail* does not, while Aberdeen, and Swindon and West Berkshire are associated with poverty by the *Daily Mail* but not the *Guardian*.

8.2 Discourses of Poverty and Place in London

Because London was so prominent in the PNCs we treated it separately (as in previous chapters). Table 8.2 shows the PNC keywords for London for each newspaper (the *Guardian*'s London PNCs were compared with the *Daily Mail's* London PNCs). We have included PNC keywords occurring a minimum of 5 times (numbers, place-names, and punctuation have been omitted). There were 241 PNC keywords for the *Guardian* and 139 for the *Daily Mail*.

Table 8.2 PNC Keywords for London when compared to the rest of the UK for the *Guardian* and the *Daily Mail* ($n \geq 5$)

Newspaper	Sig.	PNC Keywords London
Guardian	<0.01	housing, rents, affordable, private, we, councils, outer, if, move, that, new, local, inner, moving, will, government, other, homes, benefit, properties, property, impact, shelter, planning, both, residents, rented, cap, means, changes, buy, huge, transport, third, neighbourhoods, high, hostel, example, build, demand, outnumber, receive, Livingstone, officer, create, better, hotel, you, average, cheaper, not, building, the, paying, started, schemes, advice, overall, provided, foundation, fair, Amelia, sector, community, landlords, are, side, growth, low-income, with, social, what, cancelled, development, gentleman, editor, statutory, taking, would, market, these, have, services, April, such, decent, soup, legal, priced, wage, my, research, numbers, funding, one-bedroom, works, director, larger, eviction, whereas, specialist
	<0.05	friends, offer, fund, out, than, additional, letter, apply, shrink, assembly, regeneration, either, allowances, issue, might, supporting, strategy, whom, guardian, Patrick, included, evict, infrastructure, PCTS, by, rights, leave, central, only, minimum, dependent, appeal, Randeep, block, am, Wednesday, Ramesh, approach, email, Monday, economically, bite, double, cleaners, sell, is, shortage, it, places, of, claiming, provision, comes, institute, mixed, lot, aid, analysis, universal, unless, butler, wards, cope, substantial, Saturday, developments, mothers, commission, neighbouring, accounts, intention, factory, housebuilding, contract, conservative, claimant, short, deepest, unaffordable, should, recent, increasingly, renting, action, so, be, put, place, problems, hit, very, fifth, soaring, few, wales, drop, decision, earnings, driving, event, wide, movement, twitter, evidence, standards, forces, age, extended, immediately, limits, budgets, outstrip, squeezed, mansions, allow, JSA, seeing, failing, failure, department, related, conservative-run, providing, vast, funds, pushing, two-bed, federation, postcodes, accepted, win, increases, cities, vacancies, temporary, accommodation, according, now, people, least, result

(continued)

Table 8.2 (continued)

Newspaper	Sig.	PNC Keywords London
Daily Mail	<0.01	cent, per, Mr, child, constituencies, enlarge, pictured, combat, sustainably, yesterday, today, Mrs, BBC, poorest, cafe, taxpayers, district, updated, streets, Keely, store, Romanian, pupils, street, reached, baker, Ms, repossessed, slum, months, smith, men, vouchers, area, without, was, constituency, he, details, Blair, meaning, prepares, Muslim, walked, exclusive, arrived, features, Tories, blocked, Victorian, map, speaking, never, areas, worst, stage, fallen, website, house, children, claim, speech, Iain, pound, successful, benefits, jobless, mail, economy, during, forcing, top, poverty, pub, seven-bedroom, located, pledge, father, eat, culture, part-time, gang, reveals, grew, shops, Duncan, Tesco, open, heavily, believed, queue, illegal, credits, Europe, show, homeless, days, Ed, her, Miliband, while
	<0.05	lives, fact, crime, jubilee, stewards, daughter, interview, worldwide, asylum, restaurant, summer, payments, his, unemployment, revealed, in, suffering, recently, woman, labour, business, ago, she, English, daily, millions, search, sending, figures, money, hundreds, after, were, use, evictions, residential, regularly, bussed, husband

Table 8.2 shows that the *Guardian* PNC keywords with the highest log likelihood scores are very strongly associated with Housing benefits and the benefits cap (*housing, rents, affordable, private, move, moving, homes, benefit, properties, property, impact, Shelter, residents, rented, cap*). Taken together, with the *Guardian*'s wider focus on cuts, benefits, and wages, these PNC keywords are used to express the newspaper's overarching argument that high housing costs, low wages, and the government's cap on benefits mean that people are being forced to move away from London to cheaper places—a process sometimes referred to as 'social cleansing' (*move, moving, out, to, force(d), cleansing, leave, evict*). Relatedly, political organisations and individual politicians, such as London mayor Boris Johnson, Chancellor of the Exchequer George Osborne, and the London Assembly are all prominent, either for their role creating welfare-related policies (George Osborne is strongly associated with the benefits cap), or objecting to them as 'Kosovo-style social cleansing'—a phrase attributed to Boris Johnson.

Thus, the overarching discourse of poverty in London in the *Guardian* is that poverty is relative: London housing costs are more expensive than elsewhere and wages are not high enough to provide a decent standard of living (see the Living Wage Campaign, Sect. 6.3). The *Guardian* also presents a causal link between London prices and benefits receipt: as a result of high relative house prices people turn to Housing benefit, which is now capped, meaning that the unaffordability of London ultimately increases.

1. Before 2025 rents on most two-bedroom properties in the south will become unaffordable to those claiming local housing **allowance**. Within 15 years, much of London's commuter belt will become too expensive for the state to pay for the poor to live in (G news: society, Nov 2010).
2. Towns such as Chelmsford, Newbury, Bath and Maidstone would be no-go areas for those on **benefits** and all of Hertfordshire would be out of bounds. The capital would be unaffordable within a decade (G news: society, Nov 2010).
3. tight new housing benefit caps that do not increase in line with the rising **rents**, and benefit reform, has made central London increasingly inaccessible to people on low incomes (G news: society, Nov 2013).

Example (1) is framed by the claim that 'Large swaths of southern England will become off limits to Housing benefit recipients in a little more than a decade because of the government's proposed plans to cut welfare bills' (Ramesh and Sparrow 2010). Here the causality is made explicit through the use of 'because'. Furthermore, benefit cuts are deemed responsible for 'triggering a huge migration of the poor to the north' (Ramesh and Sparrow 2010), with the *Guardian* providing lists of places which it claims will become 'no-go areas' for people on lower incomes (2). The *Guardian* takes the position that those claiming Housing benefit should not be excluded from areas where rents are high (by government action); at its extreme this can be expressed as the proposition that people should not be restricted in their choice of place to live based on their economic circumstances (see Sect. 7.3). Housing benefit is positioned as a means to ensure that those who cannot afford London rents are not excluded from the city (where they are likely to work or go to school). But the benefits cap, imposed by the government, is discursively constructed as directly restricting access to high-rent areas (3) and actively contributing to relative poverty.

The *Guardian* therefore conceptualises poverty as a condition associated with the removal of opportunity from groups of people based on their economic circumstance. Individual people are not to blame for their poverty, rather poverty is the effect of structural inequality influenced by market forces, capitalism, and government endorsement of neoliberalism. The *Guardian* positions itself as pro-welfare state and implicitly draws on socialism by presenting the argument that poverty, within London in particular, would decrease with the removal of the benefits cap and the introduction of a government-mandated living wage (see Sect. 6.4).

By contrast, the PNC keywords in the *Daily Mail* do not cluster so neatly into overarching themes. The *Daily Mail* makes frequent use of statistics (*per, cent, statistics, map, economy, spokesman*), which suggest a macro-level conceptualisation of poverty as something which can be measured, endorsing the ideology that poverty is (easily) quantifiable. Despite taking poverty as something which is quantifiable, reports of large numbers in poverty and/or claiming benefits are contrasted with individual (and sometimes sensationalist) examples which are taken as representative of homogenous groups (*Mr, Mrs, Ms, he, woman, her, she, husband*). Not all individuals mentioned in relation to poverty and place are evaluated negatively (see Sect. 6.3 and the discussion of 'jobless') as actions which are seen as an embodiment of neoliberal principles are presented in a positive light. However, such examples are used contrastively with stories of individuals whose circumstances and actions are used to endorse particular negative stereotypes about the poor. As shown in (4) and (5), associations are made between receipt of benefits and being 'jobless', 'depraved', taking drugs, committing crime, and dealing in stolen goods.

4. Jobless Lee Miller, who has demanded a bigger council house for his enormous family, claims he would turn to petty crime because he has 'bills to **pay**'. The 40-year-old said he would travel to <u>London</u> and target the wealthy to provide for his children (DM news, Oct 2010).
5. The pair led a depraved lifestyle, funding their mutual crack addiction through benefits and flogging stolen goods. **Jobless** Spence

would regularly crash as Efremi's north London pad, smoking drugs for days at a time (DM news, Nov 2014).

Other trends in the London PNC keywords for the *Daily Mail* include combating child poverty (*child, sustainably, combat*) and the importance of schooling (*pupils, schools, school*), in among more general PNC keywords associated with money and employment (*poorest, vouchers, jobless, pledge* (the failure of Tony Blair's 'pledge on poverty'), *part-time, unemployment, suffering, richest*), and housing (*repossessed, house, forcing, homeless, evictions, residential, mortgage*). There is opposition to the cereal café in Shoreditch (*café, Keely, restaurant*), which shows some sympathy for those who live in one of the poorest boroughs in the UK (see Sect. 4.3). Politics and politicians are again mentioned (*Smith, Blair, Duncan, Cameron, Tories, Iain, Ed, Miliband, Labour*) but there are also groups of PNC keywords which have no parallels in the *Guardian*, such as those relating to minorities (*Romanian, Muslim, asylum*), crime (*illegal, gang, crime*), and history (*Victorian, slum*). One example which neatly contrasts the newspapers' attitudes to poverty in London is the occurrence of *one-bedroom* and *seven-bedroom* as PNC keywords in the *Guardian* and *Daily Mail* respectively. This reveals the former's preference for stories about people living in overcrowded accommodation because they cannot afford to move and the latter's tendency to report stories of (ex-migrant) benefit claimants living in large properties at the taxpayers' expense (see Sect. 7.2).

The *Daily Mail* ultimately endorses the benefits cap and other welfare reform policies, and conceptualises poverty as caused by the (in)action of (groups of) individuals who are responsible for and/or complicit in their own misfortune. The occurrence of *Romanian* as a PNC keyword relates to multiple reports of migrants sleeping rough (6), begging, and/or making children beg for them. A similar theme occurs in references to Polish migrants (7) and is generalised to 'groups of EU nationals', as in (6). Thus, at least some homelessness in London is blamed on migration rules and the free movement of EU citizens.

6. Police from Westminster regularly target Romanian **beggars** and rough sleepers in London Mrs May will also say there is a 'recurring

problem' with groups of EU nationals who set up camps in public areas in London **beg** and steal from tourists (DM news, June 2013).
7. The problem of Polish rough sleepers in the (sic) London has become so bad that last year a **homeless** charity in the capital produced a Polish-language video warning of the dangers of moving to the city without a job or means to support themselves (DM news, Feb 2014).

In terms of the *Daily Mail*'s overarching ideological position on poverty, the conclusions here must be more tentative than those posed for the *Guardian*. The *Daily Mail* does not systematically make direct links between government policies and the causes of poverty and, as such, it rejects a socially-oriented interpretation of poverty. This is evidenced through reports of individual people's circumstances, and a focus on job cuts in the private, as opposed to the public, sector: the *Daily Mail* focused more on job losses relating to declining industry than the *Guardian*, who reported more on council job losses (see Chapter 6). Ultimately, whist the *Daily Mail* does recognise that many people in London are in poverty, it treats poverty as if it is an individual characteristic. The direct causes for poverty are not high house prices and government cuts, but are implied to be the failure of government(s) to stop alleged abuse of the benefits system (by individual scroungers and, more generally, immigrants) and to increase the incentives for people to work.

8.3 Poverty in Urban Centres

Outside London, Manchester showed the biggest contrast in geographical attention between the two newspapers. Although it received similar numbers of PNCs, 232 in the *Guardian* and 241 in the *Daily Mail*, it is a cluster and hotspot in the *Daily Mail* but a cold spot in the *Guardian*. Spatial segregation analysis reveals that there are significantly more PNCs for the *Daily Mail* at $p < .05$ even with London removed from the comparison. Table 8.3 compares the PNC keywords for the two newspapers. It includes a comparison between Manchester and the rest of the UK (excl. London) for each newspaper, and a direct comparison between the newspapers. Including the former allows us to see where the two newspapers are similar, whilst the direct comparison highlights the differences.

Table 8.3 PNC Keywords for the Manchester cluster. Italicised keywords are found in both newspapers ($n \geq 5$)

Manchester	Sig.	PNC Keywords
Guardian vs UK (excl. London)	<0.01	incapacity, *conference*, city, Facebook, last, police, as
	<0.05	back, to, far, they, against, you, Britain, losses
Guardian vs *Daily Mail*	<0.01	council, as
	<0.05	city, have
Daily Mail vs UK (excl. London)	<0.01	feminist, awkwardly, t-shirt, giving, *conference*, tests, pilot, market, beggar, hospital, a, medical, scheme, anywhere, plan, get, begin, area, to, central, town
	<0.05	before, rent, top, recently, found, estate, under, fit, say, cent
Daily Mail vs *Guardian*	<0.01	cent, per, town, Mr, child, near, pilot, fit, made, his, left, help, she, also, feminist, anywhere, awkwardly, beggar, begin, hospital, t-shirt, plan, close, rent
	<0.05	being, market, area, found, money, estate, number, top, a

It is clear from the sparsity of PNC keywords that the *Guardian* has little to say about poverty in and around Manchester. The only themes that seem to emerge as distinctive for Manchester compared to the rest of the country are incapacity benefit and public sector cuts, which in this case are associated particularly with the *police*. *Council* is a PNC keyword when compared with the *Daily Mail* and is primarily associated with council cuts, while *conference* refers to political party conferences being held in the city, and *they* frequently refers to people protesting or campaigning about issues including benefit cuts, homelessness provision, and the removal of the Education Maintenance Allowance (provided to young people who remained in education post-16).

The *Daily Mail* does not just emphasise Manchester but is also concerned with towns nearby, such as Burnley and Rochdale. This emphasis is in part revealed by *town* appearing as a PNC keyword when comparing the *Daily Mail* to the *Guardian*. The most talked about of these towns is Burnley, which is discussed in relation to the trial of new fit-for-work assessments (*tests, pilot, medical, fit, found*) relating to the replacement of incapacity benefit with ESA (see Sects. 6.2 and 6.3). Rochdale is labelled (passively) as 'the most deprived area of England' and is described as a recession-hit *market town*, struggling due to the numbers of asylum seekers it has taken.

8. In the Falinge area, dubbed the 'sick-note capital of Britain', the majority of the population is on sickness **benefits**. Moreover, almost a fifth of Rochdale's population now comes from migrant communities. In nine of the town's schools, 70 per cent of the pupils speak English as a foreign language (DM news, May 2010).

In (8) a link is made between the number of people receiving sickness benefits and the number of migrants living in the area, but there is no evidence presented to suggest a direct correlation between these two variables. The *Daily Mail* leaves the link between benefits receipt and migrants implicit and further implies that there is some relationship between the languages spoken by children in the area and its relative deprivation. Whilst never stated explicitly, the underlying assumption here is that somehow migrants are to blame for the high numbers of people receiving benefits, despite the fact that, elsewhere, the *Daily Mail* notes that there are no jobs available in Rochdale. The importance of adjacency has already been noted in Chapter 7 and analysing adjacent or appended stories linked to poverty though their proximity (such as the languages spoken in schools in example 8) would be an interesting endeavour. However, such analysis is beyond the scope of current discussions of poverty and place.

Away from stories specifically referring to these two towns, places in this cluster are associated with deprivation, with *schemes* to help deprived areas and references to *child* poverty. *Plan* is used in relation to planned cuts, and *rent* and *estate* are associated with housing. As is often the case, the *Daily Mail* refers to statistics in relation to place (*per, cent, number, top*) far more than the *Guardian*. There are also stories associated with individual people (*Mr, he, she*), who are sometimes politicians but often ordinary members of the public.

Similar to Manchester, Merseyside, Birmingham, Glasgow, and Newcastle are all urban areas that have similar relative importance in the two newspapers. Table 8.4 shows the PNC keywords for Merseyside. For the *Guardian*, benefits are again a theme (*universal, credit(s), testing, system, tax*). However, in contrast to London, the benefits mentioned concern the rollout of universal credit, and tax credits, but there

Table 8.4 PNC Keywords for the Merseyside cluster. Italicised keywords are found in both newspapers ($n \geq 5$)

Merseyside	Sig.	PNC Keywords
Guardian vs UK (excl. London)	<0.01	universal, credits, Anderson, addresses, common, harder, riots, level, *deprived*, held, in, affected, *highest*, testing, combined, urban, able, claimed, study, system
	<0.05	tax, credit, *most*, *workless*, household, life, these, other, years, how
Guardian vs *Daily Mail*	<0.01	universal, other, credits, social, and, addresses, affected, says, system, tax, over, claimed, before, while, sector
	<0.05	will, life, common, public, authorities, councils, able, housing, local, council, that, under, testing, household, do, harder, riots, region, held, set, urban, credit, combined, service, spending, at
Daily Mail vs UK (excl. London)	<0.01	*highest*, *workless*, households, areas, poorest, sharp, communities, *most*, *deprived*, homes, rate, list, number, where, suggest, them, mother, cent, incapacity, need, benefits, of
	<0.05	receive, per, nearly, out, is, many, figures, no, children
Daily Mail vs *Guardian*	<0.01	cent, where, poorest, per, communities, households, Mr, number, list, incapacity, sharp, receive, suggest, nearly, mother, worst
	<0.05	benefits, losing, jobless, rate, today, areas, his, highest, top, places

are no repeated mentions of Housing benefits. There is also deprivation (*riots, deprived, urban*—often in the sense of urban dereliction, *workless, life*—usually expectancy or chances) and a strong impression of things getting worse (*harder, highest, level, affected, most*). Politics is also a theme, with *Anderson*, the mayor of Liverpool, opposing cuts to councils.

The *Daily Mail*'s PNC keywords also include a focus on benefits (*incapacity, benefits, receive*) with incapacity benefits being primary. There is also a story about a Mr. *Sharp* whose attempts to go to a job interview were thwarted by the rules around benefits (9). Here the *Daily*

Mail positions government bureaucracy as restricting this individual's access to work and depicts Mr. Sharp as someone who is being proactive and looking for a job, thus embodying the neoliberal principles the *Daily Mail* values.

9. he claims he had to pull out of the interview thanks to bizarre rules that meant he could not miss a 'Back To Work' class on the same day. **Jobcentre** staff warned Mr. Sharp, 33, from Huyton, Merseyside, that if he missed the seminar he would lose his benefit money (DM news, Oct 2010).

As with London, the *Daily Mail* draws on statistics (*homes*—used in '1 in 3 homes has no…', *rate, list, number, cent, per, figures*). The PNC keywords also evidence themes of deprivation (*deprived, workless, children, no*—in the sense of no one working) and reports on things being bad or getting worse (*communities, most, poorest, highest*)—similar themes to those found in the *Guardian*. Thus, whilst the two newspapers appear to disagree about the levels and causes of poverty in London (Sect. 8.2) they appear to have more in common when associating poverty with Liverpool.

By contrast, the PNC keywords for Birmingham (Table 8.5) reveal perhaps the biggest differences between the newspapers in all of the four major non-London clusters. Analysing the PNC keywords make it clear that the *Daily Mail*'s coverage of poverty in Birmingham is dominated by references to three high-profile stories. The first of these relates to the television programme *Benefits Street* (10), which first aired in 2014 (*Street, James, Turner, show, lives, channel, residents, benefits*). The second is a series of stories about a woman called Marie Buchan (see Chapter 7) who has eight children and receives benefits (*says, cap, three-bedroom, months*). The evaluation of Buchan is similar to that identified in Sect. 7.2 but without the emphasis on the recipient being foreign-born. The third involves a woman named Cait Reilly who took the government to court claiming that an unpaid work placement in the shop *Poundland*, which she had to do in order to keep her benefits, breached her human rights (11). These three stories contribute to *her* being a PNC keyword, and *state* is often used in relation to either *Benefits Street* or the Marie

Table 8.5 PNC Keywords for the Birmingham cluster. Italicised keywords are found in both newspapers ($n \geq 5$)

Birmingham	Sig.	PNC Keywords
Guardian vs UK (excl. London)	<0.01	*street*, *channel*, *city*, council, biggest, the, since, increase, local, already, nearly, claiming, economy, conference, *over*, paying, workers, disabled, today
	<0.05	*cut*, its, planning, rents, to, number, was, man, more, times, tory
Guardian vs *Daily Mail*	<0.01	council, local, workers, housing, this, as, constituency,
	<0.05	last, year, economy, announced, plans, under, that, now, affordable, health, minimum, rents, region, paying, before, authority, authorities, times, so, some, than
Daily Mail vs UK (excl. London)	<0.01	*street*, turner, James, Poundland, says, cap, show, lives, *channel*, three-bedroom, months, inner-city, state, her, residents, benefits, capable, where, *city*, first, *over*, set
	<0.05	seen, receive, *cut*, work, them
Daily Mail vs *Guardian*	<0.01	cent, per, James, turner, street, town, show, capable, months, benefits, where, lives, her, residents, inner-city, she, work, state, Poundland, them, three-bedroom
	<0.05	his, around, family, receive, in, says

Buchan story. There are also references to the fitness for work (*capable, receive, cut, work*) of benefits recipients in Birmingham.

10. Residents in a **deprived** Birmingham road were filmed making false welfare claims and growing cannabis in their homes (DM news, Jan 2014).
11. Mr. Johnson also criticised unemployed graduate Cait Reilly who claimed earlier this month that she is suing the Government for making her taken an **unpaid** work placement at Poundland in Birmingham. He said she 'sneered' at hardworking Britons by saying the work was 'forced labour' (DM news, Jan 2012).

12. Workshy map of Britain revealed: Thousands of incapacity benefit claimants found to be capable of working Birmingham has most **claimants** capable of work (DM news, May 2013).

The people appearing on *Benefits Street* are accused of 'false' claims and drug taking (10), Cait Reilly was described as sneering at 'hardworking Britons' by the Mayor of London, and benefits claimants in Birmingham are labelled 'workshy' and 'capable of work' (12). What unites these stories is their negative evaluation of (predominantly) able-bodied people who are represented as able to work but choose not to do so. Their receipt of benefits, therefore, is seen as illegitimate—a position which depends on an underlying ideology that benefits claimants can be easily divided into the deserving and undeserving poor. This understanding of poverty is reinforced by the contrast made between stories such as those in (10–12) and more sympathetic stories, such as (13), which concerns a National Lottery-backed food bank in Birmingham.

13. Earlier this year, reports from Birmingham's Citizens Advice Bureau revealed residents unable to **afford** their electricity bills were turning off their fridges, leading to cases of food poisoning (DM news, Sep 2011)

Here there is no explicit negative evaluation of those who have caught food poisoning, rather they are described in the article (13) comes from as 'The crippling human cost of the recession' and 'desperate families starving in poverty' (Watson 2011). Anomalously for the *Daily Mail* those accessing the foodbank are not presented as architects of their own misfortune, but rather 'the recession' is blamed for them not being able to pay their bills and buy food. Thus, those visiting the foodbank represent the deserving poor—those who face hardship through no personal failings—who are in direct contrast to benefits cheats and the 'workshy'.

The *Guardian*'s reports on poverty in Birmingham also include some PNC keywords related to *Benefits Street* (*Street, Channel*). However, it is more concerned with cuts, particularly those associated with local government (*council, local, already, workers, cut, planning*); indeed the Birmingham clusters is, in part, responsible for the focus on public sector cuts discussed in Sect. 6.4. Benefits are also a theme (*claiming*), but the focus is more on Jobseeker's Allowance than other benefits. There is also a story about a *man* setting himself on fire outside a Jobcentre when his benefits were cut. Housing is present again (*rents*) and so are wages (*paying*), particularly in relation to *disabled* people earning the minimum wage. As with Merseyside, but in a less pronounced manner, there is again a theme of things being bad or getting worse, with *number* often being used to note the extremes of poverty, to endorse the position that *times* are hard/tough.

With 99 PNCs, Glasgow is a hotspot for the *Daily Mail* but not for the *Guardian*, which has 139 PNCs in the cluster. This difference is not statistically significant using spatial segregation analysis once London is removed. Despite the numerical similarity, the different focuses of the two newspapers are revealed by the PNC keywords in Table 8.6. The *Guardian* is largely interested in the city because of Iain Duncan Smith's visit to the Easterhouse estate (see also Sect. 7.3), which is connected to his proposals for welfare reform (14) and the creation of the Centre for Social Justice (*Iain, Duncan, Smith, visit, estate, his, Centre, Social*). *Social* sometimes also occurs in relation to social deprivation or social

Table 8.6 PNC Keywords for the Glasgow cluster. Italicised keywords are found in both newspapers ($n \geq 5$)

Glasgow	Sig.	PNC Keywords
Guardian vs UK (excl. London)	<0.01	Iain, Duncan, visit, Smith, estate, life, family, when, how
	<0.05	as, now, his, new
Guardian vs *Daily Mail*	<0.01	Iain, a, I, when, social, visit, for, Duncan, smith
	<0.05	estate, there, city, you, centre
Daily Mail vs UK (excl. London)	<0.01	independent, lost, be, defence, shipyard, yards, another, capable, such, are, at, of, figures
	<0.05	some, would, this, being, including, cent, work, food
Daily Mail vs *Guardian*	<0.01	lost, per, cent, at, be, capable, defence, would, independent, including, shipyard, find, yards
	<0.05	are, such, figures, being

enterprises, a deprivation theme that also accounts for *life*, as in low life expectancy, and *family*, which is used in terms of family breakdown.

14. The occasion became known as the Easterhouse epiphany and in 2003, **Duncan Smith** announced he wanted the Conservatives to become the "party for the poor" (G news: politics, Jun 2012).

The *Daily Mail*'s PNC keywords for Glasgow draw on common discourses of benefits claimants being *capable* for *work*, as found in relation to the other cities discussed above (*work* is also used in the context of looking for work or the Department of Work and Pensions). Similarly, there is a focus on statistics (*figures, per, cent*). The *Daily Mail* also associates Glasgow with *food* banks, but this PNC keyword is accounted for by multiple instances of '1 million people are being fed from food banks such as this one in Glasgow'. Two further themes are distinctive to Glasgow. The first concerns job losses in shipyards (*lost, shipyard, yards*). The second relates to the debate about Scottish independence and its relationship to defence, particularly jobs in the defence industry (*defence, independent*). We do not find mentions of the 2014 independence debate in relation to other locations.

The final urban centre with similar geographical characteristics is the area around Newcastle, which includes Gateshead, Tyneside, and Sunderland. This area has 129 *Guardian* PNCs and 98 *Daily Mail* PNCs, making it a hotspot for both newspapers with no significant difference between them. As with Glasgow, this masks noticeable differences between the two newspapers (Table 8.7).

The *Guardian* PNC keywords come from a range of different stories and cover themes such as benefits (*paid, benefit, claimed, bedroom, housing, unemployed*), politics (*Labour, councils*), and charities and food banks (*bank, food, charity*). *She* is used to refer to individual women who lost their jobs in the public sector or were affected by the bedroom tax. The *Daily Mail* has very few PNC keywords for this cluster and does not draw on the same themes as the *Guardian* for this geographical area; food banks, for example, were not associated with Newcastle by the *Daily Mail*. However, one PNC keyword (*staff*) breaks this pattern,

Table 8.7 PNC Keywords for the Newcastle cluster. Italicised keywords are found in both newspapers ($n \geq 5$)

Newcastle	Sig.	PNC Keywords
Guardian vs UK (excl. London)	<0.01	bank, far, had, paid, benefit, food, a, go, told, claimed, against, labour, take
	<0.05	set, I, charity, bedroom, councils, workers, week, *no*, she, where
Guardian vs *Daily Mail*	<0.01	a, far, councils, labour, housing, I, benefit
	<0.05	bank, area, living, take, so, charity, set, unemployed, claimed, park, paid, had, some, year, where
Daily Mail vs UK (excl. London)	<0.01	Staff
	<0.05	his, left, by, last, *no*
Daily Mail vs *Guardian*	<0.01	–
	<0.05	Was

as it tended to be used to report on redundancies among public sector workers, a trend more commonly found in the *Guardian* (see Sect. 6.3).

The topics covered in each cluster discussed above tend to be different to those used in relation to London (Sect. 8.2). Given the dominance of London in our dataset, analysing all PNCs at the macro-level (as in the previous two chapters) can hide the nuances of place's importance in debates about poverty. The dominance of a particular location may not occur in all datasets analysed using GTA, but the preceding discussion shows the importance of analysing PNCs for a range of geographical clusters and conducting analyses at different levels of abstraction. In the final section of this chapter, we focus on the smaller, yet still significant, clusters in our data.

8.4 Poverty Away from Urban Centres

The three other areas that appear as hotspots in both newspapers, but which are away from major urban centres, are centred on Middlesbrough (including Cleveland, Redcar, and Stockton-on-Tees), Hull, and Kent and Maidstone. PNC keywords for these places are shown in Table 8.8. In each case slightly different overarching discourses are revealed.

The Middlesbrough area is used by both newspapers as an exemplar of poverty but the way this is done plays out differently in each publication. In the *Guardian* there is a discourse of supremacy for negative reasons, with terms like *highest, areas* and *where* being used to describe Middlesbrough as one of the areas with the highest levels of cuts or unemployment, or being an area where unemployment is high and/or life expectancy is low (cf. Glasgow and the *Daily Mail*, above). Unlike many other places, however, the *Guardian* makes no clear links between Middlesbrough and public sector cuts. This is anomalous and is perhaps explained (in contrast to the *Guardian's* treatment of Cornwall, see below) by the fact that Middlesbrough council is held by Labour.

The *Daily Mail* focuses on Middlesbrough as an exemplar at a far more localised level. In particular, it focuses on Limetrees Close (15) and singles out this street as a place with problems of high crime and unemployment (*Limetrees, Close, community, situated, edge, near, area*).

15. Limetrees Close is situated in the deprived community of Port Clarence, on the edge of Middlesbrough. Port Clarence suffers from a very high crime rate, and very high unemployment rate, and has suffered high levels of arson, fly-tipping and anti-social behaviour (DM news, Dec 2014).

The parallelism between 'very high crime rate' and 'very high unemployment rate' serves to indicate a perceived relationship between these two issues. Furthermore, the repetition of 'suffers/suffered' also suggests links between high unemployment and 'arson, fly-tipping and anti-social behaviour', as they are created by the same process of suffering (although the direction of any implied causality is not expressed). The links between these issues are not made explicitly, but rather by mentioning them in the same sentence, the *Daily Mail* is presenting them as linked; why mention these issues together if they are not (intended to be) connected in some way. Mentions of Limetrees Close are also linked to the second series of *Benefits Street* that was filmed nearby in Stockton (*series, average, residents*).

Table 8.8 PNC Keywords for hotspots away from major urban centres. Italicised keywords are found in both newspapers ($n \geq 5$)

Middlesbrough	Sig.	PNC Keywords
Guardian vs UK (excl. London)	<0.01	are, under, highest, areas, where, while, *average*
	<0.05	*Such*
Guardian vs *Daily Mail*	<0.01	are, there, highest, under, housing, their, from, he
	<0.05	it, to, people
Daily Mail vs UK (excl. London)	<0.01	Limetrees, situated, close, edge, Tata, products, losses, division, community, on, series, long, *average*, is, followed, across, near, area, as, job
	<0.05	child, residents, *such*, worst, an, per
Daily Mail vs *Guardian*	<0.01	–
	<0.05	close, Limetrees, losses, area, Tata, products, edge, cent, on, long, division, near, situated, per, followed, series, job, child, at
Hull	**Sig.**	**PNC Keywords**
Guardian vs UK (excl. London)	<0.01	far, into
	<0.05	in been
Guardian vs *Daily Mail*	<0.01	Been
	<0.05	into, he, at, was
Daily Mail vs UK (excl. London)	<0.01	like, find, places, to
	<0.05	Per
Daily Mail vs *Guardian*	<0.01	per, find, places
	<0.05	by, to, like
Kent*	**Sig.**	**PNC Keywords**
Guardian vs UK (excl. London)	<0.01	Town
	<0.05	homes, from, county
Guardian vs *Daily Mail*	<0.01	–
	<0.05	has, be, council, people
Daily Mail vs UK (excl. London)	<0.01	cancel, crime, month, money, I, association, police, couple, moved, last
	<0.05	house, had, to, no
Daily Mail vs *Guardian*	<0.01	money, police
	<0.05	Mr, find, couple, cancel, crime, up, moved, I

*For the Kent cluster PNC keywords are included where $n \geq 3$

There are two other themes associated with the Middlesbrough cluster which are frequently found in the *Daily Mail*. The first is concerned with particular industries, in this case job losses (and occasionally gains) at Tata Steel (*Tata, products, losses, division, long, followed, across, job*), which echoes the *Daily Mail*'s focus on industrial redundancies noted in Sect. 6.3. The second, as is a commonly-used feature of *Daily Mail* reports on poverty, is associated with statistics (*child, poverty, such, worst, per, cent*). This is not to say that the *Guardian* does not use statistics when reporting on poverty and/or specific topics such as benefits receipt or employment, but it does not use statistics as consistently as the *Daily Mail* appears to. The overarching approach employed by the *Daily Mail* appears to be to use individual (extreme) stories/examples, such as Limetrees Close, and contextualise them as if they are representative of wider statistical trends.

Both newspapers have stories about Hull being a place where people are forced to move to because of changes to Housing benefits in London: *far* is used in the *Guardian* in the context of having to move as *far* as Hull, and *like* is used by the *Daily Mail* in the context of rehousing people from London to places *like* Hull. So the distance between Hull and London is emphasised to reinforce the injustice of forced movement. Thus, for both newspapers, Hull perhaps reflects the emphasis on housing and benefits in London; Hull is present in debates about poverty precisely because it is not London. The *Daily Mail* also has its emphasis on statistics which, in this case, includes stories about Hull being one of the top ten worst *places* to *find* a job.

The Kent cluster does not have many PNC keywords, suggesting that perhaps discussions of poverty in this area are fairly typical of discussions of poverty elsewhere (outside London). That is, it is not overly associated with a particular aspect of poverty. We reduced the minimum threshold for PNC keywords for Kent to three to investigate whether there were any more minor trends in the data. However, it is only associated with familiar themes, such as the effects of council cuts in the *Guardian* (*warned, county*) and references to housing (*town, homes*). The *Daily Mail* also has stories about cuts, focusing more on the impact on crime and policing (*crime, police*), and has a story about the abuse of the benefits system, focusing on an unemployed family with five children who have been moved into a four-bedroomed housing association house (*association, couple, moved, house*).

In contrast to the apparent similarities in how the newspapers represent poverty in Kent, we conclude this section by focusing on those areas where they differ the most. Beginning with the *Guardian* (Table 8.9) we consider the locations which were hotspots for only one newspaper.

York is the clearest example of a place that the *Guardian* associates with poverty that is largely ignored by the *Daily Mail*. The reason for this was largely identified in Chapter 4, namely the *Guardian*'s focus on York attempting to make itself a poverty-free city. Chapter 4 focussed simply on PNCs around the search-term <*poverty*>. When all of our search terms are included in the analysis, the PNC keywords in Table 8.9 reveal that whilst *poverty* and *city* are particularly associated with the anti-poverty initiative, *bite* and *cuts* are associated with the impact of cuts and *living* references the living wage. Cornwall is another area that only the *Guardian* associates with poverty. Its PNC keywords reveal that the links made between poverty and place in this location are largely associated with the Conservative-controlled county council making cuts (16). The mention of which political party controls the council, combined with the choice of the verb 'imposed', makes clear who is making decisions in this situation and who, it is implied, is being unfairly acted upon ('local homeless charities' and ultimately 'rough sleepers').

16. This includes Tory-controlled Cornwall county council, which has imposed **cuts** of 40% on local homeless charities at a time when

Table 8.9 PNC Keywords for *Guardian* only clusters ($n \geq 5$)

York	**Sig.**	**PNC Keywords**
Guardian vs UK (excl. London)	<0.01	bite, poverty, living, any, city, at, not, we
	<0.05	have, says, over, cuts, year
Cornwall	**Sig.**	**PNC Keywords**
Guardian vs UK (excl. London)	<0.01	county, average, cuts, year, national, last
	<0.05	where, councils, like, I

official statistics show it has the highest number of rough sleepers in England after Westminster (G news: society, Mar 2013).

There are a number of places of interest away from major urban centres that the *Daily Mail* associates with poverty but the *Guardian* does not. These include smaller urban centres such as the clusters centred on Coventry (72 PNCs), Aberdeen (31 PNCs), and Swindon and West Berkshire (31 PNCs), which are all hotspots for the *Daily Mail* with significantly more poverty PNCs than the *Guardian*, and a larger, more rural cluster in East Anglia stretching from Cambridge to Norwich which, although it has 63 PNCs, is a cold spot in the *Daily Mail* but still has significantly more PNCs than the *Guardian*. The keywords for these four clusters are shown in Table 8.10.

Each of these places seems to have its own narrative and it is hard to identify common threads between them. The attention on Aberdeen is dominated by the pilot scheme for ESA that also led to Burnley being prominent in the *Daily Mail*. Almost all of the PNC keywords,

Table 8.10 PNC Keywords for *Daily Mail* only clusters ($n \geq 5$)

Coventry	**Sig.**	**PNC Keywords**
Daily Mail vs UK (excl. London)	<0.01	advert, city, foodbank, more, with, unemployed, free, jobs, for, vouchers, firm, make, staff, charity, school, lose, to, than, office, a, food, people
	<0.05	Their
Aberdeen	**Sig.**	**PNC Keywords**
Daily Mail vs UK (excl. London)	<0.01	tests, per, fit, if, cent, found, work, benefit, that, were, to,
	<0.05	and, will
Swindon/West Berkshire	**Sig.**	**PNC Keywords**
Daily Mail vs UK (excl. London)	<0.01	Honda, car, aged, hit, between, losses, factory, month, at, be, plant, last
	<0.05	for, will
East Anglia	**Sig.**	**PNC Keywords**
Daily Mail vs UK (excl. London)	<0.01	advertised, plus, jobseeker, only, allowance, job, pay, having, for, no
	<0.05	last, at, were, work

including *tests, per, fit, if, cent, found, work, benefit, that, were,* and *to* relate to this story. Contrastingly, there are several separate themes associated with Coventry indexing a range of attitudes to poverty. The first (*advert, city, more, with, unemployed, jobs*) involves negative evaluation of unemployed people within the city who are characterised as not looking for work. Example (17) is repeated in three different texts. The use of 'air quotes' questions the validity of the phrase 'looking for work'—it implies that people who are unemployed are not actually performing this action—whilst the mention of 10,000 people contrasted with the capitalised 'TWO' serves to reinforce the difference between the number of unemployed people and applications for a particular job. This example is taken as indicative of wider trends in the number of jobs applied for in Coventry (even though no context is provided about the types of job on offer) and serves to support ideologies of the lazy and/or idle poor.

17. Workshy Coventry? Advert for 20 **jobs** in a city with more than 10,000 unemployed 'looking for work' gets just TWO replies (DM news, Aug 2011).

There are also more sympathetic stories, one of which concentrates on schools helping parents get food from foodbanks (*foodbank, free, vouchers, charity, school, food*), suggesting that the *Daily Mail* does not apply the same level of agency to children experiencing poverty as they do to adults. Indeed, the existence of the term *child poverty* (discussed in Chapter 4) and the *Daily Mail*'s reports on the measurable number of children not bringing food to a Coventry school serves to reify the lived experience of poverty amongst a certain demographic, whilst simultaneously setting it apart from other, more abstract notions of poverty. Child poverty appears to be a phenomenon in and of itself, and investigating how this term is used in wider debates about UK poverty (independent of place) is worthy of further research. In Coventry, there are also references to redundancies, especially after the firm CityLink went into administration (*firm, staff, lose, office*), and mentions of a report by Coventry University into the white working class.

Redundancies are also a cause of the Swindon and West Berkshire cluster, particularly at the Honda car plant in Swindon (*Honda, car, hit, losses, factory, plant, will*). However, akin to the discussion of Aberdeen in Sect. 6.3, there are also more positive stories about the availability of apprenticeships for young people (*aged, between, month, last*). Finally, although the East Anglia cluster is quite diverse, the PNC keywords concentrate on two stories. The first concerns protests against a workfare scheme where jobs are offered for only Jobseekers' Allowance plus expenses (*advertised, plus, jobseeker, only, allowance, job, pay, no, work*). Whilst the *Daily Mail* does not take a clear stance on this scheme, protesters are described as a 'pressure group' and the newspaper notes that the jobs on offer were allegedly posted 'in error'. The second concerns a television programme about (migrant) fruit pickers (18).

18. A Panorama programme where the long-term **unemployed** were taken to farms in East Anglia to pick crops. The unemployed couldn't bend over to pick the vegetables, looking and sounding more like vegetables themselves, and others who were interviewed outside a JobCentre said they couldn't be bothered to get up for the wages on offer (DM news, Feb 2012).

The explicit negative evaluation 'sounding more like vegetables' and reference to the 'workshy' stereotype implied by 'couldn't be bothered' supports the *Daily Mail*'s overarching position on benefits claimants. The apparent physical inability of those concerned to pick crops, and their complaints about low wages, are not seen as legitimate. However, the article (18) is taken from (Atkinson-Small 2012) is actually an anti-immigration piece where, despite the negative evaluation of the people in (18), the social group actually blamed for workelessness are migrant workers: 'Immigration and youth unemployment go hand in hand'. In contrast to the position taken in (18), the author suggests that there are 'hundreds of thousands of British kids willing to step into these roles [fruit picking] and the tragedy is that they can't because of uncontrolled immigration'. This example highlights the importance of looking at how UK poverty is depicted within a wider context. For example, we have already seen that poverty and life expectancy are linked (cf. Glasgow, above). Here, Atkinson-Small states a causal link between immigration and unemployment rates of British-born nationals (see also the discussion of the languages spoken in Rochdale schools, above). However, this argument is never fully evidenced, as it is unclear how the reduction of migrant workers would, presumably, decrease the apparent laziness and increase the physical abilities of the people referred to in (18).

The thematic analysis of PNCs in previous chapters showed the major trends in how the two newspapers discuss poverty and place. However, the geographically-focused approach taken in this chapter has shown that the dominance of London in the PNCs somewhat overshadowed the nuances of the relationship(s) between poverty and place drawn upon in each newspaper. The clearest example of the different relationships established by the newspapers is evidenced by their focus on different types of benefit in particular areas. Not only do the two newspapers report on different benefits, their focus on particular benefits is filtered through place; discourses relating to benefits and benefit claimants are thus localised. Ultimately poverty is conceptualised as relative, with the newspapers portraying different areas of the UK as experiencing poverty in different ways. The preceding analysis is also further justification for the argument that critical analysis of media texts would benefit from a consideration of place (at multiple levels of abstraction).

8.5 Summary

There is an interesting paradox in much of what this chapter has revealed. On the one hand, the *Guardian* has more instances of both poverty search terms and place-names than the *Daily Mail*, and its interest in poverty and place (as numerically measured) far exceeds that of the *Daily Mail*. On the other hand, the *Daily Mail* seems to have a wider agenda both in terms of the places that it discusses and the discourses that it associates with those places. The *Guardian*'s coverage of poverty and place is dominated by London with a focus on housing and its apparent unaffordability in the light of low wages and benefit cuts. This comes together in stories about people being forced out of the capital due to high housing costs. Outside London, the *Guardian*'s stories often concentrate on local government cuts. Housing remains a theme, as do benefits, although it is interesting that Housing benefit seems to be seen as a London-based issue while other places are associated with other types of benefits (e.g. Incapacity Benefit in Manchester and Universal Credit in Merseyside). Charity and food banks are also important, but the *Guardian* most strongly associates these with Newcastle.

The *Daily Mail*'s construction of relationship(s) between poverty and place are more fragmentary both geographically and thematically. There are however some common threads. The *Daily Mail* concentrates on private companies far more than the *Guardian*, particularly, but not always, in relation to job losses. Examples include Tata Steel in Middlesbrough, Honda in Swindon, CityLink in Coventry, and the shipyards in Glasgow. A second theme that has a clear impact geographically is the pilots for the new ESA fitness-to-work tests, with the associated finding that many claimants are being assessed as able to work. This leads to large amounts of attention on Burnley and Aberdeen. More generally, the *Daily Mail* seems to associate poverty and place for two sets of reasons. Either there is a focus on stories about individuals or streets such as *Benefits Street* (James Turner Street) in Birmingham or Limetrees Close in Middlesbrough, or an area is discussed in very aggregate terms. The aggregation of poverty statistics and the choice to report on multiple individuals with similar circumstances (from the same street or area) serves to homogenise representations of those who are poor and/or in receipt of benefits. Stories of individuals are often negative, particularly when associated with Housing benefit and workless families with large numbers of children. London, Birmingham, and Middlesbrough are particularly associated with these stories.

There are also stories about individuals in poverty who are attempting to make the best of the situation despite difficulties which may, like in the case of Mr. Sharp in Liverpool (Sect. 8.3), be presented as caused by the inflexibility of the benefits system; in this case an individual's agency (and related neoliberal agenda) is being impeded by state-controlled conditions of welfare. By contrast, aggregate stories tend to concentrate on identifying particular places as having particular problems, which are generalised to the whole areas, and child poverty is seen as a particular concern. A similar practice can be seen in the *Daily Mail*'s reporting of alcohol dependency hotspots (cf. Chapter 7).

It is notable that some places are associated with particular issues in both newspapers, while others are treated differently. Both newspapers seem to regard Merseyside as one of the most deprived parts of the country, with *workless, deprived, highest,* and *most* featuring in the PNC keywords for both (Table 8.4) alongside references to different kinds of benefits (Universal Credit and Tax Credits in the *Guardian*, Incapacity Benefit in the *Daily Mail*). Middlesbrough also appears to be associated with deprivation by both newspapers, although in the *Guardian* this is more aggregate while the *Daily Mail* focuses on Limetrees Close in particular. At the other end of the scale, Glasgow has completely different associations in the two newspapers. The *Guardian*'s focus is dominated by Iain Duncan Smith's visit and its consequences, whilst the *Daily Mail* associates Glasgow with jobs and Scottish independence. Thus, the former endorses a position which sees Glasgow as particularly deprived and on the political radar for welfare reform, whilst the latter minimises issues of welfare.

Whilst we established in Chapters 4 and 5 that, in terms of raw hits of our queries, there was no overwhelming systematic association between poverty and place by either newspaper (although there was a stronger trend in the *Guardian*), what we have shown here is that when poverty, and its collocates, are associated with place, they tend to be used in a way which facilitates the conceptualisation of poverty as an urban phenomenon. This may be due to population density and the fact that more people living in a given area means more people could possibly experience poverty. It could also be due to the relative newsworthiness of reporting large redundancy/unemployment figures, or rates of benefits receipt in densely-populated areas, as opposed to focusing on (relatively) smaller numbers for such measures in rural areas. Nevertheless, we have shown that the links made between poverty and place are highly localised. The individualisation of poverty and place is evidenced by those stories which are repeated in a given newspaper and lead to multiple PNCs for a particular area. Although a focus on individuals was characteristic of the *Daily Mail* (a finding similar to that of Lundström (2013), see Chapter 1) the *Guardian* also reported on individuals to a lesser extent.

What we can therefore conclude is that there is no one discourse of poverty and place that is UK-wide. Rather, discourses of poverty change in relation to place and, of course, in relation to the underlying ideologies of the newspapers reporting on such places. The strong association the *Guardian* makes between poverty and York is not present in the *Daily Mail* because the latter tends to focus on areas of high poverty rates and York has a relatively low poverty rate. The *Daily Mail* also focuses on benefits receipt and uses extreme examples of benefits claimants to endorse an underlying support of Conservative-led policies to shrink the state, reflecting an adherence to ideologies of neoliberalism and capitalism. The poverty reported in York does not seem to fit this pattern. By contrast, the *Guardian* does not focus on extreme examples of benefits receipt and it does not seem to acknowledge that some families do claim large amounts. Nor does it make links between poverty and crime and/or migration. It focuses on public sector redundancies, benefits sanctions, and high house prices in order to oppose government cuts and to argue for a larger state, positions which are in keeping with its left-wing stance.

References

Atkinson-Small, J. 2012. It's Time to Pull Up the Drawbridge: Ban Immigration for Five Years and Give Our Youth a Chance. *Mail Online* 21/2/2012. http://www.dailymail.co.uk/debate/article-2104253/UK-ban-immigration-5-years-youth-chance.html. Accessed 13/3/2018.

Lundström, R. 2013. Framing Fraud: Discourse on Benefit Cheating in Sweden and the UK. *European Journal of Communication* 28 (6): 630–645.

Ramesh, R., & A. Sparrow. 2010. Housing Benefit Cuts Will 'Push Poor Out of South', Experts Warn. *Guardian* 8/11/2010. https://www.theguardian.com/society/2010/nov/08/housing-benefit-north-south-divide. Accessed 22/2/2018.

Watson, L. 2011. Lottery Hands Over £425,000 for Charity Food Bank in Birmingham. *Mail Online* 22/9/2011. http://www.dailymail.co.uk/news/article-2040024/Lottery-hands-425-000-charity-food-bank-Birmingham.html. Accessed 21/2/2018.

9
Conclusions

In the preceding chapters we have presented a new interdisciplinary method of analysis which draws together techniques from corpus linguistics, critical discourse analysis (CDA), and geographical information systems (GIS). Taking the discursive construction of UK poverty as a case study, we have provided a clear method which demonstrates how geographical text analysis (GTA) can bridge the gap between quantitative and qualitative data. We have shown how GTA facilitates comparison between the textual sources found in our corpora and official statistics associated with poverty and, by focusing on two newspapers, we have also demonstrated how GTA can be used to contrast the geographies of multiple corpora. Our analysis of place, in the form of place-names, has provided a new lens through which to analyse the language used by the mass media to discuss UK poverty.

In this final part of the book, we summarise our findings and evaluate what they can tell us about the role of place-names in discourses of poverty and place. In Sect. 9.1 we consider the similarities between the two newspapers' treatment of UK poverty, including their shared

L. L Paterson and I. N Gregory, *Representations of Poverty and Place*,
https://doi.org/10.1007/978-3-319-93503-4_9

lexical resources, their London-centric nature, and their unexpected focus on housing. Section 9.2 focuses on the nuances of the *Daily Mail*'s approach to UK poverty, whilst Sect. 9.3 does the same for the *Guardian*. In Sect. 9.4 we focus specifically on place and the patterns in the place-names used, before evaluating GTA in Sect. 9.5. We also note the limitations of the state of the art of GTA and propose some potential avenues for further research.

9.1 Trends in Newspaper Discourses of Poverty

Given their political leanings and established public images, it is no surprise that our analysis has shown that the *Daily Mail* and the *Guardian* take different stances on poverty. It was also expected that newspaper reports on UK poverty would include references to employment and benefits receipt. What is novel here is that we have shown *how* the two newspapers endorse their position on UK poverty by choosing to focus on particular topics as realised in particular geographical locations. Ultimately, the *Daily Mail* takes a right-of-centre stance that supports capitalism and neoliberal ideologies. One instance where this position is realised through allusion to place is in the example where the *Daily Mail* implied that unemployed people in Merthyr Tydfil should travel further to find work, as there were jobs available in Cardiff (Sect. 6.3). By contrast, the *Guardian* takes a left-wing view and advocates for a larger state and the common good, rather than profit, as shown in its treatment of public sector cuts in Birmingham (Sects. 6.4, 8.3) and its focus on the benefits cap in London (Sect. 7.3).

Whilst political differences such as these were to be expected, there were similarities between the two newspapers, perhaps the most prominent of which was the fact that both newspapers' coverage of poverty was London-centric. There are also similarities in the language used by the two newspapers when discussing poverty. Each had similar collocates for poverty (Sect. 5.1) and largely comparable numbers of query hits overall (although the *Guardian* did use the search terms more to talk about poverty and place). Furthermore, there was no evidence that highly evaluative terms, such as *scrounger* or *chav*, were systematically used to negatively evaluate the poor. Nor does either newspaper tend to draw on particular indexes of the working classes—such as smoking, wearing particular clothing, drinking alcohol, etc.—found elsewhere in public discourses of poverty (cf. Paterson et al. 2017, van der Bom et al. 2018).

Thus, neither newspaper engages primarily with UK poverty and place in the same way it has been portrayed through other media outlets. For example, poverty porn programming like *Benefits Street*, with its evaluative narration and editorial choices to focus on deviant behaviour, reinforces stereotypes about the undeserving poor in particular locations in England.[1] Such media representations and use of 'scrounger discourses' (see van der Bom et al. 2018) are socially powerful; references to such programmes have been used to support government positions on welfare reform (see the Hansard extract in Sect. 7.1). The newspapers' coverage of poverty is somewhat more highbrow and less sensationalist (with the potential exception of the *Daily Mail*'s use of extreme individual examples). The two newspapers do draw on stereotypes of the poor to a certain extent, but mostly this is implied, rather than comprising the explicit labelling of someone as a *scrounger* or the overt evaluation of particular behaviours and/or consumer practices. This is because the stereotypes attached to the UK poor are already well established; the newspapers assume that their readers have been exposed to such stereotypes and thus, to an extent, they have become reified and accepted as common sense.

Another unexpected finding is that reports on poverty—London-centric as they are—are dominated by references to the high cost of living and high house prices, especially in the *Guardian*. Not being able to afford (to own) a property in a major capital city does not automatically make someone poor, and there seems to be a wide level of public consensus on this; in the Breadline Britain surveys (cf. Lansley and Mack 2015) home ownership was not widely seen as an essential for having a good quality of life in twenty-first century Britain. It was not

[1]A similar trend can be found in fictional caricatures of the working classes. People tend to be represented as either feckless, as in sitcoms such as *Shameless* and the sketch show *Little Britain* (see Tyler 2008) or hardworking victims of circumstance at the mercy of government policies and an ineffectual welfare state (see Ken Loach's *I, Daniel Blake*, 2016).

expected that the affordability of housing would be such a core theme in discourses of poverty and place. However, references to housing and the cost of living (especially rents) were extremely prevalent in the co-text of the PNCs and therefore could not be ignored in our analysis. The occurrence of housing as a core theme in our data also acts as evidence for the merits of data-led research; by generating the search terms in the way that we did (using collocation to select suitable query terms, Sect. 5.1) we did not merely impose our own ideas about what concepts would be linked to poverty in language. In a similar vein, the relative absence of popular political terms such as *austerity* and *recession*, neither of which tended to occur in the PNC keywords, were surprising because we would have expected them to be drawn into debates, given the close association between government policies, welfare reform, and the overarching discourse of austerity which became popular after the 2008 recession.

The correlation of housing with other (more expected) terms relating to poverty, such as those in the Benefits, Employment, and Money subsets, begs the question about what it is to be poor in the UK. Whilst we find reports of extreme poverty in both of our corpora—and in most cases these are treated with sympathy and are underpinned by notions of the deserving poor—the majority of PNCs focused on relative poverty, particularly in terms of benefits receipt. The prevalence of reports about relative poverty supports the overarching notion that there is no such thing as a hard poverty line or threshold by which poverty can be objectively measured, yet both newspapers treated poverty as if it is (easily) measurable and quantifiable. The *Daily Mail* in particular endorses this position by its use of statistics as a matter of rule rather than exception. Despite the trend towards quantification, the discourses of poverty identified herein are evidence of its conceptualisation as a relative phenomenon, characterised not necessarily by different amounts of poverty, but different types. People are poor in London because they cannot afford expensive houses and the cost of living, people are poor in Liverpool because they are unemployed, people are poor in Birmingham because there are lots of council cuts to services, welfare, and jobs, people are poor in Rochdale because they are sick (as evidenced by high numbers of Incapacity Benefit claimants), and people are poor in

Glasgow because of sink estates, low life expectancy, and poor health profiles (see Chapter 8).

Similarly, different social groups' experiences of poverty were evaluated differently. For example, children had no agency in their own poverty and the label *child poverty* appears to refer to a particular type of poverty (a topic worthy of further investigation). Nevertheless, children were used discursively by the newspapers (the *Daily Mail* in particular) to index a particular stance on the causes of poverty: references were made to the number of children that people had and to the different languages spoken by migrant children in Rochdale (Sect. 8.3). Again, the newspaper did not need to explicitly set out the positions that people should be able to financially support the children they conceive or that migrants are to blame for fewer jobs and a higher welfare bill. These notions are implied because they are expressed elsewhere (within other media or within other articles in the *Daily Mail*) and there is an assumption that knowledge of such positions will act as a filter through which the newspaper's readership understand the preferred reading and the subtext of any given article concerning poverty.

Further supporting evidence for the position that poverty is something relative, qualitative, and abstract, as opposed to something fundamentally economic, was the fact that money terms did not always play a central role in the newspapers' reports on poverty. There was little reference to people *counting the pennies* or earning less money, suggesting that a conceptualisation of poverty based solely on economic resources is not representative of how the newspapers present this phenomenon to the wider public. When numbers are brought into reports, they tend not to relate to the specific price of goods or services, or the amount of money people have (with the exception of reports about the amounts received for Housing Benefit reported in the *Daily Mail*), rather they tended to focus on poverty in aggregate terms: the number of people claiming benefits in a particular geographical area, the employment rates for different cities, etc.

Money tended to be referred to implicitly, through references to benefits or jobs (which implies wages). When money was explicitly talked about, reports tended to focus on the Living Wage Campaign, which both newspapers ultimately endorsed albeit for different reasons: the

Guardian suggested that it would improve people's quality of life, whilst the *Daily Mail* took the position that higher wages would reduce the overall welfare bill, because it would make work more attractive than benefits receipt and would decrease the number of people drawing on Housing Benefit and particular government credit schemes. Ultimately, what underpins both newspapers' arguments is the reasoning that poverty can be alleviated (simply) by increased employment and higher wages. Thus, there are clearly points in discourses of poverty where the two newspapers agree on both its causes and its remedies. However, as was expected, there are also instances where the two newspapers are wholly dissimilar and one way their different stances on poverty is evidenced is through their choice to focus on particular aspects of poverty in particular geographical locations.

9.2 Poverty and Place in the *Daily Mail*

In the *Daily Mail*, there is a discourse of the idle poor; poverty is understood to be cause by individual laziness, and is underpinned by the notion of the undeserving poor. The newspaper takes the neoliberal stance that it is possible to get oneself out of poverty through hard work alone (and indeed there are multiple reports of people escaping poverty—see Chapter 4). Following Lansley and Mack (2015: 203) this position implies that 'inequality merely reflects differences in talent and endeavour' and, by the same token, means that economic and power differences 'with rewards at the top overstating economic contribution, and those at the bottom understating it, can be conveniently ignored'. The *Daily Mail*'s discussion of foodbanks in Birmingham (Sect. 8.3) does buck this trend somewhat and it is one of the only times the *Daily Mail* acknowledges that external forces, in this case 'the recession', have played a role in poverty rates.

The newspaper's position is realised in language though reports of individual examples, which are repeated across multiple texts. The most newsworthy examples tended to be the most extreme, such as families with large (legitimate) benefit claims. Whilst benefit fraud as a topic in its own right was not considered in this study, general deviant behaviour was implied in many reports about large benefit claims. Examples of a discourse of deviance include articles in the *Daily Mail* reporting that homeless people in London were part of migrant begging schemes (Sect. 8.2) and an article about a homeless person who lived in their mother's relatively-expensive house (Sect. 2.3).

The newspaper positively evaluates individuals who are seen to embody neoliberal principles. There are multiple reports of people going to extreme lengths to attract potential employers—such as wearing a sandwich board to advertise their availability for work (Sect. 6.3). In this example, the tone of the article is not sympathetic to the person because they are using desperate measures to find employment and/or because walking around wearing a sandwich board could be perceived as an embarrassing thing to do. Rather they are praised and presented as the antithesis of the idle poor. The *Daily Mail* positions punitive benefits policies as standing in opposition to such entrepreneurial exercises, as seen in the example where a job applicant was unable to attend a job interview because of a scheduled appointment at the Jobcentre (Sect. 8.3).

The *Daily Mail* takes the position that, if you have a welfare system for the poor, it will breed laziness and/or complacency and it will be abused. This position is evidenced in the reports of large Housing Benefit claims, the ranking of areas with the highest number (and lowest number) of benefits claimants, and reports on claiming disability benefits for stress and alcoholism (Sect. 7.2). The latter example also relates to the notion of 'luxuries' and links to flawed consumerism, by referring to the consumption of alcohol. The newspaper ultimately supports Conservative-led welfare reform policies and takes the position that cuts to benefits will be an incentive for recipients to work. It notes that there are jobs available in particular locations, such as Aberdeen, and reports that unemployment figures are falling, with the implication that jobs are available if people are willing to be flexible and/or travel (see the Cardiff example, discussed above). However, there is little real consideration of where jobs are available, and the fact that not everyone is able to move around the country for work.

The overarching notion that the benefits system is systematically abused allows the *Daily Mail* to construct UK taxpayers (who it assumes to be its readers) as the ultimate victims of poverty and the related need for the welfare state; they are the ones paying for it, while others are benefiting. Such a position supports the right-wing politics of the *Daily Mail* and the examples presented in the newspaper are given as evidence of the need for a smaller state and, relatedly, decreased taxation. This position does not, however, take into account the fact that a large majority of benefit payments relate to the state pension, and there is little to no acknowledgement in the *Daily Mail* of in-work poverty. Rather, a dichotomy between benefits recipients and 'hardworking people' is established.

The *Daily Mail* also presents UK poverty as associated with and implicitly cause by immigrants. Ultimately the blame is placed on the immigration policies of previous (Labour) governments and the UK's acceptance of immigrants from around the EU. The *Daily Mail*'s position on the relationship between poverty and immigration is reflected in their reporting of high welfare receipt in areas with large immigrant populations, reports of children speaking a range of different languages at school (here the children are implicitly indicative of a wider 'problem'), and (ex)migrants with high Housing Benefit claims. The claims reported in our PNCs are legitimate—we were focused on poverty, not criminality. However, the *Daily Mail*'s references to benefit fraud and other criminal activities in texts concerning poverty highlights that discourses do not exist in isolation. Rather, they are deployed in combination with other discourses—such as discourses of deviance—to imply (and sometimes explicitly state) links between concepts. Examining these links is beyond our focus on discourses of poverty and place, but understanding what other discourses were drawn upon in our data (discourses of criminality, anti-immigration discourses, etc.) gives an indication of the wider scope of discussion within which discourses of poverty sit.

Acknowledging these related discourses also demonstrates scope for future research. As Fairclough and Wodak (1997: 276) rightly argue, discourses 'are always connected to other discourses which were produced earlier, as well as those which are produced synchronically and subsequently'. No discourse, indexing an ideological position, is held in a vacuum independent of other semiotic resources and/or language use.

For example, discourses relating to race can link to discourses of migration, which may overlap with discourses of poverty and the undeserving poor. Whilst Fairclough and Wodak's position concerns abstract or conceptual links between discourses, GTA shows that there can also be measurable physical links between the deployment of particular ideologies and their use in relation to physical space. Thus, repeated references to poverty (or any social phenomenon) can be used to encapsulate and perpetuate particular ideologies about a particular locale.

9.3 Poverty and Place in the *Guardian*

In contrast to the *Daily Mail*, the *Guardian* takes the position that poverty is caused by societal structures, not individuals' faults or personal failings. The poor have drawn the short straw in an unequal system; they are not lazy or entitled. Fundamentally, taking this position means accepting that there is an unequal system of distribution and, relatedly, it must be accepted that to change the system would alleviate poverty. The *Guardian* positions its readers and the wider public as opposed to welfare reform, hence its coverage of anti-cuts protests. In many cases, the newspaper reports on planned demonstrations against government policy, which has the added result, not only of making their readers aware of such protests, but of publicising these demonstrations. The Conservative-led government's welfare reform policies are blamed for poverty and they are linked explicitly to place by the repetition of reports of Iain Duncan Smith visiting the Easterhouse area of Glasgow (see Sect. 9.4). Here a specific place is strongly associated with poverty and government policy.

Benefits statistics are not sensationalised to angle for welfare cuts and poverty is depicted as clustering in particular areas due to lack of opportunity, jobs, and access to resources—a discourse of disadvantage. The government is also blamed for poverty clusters in London, where the benefits cap is presented as making (parts of) London no-go areas for many people (Sects. 6.4, 7.3). Thus, it is implied that people should be allowed equal opportunity to travel, live, and work anywhere and that government policy is effectively restricting their geography (and their movement).

This is in direct contrast to the *Daily Mail*'s treatments of benefits claimants living in affluent areas (Sect. 6.4).

The *Guardian* also seems to associate the public sector—particularly Jobcentres and councils—with poverty prevention/alleviation, and it sees government initiatives, such as welfare reform, fitness to work reassessments, and changes to the benefits system as compounding poverty, rather than alleviating it. This is evidenced somewhat through repeated references to public sector cuts; more cuts equals fewer jobs equals more unemployed people (Sect. 6.3). However, it is worth considering why the *Guardian* focuses so strongly on cuts to council jobs, as opposed to the private sector job losses reported by the *Daily Mail*. The newspaper seems particularly focused on the poverty experienced (or threatening) its (largely) middle class readership, many of whom potentially work in the public sector. The *Guardian*'s related focus on poverty in relatively affluent areas was also unexpected. This focus, most clearly shown in its focus on anti-poverty initiatives in York (Sects. 4.3, 8.4), contributes to the conceptualisation of poverty as a relative, qualitative, phenomenon. It also connects poverty to shame (cf. Jo 2013) through the use of the term 'hidden poverty'. This term suggests that poverty is not what people think it is (i.e. absolute poverty or extreme relative poverty in areas of high unemployment and benefits receipt), nor is it actually what is measured by official statistics. The *Guardian* seems open to accept that people can be poor without meeting particular thresholds and, furthermore, people can be poor in areas of relatively high employment.

The *Guardian* does not draw on negative stereotypes of the poor and/or the working class when discussing poverty. However, it explicitly acknowledges negative representations of the working class in other media outlets (such as in poverty porn programming, and in right-wing newspapers) and argues that the so-called 'benefits culture' or 'benefits lifestyle' does not exist. It is sympathetic to those who use foodbanks and those receiving benefits (particularly Jobseekers Allowance and Incapacity Benefit). It rejects the idea that migrants are 'benefit tourists' who also contribute to poverty rates by taking jobs, etc. (see Sect. 7.1). The newspaper's reporting on poverty and place does not tend to mention illegitimate benefits claims; there is silence on fraud for the most part.

Additionally, no strong links are made between poverty and place and areas of high rates of migrant settlement.

Having established the ideologies drawn upon, the discourses used, and the different assumptions held implicit by each newspaper, we can argue that—based on our analysis—place is used to shape how each newspaper presents poverty to their readers. The *Daily Mail* endorses a neoliberal position and paints the poor as predominantly idle and undeserving. There are some realisations of flawed consumerism—particularly in reports about expensive London houses paid for by Housing Benefit (especially for (ex)migrant families) and in reports about people receiving benefits who are planning their wedding and buying flying lessons (Sect. 6.3)—but this was not a strong trend in the data. By contrast, the *Guardian* takes a more socialist position—advocating for a more equal distributions of wealth, but it also seeks to reinforce the concept of relative poverty, positioning it as a problem not only for the working classes, but also for those who are employed in traditionally middle class professions.

9.4 A Spotlight on Place

Both newspapers show geographical biases in their reporting of poverty that are over and above the geographical biases found in their reporting more generally (calculated using the newspapers' background geographies, Sect. 4.5). Around half of the *Guardian*'s reporting that links poverty with place focuses on places in London; for the *Daily Mail* this is around a third. Part of the reason for this is that the news agenda in both newspapers is generally London-centric—as evidenced by the background geography of each newspaper. However, even once this has been taken into account, places within London are associated with poverty more than would be expected. Outside London, there are also some clear biases. Major urban centres also tend to be particularly associated with poverty, particularly Liverpool.

Other places with high rates of poverty, be they urban peripheries, former industrial towns, or rural areas, tend to be overlooked unless there is a clear reason to talk about them. Burnley, a deprived former mill town, receives large amounts of attention because of the trial of Incapacity Benefit reassessment in the town. Middlesbrough (another deprived former industrial town) and its surrounding area are associated with poverty, at least in part, because of the second series of *Benefits Street*, and Margate, a seaside town, is linked to poverty because of Mary Portas' work there. Other locations with similar economic and poverty profiles as these three places are frequently ignored by both newspapers.

It is also interesting that even within London, places with similar poverty profiles are treated very differently. From their different perspectives, both newspapers focus on Tower Hamlets while neighbouring Newham, with similar levels of poverty and a similar demographic profile, is largely overlooked. One possible explanation for this is that Tower Hamlets consists of much of London's traditional East End and therefore has a long tradition of being associated with poverty. A second possibility is that Tower Hamlets is where wealthy London (including the City and Canary Wharf) is adjacent to deprived London, and thus the poverty is more visible.

The newspapers' focus on poverty in London, at the expense of the rest of the UK, may have significant implications for our understanding of poverty and the measures required to alleviate it. London's economy is thriving so the city has low unemployment but a serious lack of affordable housing. This means that people in London experience poverty in a very different way to people in other parts of the country where poverty is more commonly associated with industrial decline or stagnation leading to unemployment and a lack of opportunity. London is seen as the exception—it is the site of a housing crisis and it includes areas of extreme poverty—but it is reported as the rule. The media discourse, from both left- and right-wing perspectives, is dominated by London and London's problems. Added to this, decision makers, particularly politicians, are based on London and may have little experience of poverty as realised elsewhere, and the policy makers are not immune to the representations of poverty presented by the mass media. This suggests that much of the perception of poverty and responses to it are driven by London-based agendas that have limited relevance to the rest of the UK. Such a claim is evidenced by reports that when Iain Duncan Smith visited Easterhouse in Glasgow he was so shocked by what he saw that it led to significant government policy initiatives that were very different to many of the existing debates around poverty.

9.5 Evaluating Geographical Text Analysis

As well as providing a new way to interrogate the discursive construction of UK poverty, this book also has major methodological implications which have the potential to impact the analysis of any topic in human geography or other subjects where there is an interest in the geographies within texts. The methods used here allow us to identify place-names and the themes associated with them in very large corpora. While the idea of 'distant reading' of large digital corpora is not new (Moretti 2005), there has been a backlash against it which argues that such sources cannot be understood without a detailed knowledge of the source, determined by a close reading of at least parts of it (e.g. Hammond et al. 2016).

In this book, we have demonstrated that using GTA means that these two approaches—distant reading and close reading—are not incompatible. Indeed mapping allows and encourages a 'multiscale approach' (Taylor et al. in press) in which the aggregate analyses map and describe the broad patterns of where the text (or corpus) is talking about in relation to a particular theme. These maps then drive questions about why the texts in a corpus refer to these places, what is being said about them, and what places are not mentioned in the corpus. Subsequent analyses, including the close reading of concordance lines, allows researchers to answer these questions and thus develop a detailed understanding of the geography of the topic, theme, or (social) issue under study, which includes understanding how and why there are differences between places, sources, and, potentially, time points. This approach can be applied to any theme for which suitable digital corpora are available. Given the dramatic rise in the availability in digital material (Risen and Lichtblau 2013), much of it in textual form, this opens up huge potential for new forms of analysis.

As well as human geography, our approach also has significant implications for corpus linguistics and CDA. Previously, these fields have had little interaction with geography. GTA allows the researcher to first map the place-names within the text and then to conduct more sophisticated analyses based on location. The similarities and differences between the two newspapers set out above would arguably have been made visible by other methods of analysis, such as CDA or corpus-based discourse analysis, but what the present study has shown is how these underlying ideologies are promoted and endorsed by the choice of each newspaper to report on particular places. Place, something which may be seen as relatively innocuous and easily passed over in linguistic analysis, plays an important part in media-endorsed conceptualisations of what poverty in twenty-first century Britain is, what it looks like, its causes, and who is affected. As such, and as we have shown here, critical studies of social phenomena, such as poverty, can benefit greatly from a close consideration of place.

Whilst the availability of geoparsers suitable for this type of analysis is currently somewhat restricted, this is testament to the state of the art. In the first instance, we would encourage researchers interested in GTA to work interdisciplinarily with scholars who have access to such tools. Secondarily, it is hoped that as the method becomes more developed and widely-known more geoparsers (and related tools) will become available for widespread use. Additionally, it is hoped that future work describing and documenting the concordance geoparsing process will make the method more accessible to those without backgrounds in GIS and/or corpus linguistics.

Methodologically, this book provides two particular innovations. The first is the use of collocation analysis, with some manual intervention, to establish which search terms would be fruitful for the exploration of a particular theme (in a given corpus). The analysis of collocates—across multiple corpora in this instance—enables the researcher to gain a greater understanding of the language associated with a particular topic, based on a combination of prior knowledge and a systematic analysis of the corpus itself. In this book the generation of lexical collocates for <*poverty*> led to us adding a significant number of search terms that we had not previously considered as relevant to the theme of poverty and place. The second innovation is the establishing of background geographies for our corpora using a concordance geoparsed sample of instances of *the*. This allowed us to generate an understanding of the geography of each corpus as a whole without needing to geoparse them in their entirety. This, in turn, enables us to identify places that were more or less strongly associated with a particular theme than would be expected given the background geography. These two methodological innovations can be applied to any corpus for the purposes of GTA at the point of data selection (the collocation analysis) and analysis (the comparison with background geography).

There are a number of areas where our methods could be developed further. The first concerns ongoing development of the geoparser, which could lead to a more robust and trainable tool. This would decrease the need for manual checking of concordance lines. A more significant development would be to move beyond what it is currently possible to geoparse automatically. In terms of the current state of the art, a geoparser identifies place-names and thus, any subsequent analysis of geography is solely the analysis of the geography of named places. Assigning locations (and ultimately coordinates) to uses of deictic terms, such as location markers like *here* and *there*, and generic references, such as *in the city*, *the town*, or *this place*, is beyond the remit of existing geoparsers (and automatic geoparsing techniques). This potentially means that apparent differences in geography could be influenced by differences in writing style. For example, if texts from one source, show a tendency to use a proper noun, such as *Newcastle*, at the beginning of an article, but switch to deictic references throughout the rest of the article, the frequency of mentions of Newcastle would be different when compared with another source that uses *Newcastle* consistently throughout. The use of deictic terms may influence the frequency or density of place-name mentions, and this needs to be kept in mind when viewing maps generated using place-names only. Developing the ability to go beyond geoparsing place-names and to be able to handle deixis would provide valuable new abilities to GTA and would illuminate our understanding of both geographies and writing styles.

A final limitation to consider is that GTA does not take into account additional semiotic resources beyond text. Whilst this is unlikely to influence the maps generated using GTA it could have a significant impact on the analysis of discourse. As noted above, for the most part we found no trend suggesting the explicit demonization of the poor in our corpora, and we have argued that the newspapers could leave particular evaluations implicit because of their readers' wider awareness of media representations of the poor. However, implicit references within a text are not the only way that allusions to particular ideologies about poverty and the poor can be made. For example, a report about high welfare receipt in a particular area does not need to reference what benefits recipients spend their money on explicitly if the article is accompanied by an image—usually displayed prominently near the headline—which includes someone drinking alcohol, smoking a cigarette, or wearing a particular brand of clothing. Readers of online newspaper texts do not get the meaning of an article solely from the text alone. This points to a limitation of using textual data only. Whilst we have adapted textual data for use in GIS using tools from corpus linguistics, multimodal corpora are still in their infancy and, whilst we could geotag images, their content would have to be manually analysed in order to determine whether there was a relationship between images and place. This is an area for further research, but it currently lies beyond the boundaries of corpus linguisticsand GIS. Therefore, analyses using GTA must be aware that the text—although primary—is not the only semiotic resource which can index ideologies.

There is, therefore much potential for future research. Some of this is technical. As well as improved geoparsing and the ability of geoparsers to automatically cope with deixis, there are also areas where the methods used to analyse the data, from both spatial and corpus perspectives, could be further developed. More important, however, is the wider application of GTA beyond the boundaries of human geography, CDA, and applied linguistics. As stated above, the methods demonstrated herein can be applied to any research areas where there is a corpus of digital texts and an interest in the geographies they contain. This means that there is the potential for a step-change in our understanding of the geographies within texts. GIS-based analyses are quantitative by nature but, as described in this book, GTA offers the ability to apply GIS and digital methods to textual sources. This challenges the notion that such methods and tools are merely quantitative in nature, and bridges the gap between quantitative analysis and traditionally qualitative close reading approaches.

9.6 Summary

Through our exemplar analysis of UK poverty in two corpora of national newspaper texts we have demonstrated the benefits of using GTA for analysing the linguistic representation of a social phenomenon. Fundamentally, we have shown how a consideration of geography can illuminate how different aspects of a given issue are highlighted in relation to place, to concretise abstract concepts such as poverty by anchoring their lived experience in geographical space. We accepted the argument that the mass media plays a role in the construction of British society: media outlets inform us who to vote for, who to cheer for, who to vilify, and who to laugh at, newspaper articles draw our attention to stories of crime, deviance, and violence, etc. Following Fairclough (2001: 30) we note that the 'constant doses of "news" which most people receive each day are a significant factor in social control, and they account for a not insignificant proportion of a person's average daily involvement in discourse' (referring here to the production, distribution, and consumption of different texts). We have shown how the readers of each of our newspapers are being presented with a different view of what UK poverty is, where it is, what causes it, and what can alleviate it. Part of the role of a critical discourse analyst is to interrogate language in use and 'make what may be non-obvious evident' (O'Halloran 2012: 92). Our analysis of discourses of poverty and place has shown how each newspaper presents poverty but, more importantly, how their representation of poverty is filtered through the lens of place—a topic rarely explicitly and systematically considered within CDA. Ultimately the versions of UK poverty presented by each newspaper may influence their readers' opinions about the poor, their stance on poverty, and how (or indeed if) they believe UK poverty should be tackled, and by whom.

References

Fairclough, N. 2001. *Language and Power* (second edition). London: Longman.

Fairclough, N., & R. Wodak. 1997. Critical Discourse Analysis. In T. A. van Dijk (ed.). *Discourse as Structure and Process: A Multi-disciplinary Approach*. London: Sage, pp. 258–284.

Hammond, A., A. J. Brooke, & G. Hirst. 2016. Modeling Modernist Dialogism: Close Reading with Big Data. In S. Ross & J. O'Sullivan (eds.). *Reading Modernism with Machines: Digital Humanities and Modernist Literature*. Basingstoke: Palgrave, pp. 49–78.

Jo, Y. N. 2013. Psycho-social Dimensions of Poverty: When Poverty Becomes Shameful. *Critical Social Policy* 33 (3): 514–531.

Lansley, S., & J. Mack. 2015. *Breadline Britain: The Rise of Mass Poverty*. London: Oneworld.

Moretti, F. 2005. *Graphs, Maps, Trees*. Verso: London.

O'Halloran, K. 2012. Electronic Deconstruction: Revealing Tensions in the Cohesive Structure of Persuasion Texts. *International Journal of Corpus Linguistics* 17 (1): 91–124.

Paterson, L. L., D. Peplow, & K. Grainger. 2017. Does Money Talk Equal Class Talk? Audience Responses to Poverty Porn in Relation to Money and Debt. In A. Mooney & E. Sifaki (eds.). *The Language of Money and Debt: An Interdisciplinary Approach*. Basingstoke: Palgrave, pp. 205–232.

Risen, J., & E. Lichtblau. 2013. How the U.S. Uses Technology to Mine More Data More Quickly. *New York Times* 8/6/2013.

Taylor, J. E., I. N. Gregory, & C. Donaldson. in press. Combining Close and Distant Reading: A Multiscalar Analysis of the English Lake District's Historical Soundscape. *International Journal of Humanities and Arts Computing*.

Tyler, I. 2008. 'Chav mum, chav scum': Class Disgust in Contemporary Britain. *Feminist Media Studies* 8 (1): 17–34.

van der Bom, I., L. L. Paterson, K. Grainger, & D. Peplow. 2018. 'It's Not the Fact They Claim Benefits but Their Useless, Lazy, Drug Taking Lifestyles We Despise': Analysing Audience Responses to Benefits Street Using Live Tweets. *Discourse, Context & Media* 21: 36–45.

References

Altheide, D. L. 2000. Tracking Discourse and Qualitative Document Analysis. *Poetics* 27 (4): 287–299.

Atkinson-Small, J. 2012. It's Time to Pull up the Drawbridge: Ban Immigration for Five Years and Give Our Youth a Chance. *Mail Online* 21/2/2012. http://www.dailymail.co.uk/debate/article-2104253/UK-ban-immigration-5-years-youth-chance.html. Accessed 13/3/2018.

Baker, P. 2006. *Using Corpora in Discourse Analysis*. London: Continuum.

Baker, P., C. Gabrielatos, M. KhosraviNik, M. Kryzanowski, T. McEnery, & R. Wodak. 2008. A Useful Methodological Synergy? Combining Critical Discourse Analysis and Corpus Linguistics to Examine Discourses of Refugees and Asylum Seekers in the UK Press. *Discourse and Society* 19 (3): 273–306.

Baker, P., & T. McEnery (eds). 2015a. *Corpora and Discourse Studies*. Basingstoke: Palgrave.

Baker, P., & T. McEnery. 2015b. Who Benefits When Discourse Gets Democratised? Analysing a Twitter Corpus Around the British Benefits Street Debate. In P. Baker & T. McEnery (eds.). *Corpora and Discourse Studies: Integrating Discourse and Corpora*. Basingstoke: Palgrave, pp. 244–265.

L. L Paterson and I. N Gregory, *Representations of Poverty and Place*,
https://doi.org/10.1007/978-3-319-93503-4

Ballinger, L. 2009. Taxpayers Pay £1,600-a-Week for Family of Ex-asylum Seekers to Live in Luxury Five-Storey Home. *Mail Online* 20/11/09. http://www.dailymail.co.uk/news/article-1231795/Taxpayers-pay-1-600-week-family-ex-asylum-seekers-live-luxury-storey-home.html. Accessed 22/1/2018.

Bauman, Z. 2004. *Work, Consumerism and the New Poor.* Buckingham: Open University Press.

Bednarek, M. 2006. *Evaluation in Media Discourse: Analysis of a Newspaper Corpus.* New York: Continuum.

Bennett, J. 2012. 'And What Comes Out May Be a Kind of Screeching': The Stylisation of Chavspeak in Contemporary Britain. *Journal of Sociolinguistics* 16 (1): 5–27.

Berman, M. L., R. Mostern, & H. Southall. 2016. Introduction. In M. L. Berman, R. Mostern, & H. Southall (eds.). *Placing Names: Enriching and Integrating Gazetteers.* Bloomington: Indiana University Press, pp. 1–11.

Besag J., & J. Newell. 1991. The Detection of Clusters in Rare Diseases. *Journal of the Royal Statistical Society Series A* 154: 143–155.

Biber, D., S. Conrad, & R. Reppen. 1994. Corpus-Based Approaches to Issues in Applied Linguistics. *Applied Linguistics* 15 (2): 169–189.

Biressi, A. 2011. 'The Virtuous Circle': Social Entrepreneurship and Welfare Programming in the UK. In H. Wood & B. Skeggs (eds.). *Reality Television and Class.* London: British Film Institute/Palgrave Macmillan, pp. 144–155.

Block, D. 2013. *Social Class in Applied Linguistics.* London: Routledge.

Bourdieu, P. 1986/2010. The Forms of Capital. In I. Szeman & T. Kaposy (eds.). *Cultural Theory: An Anthology.* Oxford: Wiley Blackwell, pp. 81–93.

Bourdieu, P., & L. Wacquant. 2004. Symbolic Violence. In N. Scheper-Hughes & P. Bourgois (eds.). *Violence in War and Peace: An Anthology.* Oxford: Blackwell, pp. 272–274.

Breit, E. 2010. On the (Re)construction of Corruption in the Media: A Critical Discursive Approach. *Journal of Business Ethics* 92 (4): 619–635.

Brezina, V. 2018. *Statistics in Corpus Linguistics: A Practical Guide.* Cambridge: Cambridge University Press.

Chainey, S., & J. Ratcliffe. 2005. *GIS and Crime Mapping.* Chichester: Wiley.

Chambers, R. 2006. What Is Poverty? Who Asks? Who Answers? Poverty in Focus. International Poverty Centre: United Nations Development Programme. http://www.ipc-undp.org/pub/IPCPovertyInFocus9.pdf. Accessed 23/9/2015.

Conrad, S. 2002. Corpus Linguistic Approaches for Discourse Analysis. *Annual Review of Applied Linguistics* 22: 75–95.

Cooper, D., & I. Gregory. 2011. Mapping the English Lake District: A Literary GIS. *Transactions of the Institute Of British Geographers* 36 (1): 89–108.

Cope, M., & S. Elwood (eds). 2009. *Qualitative GIS: A Mixed Methods Approach*. London: Sage.

Cresswell, T. 2004. *Place: A Short Introduction*. London: Blackwell.

Cromley, E. K., & S. L. McLafferty. 2012. *GIS and Public Health*. London: Guilford.

DeMers, M. 2008. *Fundamentals of Geographical Information Systems* (fourth edition). Chichester: Wiley.

Department for Communities and Local Government. 2017. Policy Paper: 2010 to 2015 Government Policy: Support for Families. https://www.gov.uk/government/publications/2010-to-2015-government-policy-support-for-families/2010-to-2015-government-policy-support-for-families. Accessed 2/11/2017.

Diggle P., P. Zheng, & P. Durr. 2005. Nonparametric Estimation of Spatial Segregation in a Multivariate Point Process: Bovine Tuberculosis in Cornwall, UK. *Journal of the Royal Statistical Society Series A* 54: 645–658.

Donaldson C., I. N. Gregory, & J. E. Taylor. 2017. Locating the Beautiful, Picturesque, Sublime and Majestic: Spatially Analysing the Application of Aesthetic Terminology in Descriptions of the English Lake District. *Journal of Historical Geography* 56: 43–60.

Dorling, D., & D. Fairburn. 1997. *Mapping: Ways of Representing the World*. Harlow: Longman.

Dorling, D., R. Mitchell, M. Shaw, S. Orford, & G. Davey Smith. 2000. The Ghost of Christmas Past: Health Effects of Poverty in London in 1896 and 1991. *British Medical Journal* 321: 1547–1551.

Dreier, P. 2005. How the Media Compound Urban Problems. *Journal of Urban Affairs* 27 (2): 193–201.

DWP. 2015. Fraud and Error in the Benefits System. https://www.gov.uk/government/uploads/system/uploads/attachment_data/file/575407/fraud-and-error-stats-release-2015-16-final-estimates.pdf. Accessed 13/8/2016.

DWP. 2016. Freedom of Information Requests 2016-398/2026-397. https://www.gov.uk/government/uploads/system/uploads/attachment_data/file/502566/389-397-2016.pdf. Accessed 13/11/2016.

DWP. 2018. Housing Benefit Caseload Statistics. https://www.gov.uk/government/uploads/system/uploads/attachment_data/file/659362/housing-benefit-caseload-data-to-august-2017.ods. Accessed 23/3/2018.

Fairclough, N. 2001. *Language and Power* (second edition). London: Longman.
Fairclough, N., & R. Wodak. 1997. Critical Discourse Analysis. In T. A. van Dijk (ed.). *Discourse as Structure and Process: A Multi-disciplinary Approach*. London: Sage, pp. 258–284.
Fotheringham, A. S. 1997. Trends in Quantitative Methods I: Stressing the Local. *Progress in Human Geography* 21: 88–96.
Fotheringham, A. S., & F. Zhan. 1996. A Comparison of Three Exploratory Methods for Cluster Detection in Spatial Point Patterns. *Geographical Analysis* 28: 200–218.
Fotheringham, A. S., C. Brusdon, & M. Charlton. 2000. *Quantitative Geography: Perspectives on Spatial Data Analysis*. London: Sage.
Fukuda-Parr, S. 2006. The Human Poverty Index: A Multidimensional Measure. *Poverty in Focus*. International Poverty Centre: United Nations Development Programme. Online. http://www.ipc-undp.org/pub/IPCPovertyInFocus9.pdf. Accessed 11/11/2015.
Galbraith, J. K. 1958. *The Affluent Society*. London: Penguin.
Geonames. n.d. Geonames Homepage. http://www.geonames.org. Accessed 11/7/2017.
Getty Research Institute. n.d. Getty Thesaurus of Geographic Names. Online. http://www.getty.edu/research/tools/vocabularies/tgn. Accessed 11/7/2017.
Goodchild, M. F. 1992. Geographical Information Science. *International Journal of Geographical Information Systems* 6: 31–45.
Gordon, D. 2006. The Concept and Measurement of Poverty. In C. Pantazis, D. Gordon, & R. Levitas (eds.). *Poverty and Social Exclusion in Britain*. Bristol: The Policy Press, pp. 29–70.
Gordon, D. 2011. Consultation Response: Social Mobility and the Child Poverty Review. *Policy Response Series* 2, PSE 2011, pp. 4–5. http://www.poverty.ac.uk/pse-research/pse-uk/policy-response.
Gov.UK. n.d. Benefit Cap. https://www.gov.uk/benefit-cap. Accessed 23/11/2017.
Gregory, I. N. 2009. Comparisons Between Geographies of Mortality and Deprivation from the 1900s and 2001: Spatial Analysis of Census and Mortality Statistics. *British Medical Journal* 339, b3454: 676–679.
Gregory, I. N., & C. Donaldson. 2016. Geographical Text Analysis: Digital Cartographies of Lake District literature. In D. Cooper, C. Donaldson, & P. Murrieta-Flores (eds.). *Literary Mapping in the Digital Age*. Abingdon: Routledge, pp. 67–87.

Gregory, I. N., C. Donaldson, P. Murrieta-Flores, & P. Rayson. 2015. Geoparsing, GIS and Textual Analysis: Current Developments in Spatial Humanities Research. *International Journal of Humanities and Arts Computing* 9: 1–14.

Gregory, I. N., K. Kemp, & R. Mostern. 2003. Geographical Information and Historical Research: Current Progress and Future Directions. *History and Computing* 13: 7–22.

Grover, C., R. Tobin, K. Byrne, M. Woollard, J. Reid, S. Dunn, & J. Ball. 2010. Use of the Edinburgh Geoparser for Georeferencing Digitized Historical Collections. *Philosophical Transactions of the Royal Society A* 368: 3875–3889.

Hammond, A., A. J. Brooke, & G. Hirst. 2016. Modeling Modernist Dialogism: Close Reading with Big Data. In S. Ross & J. O'Sullivan (eds.). *Reading Modernism with Machines: Digital Humanities and Modernist Literature*. Basingstoke: Palgrave, pp. 49–78.

Hansard. 2014. Topical Questions, 13 January, Vol. 573. https://hansard.parliament.uk/Commons/2014-01-13/debates/14011313000007/WorkAndPensions. Accessed 4/1/2018.

Hardie A. 2012. CQPweb—Combining Power, Flexibility and Usability in a Corpus Analysis Tool. *International Journal of Corpus Linguistics* 17: 380–409.

Hardt-Mautner, G. 1995. Only Connect. Critical Discourse Analysis and Corpus Linguistics. *UCREL Technical Papers* 6. http://ucrel.lancs.ac.uk/papers/techpaper/vol6.pdf. Accessed 18/10/2009.

Heywood, I., S. Cornelius, & S. Carver. 2011. *An Introduction to Geographical Information Systems* (fourth edition). Pearson: Harlow.

Ipsos MORI. 2013. Perceptions Are Not Reality. https://www.ipsos.com/ipsos-mori/en-uk/perceptions-are-not-reality. Accessed 15/7/2016.

Jackson, J. 2016. Independent, Mirror, Express and Star Suffer Sharp Fall in Traffic. *The Guardian* 17/3/2016. https://www.theguardian.com/media/2016/mar/17/independent-mirror-express-and-star-suffer-sharp-fall-in-traffic. Accessed 12/5/2017.

Jiang, H., & J. R. Eastman. 2010. Application of Fuzzy Measures in Multi-criteria Evaluation GIS. *International Journal of Geographical Information Science* 14 (2): 173–184.

Jo, Y. N. 2013. Psycho-social Dimensions of Poverty: When Poverty Becomes Shameful. *Critical Social Policy* 33 (3): 514–531.

Katz, M. B. 2013. *The Undeserving Poor* (second edition). Oxford: Oxford University Press.

Kennedy, G. D. 1998. *An Introduction to Corpus Linguistics*. London: Longman.

Kress, G. 1994. Text and Grammar as Interpretation. In U. Meinhof & K. Richardson (eds.). *Text, Discourse and Context: Representations of Poverty in Britain*. London: Longman, pp. 24–47.

Kress, G., & T. van Leeuwen. 2001. *Multimodal Discourse: The Modes and Media of Contemporary Communication*. London: Arnold.

Kulldorf, M. 1997. A Spatial Scan Statistic. *Communications in Statistics: Theory and Methods* 26: 1481–1496.

Kwan, M-P. 2008. From Oral Histories to Visual Narratives: Re-Presenting the Post-September 11 Experiences of the Muslim Women in the United States. *Social and Cultural Geography* 9 (6): 653–669.

Lansley, S., & J. Mack. 2015. *Breadline Britain: The Rise of Mass Poverty*. London: Oneworld.

Lee, P. 1999. Where Are the Deprived? Measuring Deprivation in Cities and Regions. In D. Dorling & S. Simpson (eds.). *Statistics in Society*. London: Arnold, pp. 172–180.

Lister, R. 2004. *Poverty*. Cambridge: Polity Press.

Lloyd, C. D. 2011. *Local Models for Spatial Analysis* (second edition). Boca Raton, FL: CRC Press.

Lo, C. P., & A. K. W. Yeung. 2007. *Concepts and Techniques of Geographical Information Systems* (second edition). Toronto: Pearson.

Lorenzo-Dus, N., & S. Marsh. 2012. Bridging the Gap: Interdisciplinary Insights into the Securitization of Poverty. *Discourse and Society* 23 (3): 274–296.

Lundström, R. 2013. Framing Fraud: Discourse on Benefit Cheating in Sweden and the UK. *European Journal of Communication* 28 (6): 630–645.

Mack, J., & S. Lansley. 1985. How Poor Is Too Poor? Defining Poverty. In J. Mack & S. Lansley (eds.). *Poor Britain*. London: George Allen & Unwin.

Malpas, J. E. 1999. *Place and Experience: A Philosophical Topography*. Cambridge, MA: MIT Press.

Mautner, G. 2007. Mining Large Corpora for Social Information: The Case of Elderly. *Language in Society* 36 (1): 51–72.

Mautner, G. 2009. Checks and Balances: How Corpus Linguistics Can Contribute to CDA. In R. Wodak & M. Meyer (eds.). *Methods of Critical Discourse Analysis*. London: Sage, pp. 122–143.

McCarthy, M., & R. Carter. 2004. Focus-on Issue: Corpus Linguistics (Part I)—Introduction. *Journal of Pragmatics* 36 (2): 147–148.

McKay, S. 2004. Poverty or Preference: What Do 'Consensual Deprivation Indicators' Really Measure? *Fiscal Studies* 25 (2): 201–223.

McKenzie, L. 2015. *Getting By: Estates, Class and Culture in Austerity Britain.* London: Polity Press.

Meinhof, U. 1994. From the Street to the Screen: *Breadline* Britain and the Semiotics of Poverty. In U. Meinhof & K. Richardson (eds.). *Text, Discourse and Context: Representations of Poverty in Britain.* London: Longman, pp. 65–92.

Misturelli, F., & C. Heffernan. 2011. The Language of Poverty: An Exploration of the Narratives of the Floor. *Sustainable Development* 19 (3): 206–222.

Moretti, F. 2005. *Graphs, Maps, Trees.* Verso: London.

Morgan, O., & A. Baker. 2006. Measuring Deprivation in England and Wales Using 2001 Carstairs Scores. *Health Statistics Quarterly* 31: 28–33.

Morris, R., & V. Carstairs. 1991. Which Deprivation? A Comparison of Selected Deprivation Indexes. *Journal of Public Health Medicine* 13 (4): 318–326.

Murrieta-Flores, P., A. Baron A., I. N. Gregory, A. Hardie, & P. Rayson. 2015. Automatically Analysing Large Texts in a GIS Environment: The Registrar General's Reports and Cholera in the Nineteenth Century. *Transactions in GIS* 19: 296–320.

Newton, J. 2015. More Than 100,000 Benefit Claimants Across the UK Are Being Handed £100 a Week After Being Assessed as Unable to Work Because of Addiction, Obesity and Stress. *Mail Online* 22/5/15. http://www.dailymail.co.uk/news/article-3006248/More-100-000-benefits-claimants-UK-handed-100-week-assessed-unable-work-addiction-obesity-stress.html. Accessed 14/3/2018.

Noble, M, G. Wright, G. Smith, & C. Dibben. 2006. Measuring Multiple Deprivation at the Small-Area Level. *Environment and Planning A* 38: 169–185.

O'Halloran, K. 2012. Electronic Deconstruction: Revealing Tensions in the Cohesive Structure of Persuasion Texts. *International Journal of Corpus Linguistics* 17 (1): 91–124.

OED. 2017. Poverty, n. *OED Online.* www.oed.com/view/Entry/149126. Accessed 2/11/2017.

ONS. 2014. 2011 Census Glossary of Terms. https://www.ons.gov.uk/ons/guide-method/census/2011/census-data/2011-census-data/2011-first-release/2011-census-definitions/2011-census-glossary.pdf. Accessed 24/2/2017.

ONS. 2016a. Unemployment Rate: Sourced from the Labour Market Statistics Time Series Dataset. https://www.ons.gov.uk/employmentandlabourmarket/peoplenotinwork/unemployment/timeseries/mgsx/lms. Accessed 2/12/2016.

ONS. 2016b. Statistical Bulletin: UK Labour Market: Nov 2016. https://www.ons.gov.uk/employmentandlabourmarket/peopleinwork/employmentandemployeetypes/bulletins/uklabourmarket/november2016. Accessed 2/12/2016.

ONS. n.d.(a) Unemployment. https://www.ons.gov.uk/employmentandlabourmarket/peoplenotinwork/unemployment. Accessed 2/1/2018.

ONS. n.d.(b) Households by Combined Economic Activity Status of Household Members by Local Authority: Table A1 LA. https://www.ons.gov.uk/employmentandlabourmarket/peoplenotinwork/unemployment/datasets/householdsbycombinedeconomicactivitystatusofhouseholdmembersbylocalauthoritytablea1la/current. Accessed 24/2/2017.

Openshaw, S. 1984. *The Modifiable Areal Unit Problem. Concepts and Techniques in Modern Geography 38*. Norwich: Geo Books.

Openshaw, S. 1997. The Truth About Ground Truth. *Transactions in GIS* 2: 2–24.

Openshaw, S., M. Charlton, C. Wymer, & A. Craft. 1987. A Mark 1 Geographic Analysis Machine for the Automated Analysis of Point Data Sets. *International Journal of Geographical Information Systems* 1: 335–358.

Ordnance Survey. 2014. The National Grid FAQs. https://www.ordnancesurvey.co.uk/support/the-national-grid.html. Accessed 19/2/2016.

Orpin, D. 2005. Corpus Linguistics and Critical Discourse Analysis: Examining the Ideology of Sleaze. *International Journal of Corpus Linguistics* 10 (1): 37–61.

OSF. 2014. *A Report on Six European Cities: Europe's White Working Class Communities*. New York: Open Society Foundations. http://www.opensocietyfoundations.org/sites/default/files/white-working-class-overview-20140616.pdf. Accessed 19/6/2014.

Pantazis, C., D. Gordon, & P. Townsend. 2006. The Necessities of Life. In C. Pantazis, D. Gordon, & R. Levitas (eds.). *Poverty and Social Exclusion in Britain*. Bristol: The Policy Press, pp. 89–122.

Paterson, L. L. Forthcoming. Electronic Supplement Analysis of Multiple Texts: Exploring Discourses of UK Poverty in Below the Line Comments.

Paterson, L. L., L. Coffey-Glover, & D. Peplow. 2016. Negotiating Stance Within Discourses of Class: Reactions to *Benefits Street. Discourse & Society* 27 (2): 195–214.

Paterson, L. L., D. Peplow, & K. Grainger. 2017. Does Money Talk Equal Class Talk? Audience Responses to Poverty Porn in Relation to Money and Debt. In A. Mooney & E. Sifaki (eds.). *The Language of Money and Debt: An Interdisciplinary Approach*. Basingstoke: Palgrave, pp. 205–232.

Pickles, J. (ed.). 1995. *Ground Truth: The Social Implications of Geographic Information Systems*. New York: Guilford Press.

Pleiades. n.d. Pleiades. https://pleiades.stoa.org. Accessed 11/7/2017.

Porter, C., P. Atkinson, & I. N. Gregory. 2015. Geographical Text Analysis: A New Key to Nineteenth-Century Mortality. *Health and Place* 36: 25–34.

Potts, A., M. Bednarek, & H. Cape. 2015. How Can Computer-Based Methods Help Researchers to Investigate News Values in Large Datasets? A Corpus Linguistic Study of the Construction of Newsworthiness in the Reporting on Hurricane Katrina. *Discourse & Communication* 9 (2): 149–172.

Ramesh, R., & A. Sparrow. 2010. Housing Benefit Cuts Will 'Push Poor Out of South', Experts Warn. *The Guardian* 8/11/2010. https://www.theguardian.com/society/2010/nov/08/housing-benefit-north-south-divide. Accessed 22/2/2018.

Rayson, P. 2008. From Keywords to Semantic Domains. *International Journal of Corpus Linguistics* 13 (4): 519–549.

Rayson P., D. Archer, S. Piao, & T. McEnery. 2004. The UCREL Semantic Analysis System. *Proceedings of the Beyond Named Entity Recognition Semantic Labelling for NLP Tasks Workshop, Lisbon, Portugal, 2004*, pp. 7–12.

Reibel, M. 2007. Geographic Information Systems and Spatial Data Processing in Demography: A Review. *Population Research Policy Review* 26: 601–618.

Richardson, J. E. 2006. *Analysing Newspapers: An Approach from Critical Discourse Analysis*. Basingstoke: Palgrave Macmillan.

Risen, J., & E. Lichtblau. 2013. How the U.S. Uses Technology to Mine More Data More Quickly. *New York Times* 8/6/2013.

Robinson, A. H., J. L. Morrison, P. C. Muehrcke, A. J. Kimerling, & S. C. Guptil. 1995. *Elements of Cartography* (sixth edition). Chichester: Wiley.

Rowlingson, B. 2015. *Spatial Segregation Analysis.* Personal Communication.
Rupp, C. J., P. Rayson, I. N. Gregory, A. Hardie, A. Joulain, & D. Hartmann. 2014. Dealing with Heterogeneous Big Data When Geoparsing Historical Corpora. *Proceedings of the 2014 IEEE Conference on Big Data*, pp. 80–83.
Rushton, G. 2003. Public Health, GIS, and Spatial Analytic Tools. *Annual Review of Public Health* 24: 43–56.
Sack, R. 1997. *Homo Geographics.* Baltimore: Johns Hopkins University Press.
Scheuer, J. 2003. Habitus as the Principle for Social Practice: A Proposal for Critical Discourse Analysis. *Language in Society* 32 (2): 143–175.
Schuurman, N. 2006. Formalization Matters: Critical GIS and Ontology Research. *Annals of the Association of American Geographers* 96 (4): 726–739.
Siebert, L. J. 2000. Using GIS to Document, Visualize, and Interpret Tokyo's Spatial History. *Social Science History* 24 (3): 537–574.
Simon, R., L. Isaksen, E. Barker, & P. de Soto Canamares. 2016. The Pleiades Gazetteer and the Pelagios Project. In M. L. Berman, R. Mostern, & H. Southall (eds.). *Placing Names: Enriching and Integrating Gazetteers.* Bloomington: Indiana University Press, pp. 97–109.
Skeggs, B., & H. Wood (eds). 2011. *Reality Television and Class.* London: British Film Institute/Palgrave Macmillan.
Slack, J. 2010. Migrants ARE Driving Down Wages of the Poor, as Equalities Watchdog Blames East European Influx. *Mail Online* 18/1/10. http://www.dailymail.co.uk/news/article-1244060/Migrants-ARE-driving-wages-poor-equalities-watchdog-blames-East-European-influx.html. Accessed 15/1/2018.
Southall, H. R., R. Mostern, & M. L. Berman. 2011. On Historical Gazetteers. *International Journal of Humanities and Arts Computing* 5: 127–145.
Stubbs, M. 2001. Texts, Corpora, and Problems of Interpretation: A Response to Widdowson. *Applied Linguistics* 22 (2): 149–172.
Tanner, S., T. Munoz, & P. H. Ros. 2009. Measuring Mass Text Digitization Quality and Usefulness: Lessons Learned from Assessing the OCR Accuracy of the British Library's 19th Century Online Newspaper Archive. *DLib Magazine* 15 (7/8).
Taylor, J. E., I. N. Gregory, & C. Donaldson. in press. Combining Close and Distant Reading: A Multiscalar Analysis of the English Lake District's Historical Soundscape. *International Journal of Humanities and Arts Computing.*
Tognini-Bonelli, E. 2001. *Corpus Linguistics at Work.* Amsterdam: John Benjamins.

Townsend, P., P. Phillimore, & A. Beattie. 1988. *Health and Deprivation: Inequality and the North*. London: Routledge.

Turvill, W. 2015. National Newspaper Circulations, May 2015: Mail on Sunday Overtakes Sun on Sunday, Times Remains Only Growing Title. http://www.pressgazette.co.uk/national-newspaper-circulations-may-2015-mail-sunday-overtakes-sun-sunday-times-remains-biggest-growing/. Accessed 15/1/2016.

Tyler, I. 2008. 'Chav mum, chav scum': Class Disgust in Contemporary Britain. *Feminist Media Studies* 8 (1): 17–34.

UN. 1995. The Copenhagen Declaration and Programme of Action. *World Summit for Social Development*, 6–12 March. New York: United Nations.

Unwin, D. 1995. Geographic Information Systems and the Problem of 'Error and Uncertainty.' *Progress in Human Geography* 19: 549–558.

van der Bom, I., L. L. Paterson, K. Grainger, & D. Peplow. 2018. 'It's Not the Fact They Claim Benefits but Their Useless, Lazy, Drug Taking Lifestyles We Despise': Analysing Audience Responses to Benefits Street Using Live Tweets. *Discourse, Context & Media* 21: 36–45.

Watson, L. 2011. Lotterty Hands Over £425,000 for Charity Food Bank in Birmingham. *Mail Online* 22/9/2011. http://www.dailymail.co.uk/news/article-2040024/Lottery-hands-425-000-charity-food-bank-Birmingham.html. Accessed 21/2/2018.

Wodak, R. 1999. Critical Discourse Analysis at the End of the 20th Century. *Research on Language and Social Interaction* 32 (1–2): 185–193.

Wodak, R. 2001. What CDA Is About—A Summary of Its History, Important Concepts and Its Development. In R. Wodak & M. Meyer (eds.). *Methods of Critical Discourse Analysis*. London: Sage, pp. 1–13.

Wodak, R., & M. Meyer. 2009. Critical Discourse Analysis: History, Agenda, Theory and Methodology. In R. Wodak & M. Meyer (eds.). *Methods of Critical Discourse Analysis* (second edition). London: Sage, pp. 1–33.

Wong, D. 2009. The Modifiable Areal Unit Problem. In A. S. Fotheringham & P. A. Rogerson (eds.). *The Sage Handbook of Spatial Analysis*. London: Sage, pp. 105–124.

Wood, H., & B. Skeggs (eds). 2011. *Reality Television and Class*. London: British Film Institute/Palgrave Macmillan.

Index

L. L Paterson and I. N Gregory, *Representations of Poverty and Place*,
https://doi.org/10.1007/978-3-319-93503-4